Language as a Human Problem

Essays by Morton Bloomfield
Roger Brown
Courtney B. Cazden
Charles Ferguson
Einar Haugen
David G. Hays
Dell Hymes
Martin Kay
Edward L. Keenan
Paul Kiparsky
D. Terence Langendoen
Eric H. Lenneberg
William G. Moulton
Peter Strevens
Karl V. Teeter
Eric Wanner
Calvert Watkins

Language as a Human Problem

Edited by MORTON BLOOMFIELD *and* EINAR HAUGEN

 LUTTERWORTH PRESS • *Guildford and London*

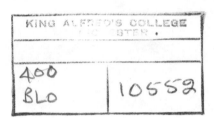
First published in Great Britain 1975

ISBN 0 7188 2241 2

Copyright © 1973, 1974 by the American Academy of Arts and Sciences

With one exception, articles previously appeared in
the summer 1973 edition of *Daedalus*.

First published in book form in the United States of America in 1974
by W. W. Norton & Company, Inc.

Contents

EINAR HAUGEN

Foreword

THIS VOLUME was conceived as focusing on those language problems that touch human life rather than on the techniques and goals of current linguistics, which are often highly abstract and esoteric. Contributors were invited who were known to be doing research on various language problems both inside and outside the special field of linguistics. Our contributors are all linguists in the widest sense, but many of them are housed in departments of English, psychology, philosophy, anthropology, or education. A background for this common focus of interest is provided in an introduction by *Morton Bloomfield*, who surveys the history of language study in its long progression from folk-wisdom to scientific linguistics.

The remaining essays fall naturally into three major sections which we have called "The Variety of Language," "The Learning of Language," and "The Functions of Language." The variety of language is at once an appalling and an appealing aspect of human life, one that constantly obtrudes itself on the attention of the traveler and the scholar. One cognitive problem we encounter when we approach it is that most people acquire their language in childhood so that their performance of it is mostly below the level of consciousness. There is no tradition of general linguistics in our schools and rarely any awareness of the structure and form of language even among well-educated speakers. It is therefore appropriate to open with an insightful essay on the basic facts about the "nature of language," offered by linguist *William G. Moulton*. For all its deceptive simplicity, this is an indispensable *janua linguarum:* a gateway to linguistic understanding.

From time to time the variety of language erupts as a problem on the political scene as well, demanding solutions for which our leaders are ill prepared. Drawing on his wide experience as a student of Arabic and Indic languages and as an observer of language policy development in Egypt, India, Africa, and the Americas, *Charles Ferguson* shows how linguistic scholarship in the field of *sociolinguistics* is coming to grips with problems of variation. By establishing such concepts as *language variation* and *language repertoire*, he says, it may be possible to overcome the notion that all language is or should be homogeneous, and to encourage an understanding

of the problems that arise when the patterns of language usage are undergoing rapid change. One of the symbols of language variation is the Hebrew
tale of the tower of Babel, and in my own essay on the "Curse of Babel" I
point to the value of bilingualism in overcoming the "curse." The language
problems of American Indians, Chicanos, and blacks have parallels in other
parts of the world, and I advise Americans to look at one such parallel, that
of northern Sweden, where Lapps, Finns, and Swedes live in an uneasy linguistic symbiosis not unlike our own.

The whole problem of inequality among speakers due to their various
speech is explored with exemplary thoroughness and incision by *Dell Hymes,*
whose concept of the *ethnography of speaking* has been a most fruitful idea
in recent anthropology. *Karl V. Teeter* explores the same concept further in
assessing the respective roles of anthropologists and linguists in studying
language behavior. While some linguists have restricted their concern to "the
speaker's *knowledge* of his language," Teeter emphasizes that knowledge is
not enough: speakers must also have what he calls *command,* or mastery of
language use in all possible situations.

Behind the often confusing variety of language there is of course a history,
which may help to account for the human babel in something more than
mythical terms. *Calvert Watkins,* from his rich store of knowledge concerning the Indo-European languages, brings us examples of how variations observable in the present can shed light on the process of linguistic change
itself. Language repertoire is not only synchronically varied, but even within
one society there are older, archaic forms that may be indicators of the direction in which a language is evolving in the future.

The key to language change, repeatedly emphasized in these papers, is of
course the learning of language anew by each generation of speakers. It is
therefore appropriate that our second section should deal with problems of
learning. *Eric H. Lenneberg* considers what clinical psychology can offer us
on the way language is stored in the brain. Since the *cerebral activity states*
that trigger language use cannot be observed directly, evidence must be
drawn from aphasiology, the study of the brain lesions which produce abnormal language behavior. The awesome complexity of the brain has left
abundant room for speculation, and so far, attempts to localize specific linguistic operations in the brain itself have been in vain. The most striking fact
emerging from such efforts is that the brain is not a passive "conveyor of
information" or a "channel," but a highly active object.

This insight is further confirmed by the pioneering researches of psychologist *Roger Brown,* originally stimulated by Chomsky's emphasis on
the creativity of the language user. By taping, transcribing, and analyzing
the first sentences of small children, from "That doggie" to "Hit ball," Brown
and his associates have been able to document the stages in the child's
language learning process more precisely than ever before. Their early attempts to interpret these in such terms as "telegraphic speech" or "pivot

grammar" have been replaced by an attempt to take into account what the child intends to express, as every mother knows it. Children's sentences grow longer and grammatically more complex as the children grow older, gradually and without teaching, not as mere imitation of what they hear, nor only as a response to social pressures, but also as an unfolding of their inborn human potentiality.

Educationist *Courtney B. Cazden* points out the paradox that language can be learned by children, but not taught to them. Explicit teaching is often more confusing than helpful, so emphasis must be placed on making the environment of learning such that the child wants to learn. Only after a person is past the watershed of puberty, when his natural aptitude for language learning is weakened, can second language teaching be done effectively by explicit rule. This is the theme of *Peter Strevens'* paper, which surveys the various "methods" that have been the fetish of language teaching. He rejects the idea that any single method of teaching can be the most effective one in all learning situations, and lists the dimensions of language learning: pupil age, educational aims, free will, present proficiency, language of instruction, and perspective. Language teaching, he tells us, is moving away from a teacher-centered to a learner-centered approach.

Once learned, language functions in a fascinating multitude of ways. *Eric Wanner* tries to account for the way in which language conveys meaning: the signals of speech are in fact quite inadequate for a machine to decode unless a machine could be built to interpret signals in the same way the human brain does it. Not only is the phonetic signal itself often scrambled and degenerate, but the brain must interpret the *deep structure* that lies behind the surface of every sentence. The listener brings to the speech act an inside-out process that is scarcely understood at all, though it reflects a powerful ability that is peculiarly human. *Edward L. Keenan* shows how language can be used to overcome its own weaknesses through the methods of formal logic. Having been developed to eliminate the ambiguities and redundancies of natural language, logic can now be used to analyze natural language and show how a pair of languages like Hebrew and English differ systematically in what they are able to express.

There are thinkers like Paul Goodman who reject the "calculus" of this kind of analysis, and *D. Terence Langendoen* explicates the difference in stance between Goodman and a grammarian like Chomsky. Chomsky wants to account for *grammaticality* and the *conventional* meaning of a sentence, while Goodman wishes to go beyond that and account also for *acceptability* and *conversational* meaning. Langendoen sees no real conflict here and rejects the idea that the interpretation of a sentence in its actual context depends on its grammar. He does not say that research on grammaticality should be abandoned, but rather that new research should be opened in the area of acceptability and intelligibility.

That language is indeed crucial in interpersonal relationships is the thesis also of *David G. Hays*, who reports on a body of research on conversations that would seem to be an answer to Goodman's plea. The current metaphor for simpler conversational exchanges is one that depends on the computer: in our verbal intercourse we are *programmed* with various images and routines that enable us to cope with the social situations that face us. *Martin Kay* brings this metaphor into focus by asking how actual computers can be used in the treatment of linguistic data. He discusses in some detail the débacle of machine translation which wasted millions of the taxpayers' dollars to little purpose and impeded the progress of serious research in the field. One of the startling but somehow comforting facts that Kay brings out is that, in one case, human translators turned out 450 words per hour, while editors who had to work over the machine output produced only 400 words. Kay suggests that other approaches to machine translation are possible and speculates as to the prospects that computers can be made to mimic human behavior with artificial intelligence and syntactic processors.

By universal consent the highest functions of language are those of poetry, but even here, as *Paul Kiparsky* demonstrates, there are recurrent patterns that turn out to be basically linguistic. While the constants of poetic form are ordinarily thought to reside chiefly in sound patterns, Kiparsky applies the principles of generative grammar to suggest that they are deeply associated with the very structure of language itself.

If these papers have any theme in common, it is that the human faculty of language is man's chief glory and mystery, and that we can approach the study of it only in a spirit of lively curiosity and deep reverence.

MORTON BLOOMFIELD

Introduction

LANGUAGE IS OUR all-encompassing medium, almost certainly the oldest means of communication and expression, one which is both central to and pervasive in the realm of all human thought. It is the basis of whatever social cohesion we can attain. It determines in large measure the way we look at the world; it enables us to control it. It links the past intimately with the present and makes possible at least some continuity into the future. It possesses magic and hypnotic power. It may elevate and depress. We cannot escape its influence even by silence. We need it to grasp things intellectually and to get others to do so. We cannot avoid it even when we talk about it. To a large extent, it defines our very humanity.

Being human involves, in a curious way, a turning back on oneself. We are both inside and outside our bodies and culture at the same time. The primal pattern for this duality is language itself, which is both within and without us at the same time and can itself be its own object and subject. As someone put it at the *Dædalus* conference held in May 1972 at the House of the Academy, language is at the same time both a problem and a resource. Or to put it another way, language must use itself to solve the problem of being itself.

A major goal of this issue is to present in the broadest sense of the term, *the anthropology and psychology of communication.* This is *a* goal, but we have others. We wish to emphasize the problems facing linguistics in its manifold forms as it strives to understand language and to make it more sensitive to the human problems it creates. We are just now beginning to examine scientifically the realities of language communication: under what conditions, internal and external, it takes place, and how it modifies and affects the human condition and the realities of social life and is modified and affected by them. Although the study of language cannot be confined to its own system and rules, language itself is, nevertheless, a system. It is *both* a system and an interaction with an environment; one cannot be completely reduced to the other. To keep these oppositions and similarities in mind at the same time calls for the greatest intelligence and understanding.

The new awareness of the social and psychological dimensions of communications now becoming evident is taking the subject out of the realm of intuition and folk wisdom. The topic is being looked at in a new hard way. It recalls its ancient predecessor—rhetoric. Rhetoric, unlike the ancient language disciplines of grammar and language philosophy, was always concerned with the communication situation, with the effect of speech upon an audience and how to control and obtain those effects for various purposes good and bad. But although rhetoric has something in common with the *anthropology and psychology of communication* in that both are concerned with the practical effects of speech, the latter is broader and more subtle in its approach, recognizing a variety of causes and effects as well as such matters as feedback and self-awareness, nor is it limited to judging the effectiveness of language use.

A brief review of the history of linguistics may help us to see the continuity of language problems. The systematic study of language began with the Greeks. No doubt an interest in language had existed from early times. There is certainly evidence for it in the invention of writing. Many alphabets presuppose some knowledge of grammar. The play on language characteristic of much oral literature and the word magic in charms and riddles also argue that a fascination with words and syntax existed from the earliest of times. But as far as we know, the Greeks, with their scientific attitude toward life and nature, created the first written and systematic grammar in our tradition. In India in the fourth century B.C., Panini wrote a more scientific grammar than any written by Greeks, but it remained unknown in the West until the nineteenth century. There may be lost Babylonian or Egyptian grammars. But as far as the science of linguistics is concerned, the Greek creation of grammars is the decisive step. Interest in grammar arose out of the question—one which has, as we shall see, continually exercised Western man—whether languages were *natural* or *conventional,* a question connected in early Greek thought with the more general dispute over the boundaries of nature (φύσις) and of law or convention (νόμος). In the fifth century, Protagoras of Abdera began to discuss language and to classify parts of speech, inflections, moods, and so forth. From the partially preserved record of his grammatical work, it is believed that he was concerned with this issue of nature and convention. Certainly the dispute raged in the fifth century during his time.

In order to settle this debate it was necessary to discover the regularities of speech so that one could judge whether they corresponded to the regularities of the human mind or not. The problem of words, their sounds and significations, was also involved in the matter. Plato's *Cratylus,* a most enigmatic dialogue, deals with these and related subjects. The notion of parts of speech aided philosophers in their exploration of reason in action and of the human mind. Thus even after it was established as a separate subject, grammar continued to maintain its connection, although in some periods rather tenuously, with philosophy. And one of its perpetual concerns has been the natural-conventional controversy.

The Stoics were especially active in making grammar a definite part of philosophy. They set the matrix of linguistic discussions for some 2,000 years. They distinguished the sign from that which is signified and expanded parts of speech from Plato's and Aristotle's three to four. They laid the basis for the study of speech sounds. But above all, they were interested in general linguistic questions including the relation of logic and grammar, and, of course, in language as natural or conventional.

The Alexandrine grammarians, especially Dionysius Thrax (late second century B.C.) and later Apollonius Dyscolus (second century A.D.), wrote simple and effective description of languages in the form of rules (with exceptions), in effect making grammar a discipline in its own right. In Hellenistic times, rhetoricians and grammarians used grammar to inculcate ideas of correctness, style and effectiveness in language use. The Romans carried on these interests and, mainly through Donatus and Priscian (not to speak of the rhetoricians), passed them on to the Middle Ages. Although they were not terribly original, these grammarians were great classifiers. Thus grammar tended in the later classical period and early Middle Ages to become a handmaiden of rhetoric, and grammarians emphasized its practicality. Grammar, it was said, was the gateway to all learning. However, its ties with philosophy were never completely cut.

The notion of rules, first developed by the Greeks, implied some rationality in language, and the idea of reason was central to medieval thinking on the subject. It was not, however, until the period of high scholasticism that philosophy returned in full and original measure to language; and a group of scholastic philosophers, Boethius of Dacia (Denmark) and Thomas of Erfurt in particular, seriously began again to see if the human mind could be illuminated by a knowledge of grammar and especially of the parts of speech. They distinguished form or grammatical words (*syncategorematic* words) from referential words (*categorematic* words). They founded what was known as speculative grammar. They believed in universal grammar and felt that all languages reflected certain immutable categories of the human mind and the world, particularly notions like substance and accident, and logical categories like mode, predicament, and signification. They felt that all languages were substantively the same, that they varied only accidentally. Grammar was regarded as a branch of logic rather than of rhetoric. These *modistae,* as they were called, raised interesting questions, but there has been a tendency to overestimate their importance. Even in the Middle Ages, they did not meet with universal acclaim. Furthermore, they flourished only in the period of high scholasticism. The rise of nominalism in the later Middle

Ages destroyed the philosophical realism on which their philosophical grammar rested. Through it all, teachers and rhetoricians kept open an interest in the realities of communication.

The first signs of comparative grammar arose in the Islamic world where the similarities of Arabic and Hebrew did not escape the notice of Hebrew grammarians and where Arab grammarians turned, stimulated by Greek grammarians, to classifying the language of the Koran. But speculation on comparative linguistics and on linguistic relativity really began to expand only with the Renaissance. Exploration opened up the world and provided much more material to work on, and the rise of the secular urban spirit contributed to the desire to know and understand language as it existed.

The late medieval and Renaissance period saw the rise in the West of several vernaculars to the level of full-fledged languages, capable of communicating serious religious and scientific matters and of displaying "high style," up to then confined in the West to Latin. Tentative attempts were made during this period to classify languages. The major Western languages—English, French, Dutch, German, Spanish and Italian—were preparing to take over and in some cases actually did take over their full functions. These developments necessitated the creation of grammars, dictionaries and new vocabulary, which, in various ways and degrees, was more or less completed by 1700 or 1750. By 1750, these vernaculars had conquered.

The geographic discoveries, the deepening interest in the classics, the rise of Protestantism, commercialism, and the secular spirit all had their impact on language and on man's conception of language. The gradual death of Latin as an international language made substitutes like French, Italian, and later English necessary, whereas previously they had only served as alternative languages. Newton still felt he had to write his scientific works in Latin, but Priestley and Herschel, at the end of the same century, never hesitated to write in English. The French Academy (founded in 1635) had as one of its main functions the "upgrading" of the French language. In England these matters were left to lexicographers and grammarians. Italy had had its own language academy since the sixteenth century. The political power of countries is an important element in spreading a particular language. The dominance of English today is no doubt due to the political and economic power of England and the United States.

The seventeenth and eighteenth century philosophers, led by Descartes and Leibnitz, explored the notion of a "universal grammar," a notion expressing in new ways the superiority of nature over convention. The rhetorical and pedagogical tradition, imitative of Greece and Rome, which had so dominated the late Middle Ages, receded somewhat in the eighteenth century. Its continued popularity was insured, however, by the rise of an uncertain and increasingly literate bourgeois class who know how to speak and write "correctly." Attempts to combine t osophical and rhetorical traditions may be found in some seve and eighteenth century grammars, notably those of Port Royal, produced by French grammarians of a Jansenist cast, interest in which has been renewed in recent years due to Chomsky. These grammars and logics attempted to discover the inner rules of thought as revealed in language or, more practically, the way in which language reflects universal ideas and concepts of the human mind. These grammarians suffered from their lack of knowledge of non-Indo-European languages, a knowledge which might have made them more aware of the complexity of their task. When we read some of the eighteenth century *philosophes* on language, we might almost believe ourselves back in the high Middle Ages. Yet the clarity of their thought and their sense of style certainly make them more pleasant reading than thirteenth and fourteenth century speculative grammarians.

However, there was also an empiricist and objective strain in language speculation in the eighteenth century which is the ancestor of modern structuralist and behaviorist approaches. The ancient *conventionalists* found their eighteenth century descendents in Locke and Hume.

Modern linguistics began in 1786 when Sir William Jones suggested that Sanskrit, Greek, Latin, and possibly other languages had a common ancestry. The problem of the universality of language was suddenly historicized, as befitted the rise of the historical age. The question for most linguists was what this original ancestor was like. If it no longer existed, it could perhaps be reconstructed. Facts and hypotheses based on facts were needed. The universality of the human mind was ignored or minimized in the search for actual language similarities. The surface is what counts, they argued.

Again a shift on the perpetual issue of *physis* versus *nomos* took place, and language, for the most part, was proclaimed by the linguists as conventional, even though users of language persisted, as men tend to do, in their *natural* attitude towards their own languages. The historical approach and the quest for origins in every field thus affected the study of language, giving rise to historical and comparative linguistics.

The sense of excitement in these early comparative philologists, as decipherments and new discoveries came in and new hypotheses were put forward, and their feeling that mankind was close to a unified knowledge of the human race in which language, mythology, thought, science and culture were all to be combined in a glorious synthesis, make one think that here is a continuation of the old hermetic tradition which flourished on the widespread notion that profound secrets of the human race were hidden in ancient traditions and rites. This feeling surfaced in the eighteenth century in Boehme, Swedenborg and Blake, in the Illuminati, and in the Masonic movement. The relationship between these underground movements and philosophies and the rise of historical and comparative linguistics is an aspect of the history of linguistics which is still unexplored. Although Jones, Grimm, Rask and Bopp transformed language from a rationalistic to a historical science, the fact that they were not untouched by this excitement is evidenced by the title of Friedrich von Schlegel's book, *Ueber die Sprache and Weisheit der Inder* (1808). Language and wisdom go together.

Since the early nineteenth century the study of language presents a continuing story of competing and, in some cases, complementary schools. Despite their serious differences, however, they were more or less united, until Chomsky came along, in regarding language as conventional and arbitrary. Although its victory was never absolutely complete, the historical school certainly dominated until the First World War.

The practical side of language, it must be remembered, still continued to be of absorbing interest to the general public while the linguists pursued the quest into origins, debated whether linguistic and grammatical "laws" had exceptions or not, produced great dictionaries and grammars (often historically organized), edited older texts, opened up medieval linguistic studies, and so forth.

The great historical linguists, many of them German, continued to explore the by-paths and main roads of the diachronic approach to languages which enabled them to create ancestor languages like proto-Indo-European, proto-Semitic, proto-Dravidian, and so forth. The explanatory power—and it was considerable—of these Ur-language theories was exploited to the full after Rask, Bopp and Grimm, by linguists like Diez, Zeuss, Miklosich and Schleicher and continued throughout this period in the great synthesizing works of Karl Brugman (1849-1919) and Hermann Hirt (1865-1936). Discoveries of Tocharian and Hittite in our century added new languages to the Indo-European family.

Around 1870 a new school, still primarily historical, arose, called the *Neogrammarian,* which emphasized the collection of data and the application of strict scientific criteria to the organization of language facts both present and past. Their interest in rules and their status foreshadows the synchronic and grammarian interests of our time.

The most important bridge to modern linguistics was Ferdinand de Saussure, a Swiss professor at the University of Geneva. Although not a Neogrammarian in the strict sense of the word, his interest in language as a system, his distinction between *parole* (speech) and *langue* (language) between the synchronic and diachronic study of language all contributed to the passing of the great dominance of historical linguistics in language study. Nevertheless, he himself made brilliant contributions to historical linguistics and to the study of style.

Linguists began to show more and more interest in language as a system but found meaning and psychology less tractable to systemization than phonology and morphology. Anthropology, with its stress on field work and the collecting and classifying of data, began to extend in amazing ways our knowledge of primitive languages. In the 1920's and 1930's the influence of Boas, Malinowski and Sapir in anthropological linguistics became marked and abetted the rise of what has been called structural linguistics in America. Sapir always maintained, however, an interest in general linguistic ideas as well as in particular languages. Leonard Bloomfield reinterpreted and synthesized their ideas in the light of the then dominant behaviorism in the social sciences, and added original ideas of his own in *Language* (1933), a landmark in linguistics.

About 1955, there were in the Western world various linguistic schools and dominant figures:

1) Historical linguistics (or comparative linguistics), centered in Germany, still flourished but was no longer the dominant approach.

2) Structural linguistics (perhaps positivist linguistics is a better name for it) as presented by Bloomfield and his followers was a powerful and influential school which stressed surface rather than inner structure, emphasized formal criteria of definition, and was suspicious of meaning and "mentalism" in explaining languages.

3) The Dane, Hjelmslev, had developed a special type of language analysis called *glossematics*, heavily emphasizing formal analysis.

4) Firth, an Englishman much influenced by Malinowski, dominated English linguistics with a system which, interestingly enough, stressed the communication situation, a stress also found in Dutch linguistic thinking of the time.

5) André Martinet in France developed a system of linguistic functionalism.

6) Roman Jakobson, a leading light in the Prague School, brought his ideas to America in the early 1940's. The Prague School in the 1920's and 1930's had developed its own type of structuralism but was more or less destroyed by the war. With his versatility and genius, Jakobson had an enormous impact on American linguistics and made contributions to historical linguistics, grammar, stylistics, phonology, poetics, aphasia, semiology, coding and practically every aspect of the subject of language. He was a major influence on Chomsky and his collaborator Morris Halle.

In 1957 Noam Chomsky published *Syntactic Structures* in which he calls for a new program of linguistic study and dismisses the attempt to understand language by studying only its surface manifestation. He argues for the importance of understanding the internal rules which govern language use, and stresses the role of *competence* as distinguished from *performance*. He sees language as a set of inner rules which generates by application to speech sounds all the correct sentences of a language and none of the incorrect sentences. Chomsky shows how linguistics need not be positivistic in order to be scientific, how objective criteria for deep structure and rules can be set up (Does it and do they generate all the correct sentences and none of the incorrect sentences?). Language is an internal system of rules using recurrence, division, and transformation, a process which links meaning (semantics) with sound (phonology). Furthermore, Chomsky stresses the universal element in languages and argues for a kind of universal grammar. Once again, even with the distinctions Chomsky made between language universals and particular languages, we are back to philosophy and the old problem of *physis/nomos*, this time with the stress on *physis, nature,* rather than *convention.*

Chomsky's own background and the influences on him still await investigation. It is clear that modern logic and the effects of computer science have had their impact on his thought. His own teacher in linguistics at the University of Pennsylvania was Zelig Harris, a structuralist Semitic scholar with a strong interest in general linguistics whose writings in the early 1950's about transformations must have influenced Chomsky.

None of the other schools has disappeared, but Chomskyan linguistics has become the dominant force in our time in the study of language, even influencing in many ways schools opposed to it. This revolution with all its implications for philosophy, psychology, poetics, sociology, and so forth is still with us. It is still too early really to evaluate its total effect and meaning. But that it has been and still is extensive there can be no doubt. However, it is doubtful whether the ideal of an existentially indifferent set of rules, somewhat like mathematics, can do full justice to the living reality of speech. This volume is pointing to other problems in language and above all to the language context.

This volume then concentrates on the human problems of language and tries to identify some of them and to indicate what is being done about them. The rise of ethnic consciousness and militancy as well as a general dissatisfaction with the "way things are" have led to a new stress on what may be called applied linguistics and the social dialect problems. The notion of the *speech situation* and the influence in particular of the *speech act* as described by the Oxford philosopher, J. L. Austin, and later by John Sears, have also helped to change the emphases of the early sixties. Problems of literacy, translation, bilingualism, language teaching, language and nationalism, the role of dialects, and so forth have become urgent and some of our best minds have begun to turn toward these matters.

Although earlier in 1966 I had thought that this volume, then being thought about, should be devoted to transformational-generative grammar (T-G), it is now clear that the *anthropology of communication* has more need of informed attention. The present situation in Chomskyan linguistics is confused. The intellectual drive and stimulus of the T-G movement have slowed down somewhat, and the Chomsky epigones are quarrelling among themselves and with the master. New bold steps are not coming out of M.I.T. Chomsky has been a great force in our time and is a very great linguist, but other questions than his can be asked of language. Furthermore, seven years have produced a wider knowledge of T-G and several useful books explaining it have appeared. The need for a general introduction to the topic is no longer as necessary as it once was.

Hence when Einar Haugen suggested that our topic be *Language as a Human Problem* rather than some aspect of pure linguistics, I was only too willing to accept the proposal. Stephen Graubard then agreed to go ahead and, with his great help, together with that of the Ford Foundation, plans were laid for a preliminary planning session in May 1971 to be followed by a fuller meeting a year later, both at the House of the Academy in Brookline, Massachusetts. This volume is the result of these meetings. Our subject then is language and not linguistics, except insofar as linguistics has language as its subject matter. The main emphasis, in other words, is to be on that marvelous, complex instrument of communication, expression and humanity, *language,* rather than on an academic subject, linguistics.

If we look at the topics dealt with here, our hearts may well sink at the problems in psychology, sociology and education that face us. This issue merely looks in an up-to-date fashion at what we have still to do. But if asking the right questions is the key to progress in the sciences and humane disciplines, then perhaps what we are doing here may be of great importance in the future.

Even here, we have not been able to ask all of the questions we should want to know about. Sensitivity and intuition are still important guides to the study of language. False questions have been asked in the past, time wasted on will-o'-the-wisps, and more questions (and more answers) will no doubt be thrown into the trash-cans of history, as the Marxists say. Yet only by accurate knowledge, by good sense and human understanding, will we be able to separate the wheat from the chaff. If this volume contributes somewhat to sensitive judgment, we will have contributed something to the clarification of language as a human problem.

THE VARIETY OF LANGUAGE

WILLIAM G. MOULTON

The Nature of Language

LANGUAGE IS A wonderfully rich vehicle for communication. We can use it to convey wishes and commands, to tell truths and to tell lies, to influence our hearers and to vent our emotions, and to formulate ideas which could probably never arise if we had no language in which to embody them. We can even use language to communicate with ourselves; in fact, such self-communication seems to constitute much of what we call "thinking." In our own particular culture, such "talking to oneself" is permissible as long as we do it silently; it becomes a problem only if we are caught doing it out loud.

Paradoxically, the very richness of language as a communication system is the source of many human problems. Every language exists in many styles; it offers different ways of speaking and writing appropriate for different occasions. We use one style in speaking with close friends our own age, a style that connotes comradeship and familiarity; and this style has different sub-varieties depending on whether we are talking man to man, woman to woman, man to woman, or woman to man. We use quite another style when we are being interviewed for a job, a style that implies respect and perhaps just a bit of deference. And we use still other styles in public address, in religious services, with people older or younger than we, and so on and on. Though such differences in style are extremely subtle (and still very poorly understood), children start to learn them at a surprisingly young age. First-graders have already learned enough to use one style with their playmates, another style with their teachers, and perhaps still another style with their parents.

These many styles, for all their communicative richness, contain many pitfalls. For woe to him who uses a style that does not fit the occasion. If we use the style of respect and deference with a close friend, all sense of comradeship and familiarity is lost. If we use our familiar style at a job interview, we will almost certainly not get the job. And if a man speaks to a man in the style that is appropriate only for a man speaking to a woman—the reader can imagine the consequences.

Every language, provided it has more than a minute number of speakers,

3

also has another source of richness: it exists in many different geographical and social varieties. We all know that a Bostonian speaks differently from a San Franciscan, and a Houstonian differently from a Chicagoan; and that, in all four of these cities, people in the professions speak differently from day laborers. In our own country, geographical differences usually create only minor human problems. The adult Atlantan who moves to Seattle will, in speech, usually remain forever a "southerner," and will perhaps want to remain so, but this will not prevent him from becoming a successful doctor or lawyer, or from being invited to join the country club. Social differences, on the other hand, can lead to human problems that are far more serious—even tragic. The lower-class speaker who, for whatever reason, is unable to learn middle-class English will generally be barred forever from holding a middle-class job; and he will almost certainly not be invited to join the country club. Few of the readers of these lines would be inclined to engage the services of a doctor or lawyer who said such things as "I seen him when he done it"; and probably still fewer would be inclined to invite him to join the country club—despite the fact that they can understand him just as well as if he said, "I saw him when he did it." Such observations may not place American society in a particularly attractive light; yet our own language prejudices can be matched over and over again in other parts of the world, and often in far more extreme form.

Is there any sense in which we can say that such geographical and social differences "enrich" a language—or its speakers? There surely is; for they provide all speakers of a given geographical or social variety with a kind of solidarity which they would otherwise lack. Most readers of these lines—Americans from the professional class—will probably have experienced only a pale reflection of this sense of solidarity. This is the warm or affectionate feeling that many of us sense when, after an absence of years, we return to our home towns and hear again the variety of English that we learned in our childhood. A more striking example in our own country is the sense of solidarity which speakers of black English feel when they encounter other speakers of black English. Still more striking examples are provided in many other parts of the world. In German-speaking Switzerland, everyone uses dialect, the local variety of German, for all normal daily communication, and High German, the standard variety of German, only on special formal occasions. This use of dialect gives to the German-speaking Swiss a very precious sense of solidarity. They do not feel themselves to be Germans; they do not wish to be thought of as Germans; and their special Swiss variety of German, in its many different subvarieties, is a most valuable means of preserving their strongly felt emotional need for independence.

Though the linguist recognizes the communicative richness of these many styles and varieties, he typically works rather narrowly and concentrates primarily on what he considers the central function of language: that of conveying information from a speaker to a hearer, in whatever style or variety. Even viewed as a communication system in this narrower sense, however, language shows a richness that presents many human problems. In one respect, each language gives its speakers unbounded freedom: it permits them to say and understand quite literally an unlimited number of sentences; and most are sentences that have probably never been spoken or heard or written or read before: take, for example, the sentences in this or any other book. But in other respects each language keeps its speakers in slavish bondage, namely by the semantic way in which sentences must reflect the world of experience outside of language, and by the grammatical way in which sentences must be constructed. Consider the simple matter of asking a person what his name is. In English we say: "What's your name?" In French one must say what sounds to us like "How you call you?" (*Comment vous appelez-vous?*), in Italian, "How self calls?" (*Come si chiama?*), in Spanish, "How self calls you?" (*¿Cómo se llama usted?*), and in Russian, "How you they call?" (*Kak vas zovut?*). Or consider, in German, the grammatical baggage that must be included with every noun: it must be either masculine (*der Mann* "the man," *der Löffel* "the spoon"), or feminine (*die Frau* "the woman," *die Gabel* "the fork"), or neuter (*das Kind* "the child," *das Messer* "the knife").

Because, as children, we learn such matters outside of awareness, we usually do not notice them in our native language; or, if we do, we consider them *natural*. The tyranny of English nearly always forces us to mark a noun as either singular ("dog," "man") or plural ("dogs," "men"). There is nothing *natural* about this; many languages have no such singular/plural distinction in nouns, or use it only optionally. In addition, English usually forces us to mark every verb as either present ("talk," "see") or past ("talked," "saw"). There is again nothing *natural* about this; in many languages such a present/past distinction is totally lacking.

In one sense, then, a language liberates us; it permits us to send an unlimited number of messages and thus serves as a vehicle for our endless thoughts. But in another sense it enslaves us: it forces us to communicate our thoughts in strictly regulated ways. Does language thereby also regulate our thoughts? Does the medium influence the message? Perhaps; though since language is the only medium we have to express our thoughts, or to speculate about them, it is hard to say. But there are a few weak indications. As speakers of English, we find it hard to understand the sentence, "The wolf killed the sheep," with a noun "sheep" that is neither singular nor plural—because of the fact that, in this rare case, there is no signal to tell us which it might be. Similarly, we find it hard to understand the sentence, "The men put on their hats," with a verb "put" that is neither present nor past—because of the fact that, in this rare case, there is again no signal to tell us which it might be. It seems to be a fact that, because English forces us to signal the distinction between singular and plural in *most* nouns, and the distinction between present and past in *most* verbs, we then go on to feel the need for these distinctions in *all* nouns, and in *all* verbs. Speakers of languages which lack these compulsory distinctions might well say that, in our view of the world outside of language, we speakers of English are *obsessed* with the notions of number (singular vs. plural) and of tense (present vs. past).

The above remarks are intended to serve only as an introduction to the many human problems connected with language; further examples will be given in the other essays in this volume. The remainder of this introductory essay will be devoted to a discussion of what is perhaps the greatest human problem of all: How have human beings been able to design those many communication systems that we call "languages"—systems that can be used for sending and receiving messages? We shall ask, and try to answer, such questions as these: How do communication systems in general work? How do communication systems of the particular sort called "languages" work? What are the design features that seem to be common to all human languages?

Of all the communication systems used by human beings, language is by far the most ingenious, flexible, and productive. Most communication systems can be used to send and receive only a very limited number of messages. Human language, on the other hand, can be used to send and receive an unlimited number of messages; there is simply no end to the number of things we can say, in any language. A communication system with this unlimited capacity is ingenious indeed. We shall be particularly concerned with the design features which make possible this extraordinary productivity.

Communication Systems

The simplest type of communication system is one which provides only for a single *message*, through the association of a single *meaning* with a single *symbol:*

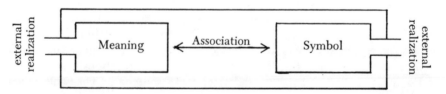

An example of such a simple communication system is the humble "barber pole language." Here there is just one symbol, the familiar red-white-and-blue pole; just one meaning, something like "place where a man can get a shave and haircut"; and hence just one message through the association of the meaning and the symbol.

In the above diagram we have twice written "external realization" to show that any communication system must be connected, at two ends, with the world outside the system. The *symbol* must be perceivable by one of the five senses outside the system (the barber pole is a visual symbol); and the *meaning* must refer to something outside the system (here, to a barbershop). In the case of human language, it is easy to describe the external realization of the symbols we use: they are realized in *sound,* and are therefore auditory symbols. It is far more difficult to describe those external things that the meanings of human language messages refer to. Should we say that they refer to thoughts, ideas, concepts? Could these thoughts, ideas, concepts exist if there were no language to embody them? We immediately get ourselves involved in difficult philosophical questions. The fact of the matter seems to be that, in English, we simply have no term which properly sums up all the things human beings talk about when they use language. For want of a better term, we shall use the word *experience.* But this should be interpreted in the widest possible sense. It includes not only matters of direct experience, "It's hot today," but also fictitious statements, "St. George slew the dragon"; factually incorrect statements, "George Washington was a Frenchman"; questions, "Who is that?" and commands, "Give me the book"—in short, all the kinds of things that we say when we use language.

Symbols

Communication in the "barber pole language" has just one meaning, and hence needs only one symbol. If we now wish to devise a system with further meanings, we must of course devise further symbols. But how? One method is to use symbols that are unitary and indivisible and have no internal structure. This is what we do in "traffic light language": we use one unitary symbol *red* for the meaning "stop," a second unitary symbol *amber* for the meaning "caution," and a third unitary symbol *green* for the meaning "go."

There is, however, a more ingenious and economical way of devising further symbols. Instead of making them unitary and indivisible, we can give them an internal structure by building them out of component parts. Most simply, we can choose some single element, use one occurrence of it as the symbol for one meaning, two occurrences of it as the symbol for a second meaning, three occurrences of it as the symbol for a third meaning, etc. This, Longfellow tells us, is what Paul Revere did:

> He said to his friend, "If the British march
> By land or sea from the town to-night,
> Hang a lantern aloft in the belfry arch
> Of the North Church tower as a signal light—
> One, if by land, and two, if by sea."

In this system the lantern as such is not a symbol, but a meaningless element. It can, however, be used in two arrangements. Used once, it is the symbol for "by land"; used twice, it is the symbol for "by sea."

This device of using meaningless elements in different arrangements so as to provide symbols for different meanings is simple and economical. It is also enormously powerful and productive. Because we shall need to refer to it again and again, let us give it a name. Let us call it the *structural principle*: the simple device of building larger elements out of smaller ones.

The Morse code provides an interesting example of the power of the structural principle. Here we need symbols for some forty-odd meanings: one each for the twenty-six letters of the alphabet, for the ten digits, and for a handful of punctuation marks. Building these forty-odd symbols out of arrangements of a single element (as in Paul Revere's language) would be uneconomical; it could lead to such monstrosities as a symbol consisting of forty-odd elements in a row. Suppose, instead, that we increase the number of meaningless elements from one to two—surely a very modest increase. In the Morse code these two meaningless elements are the *dot* and the *dash*. Symbols are then built out of sequences of 1, 2, 3, 4, 5, or 6 of these elements. Examples: · for E, ·– for A, –·· for D, –··· for B, ··–––– for 2, ·–·–·– for "comma." Note the power of the device: just two elements, the *dot* and the *dash*, arranged in strings one to six elements in length, can provide no less than 126 symbol shapes—far more than the Morse code actually needs:

1 element in length	2	2
2 elements in length	2 × 2	4
3 elements in length	2 × 2 × 2	8
4 elements in length	2 × 2 × 2 × 2	16
5 elements in length	2 × 2 × 2 × 2 × 2	32
6 elements in length	2 × 2 × 2 × 2 × 2 × 2	64
	Total available symbol shapes	126

The Morse code also uses, in a somewhat different way, a third element; the *pause*. A single pause serves to separate symbols; and, since it does not refer to anything outside the system, it is not a symbol. But a double pause *does* refer to something outside the system and therefore *is* a symbol: it symbolizes the space that is used to separate words in writing.

How do human languages devise symbols for meanings? Like Paul Revere and the Morse code, they use the structural principle; but they vastly increase its power by increasing the number of elements. These elements, realized in sound as vowels and consonants, are what the linguist calls *phonemes*, from Greek *phōné* "sound."

Consider the example of English. To symbolize the meaning "plural," as in "hats," we use the single phoneme /s/; for "at" we use two phonemes,

/æt/; for "fish" three phonemes, /fiš/; for "chest" four phonemes, /čest/; for "thrift" five phonemes, /Ɵrift/; for "glimpse" six phonemes, /glimps/; and so forth. In order to distinguish phonemic symbols from the letters of ordinary spelling, linguists write them between slant lines: / /. Just what particular symbols are used—/æ/ for the vowel of "at," /š/ for the final consonant of "fish," /č/ for the initial consonant of "chest"—is of no theoretical importance. If a language has, like English, more than twenty-six phonemes, one has to go beyond the twenty-six letters of the alphabet. In doing so, one tries as far as possible to choose symbols which are easy to write, type, print, and read.

Some idea of the power of this device can be given by the following statistics. Standard English has twenty-four consonants and, depending on the variety of English, around sixteen vowels and diphthongs. So let us accept forty as an approximate figure for the number of meaningless elements, *phonemes*, out of which symbols can be built. (Forty phonemes is not an extreme number. Many languages have more than this, and many have fewer.) Let us assume further that, as in the Morse code, up to six such elements can be strung along in a row in any symbol. (For English this is actually an understatement. The symbol /kənetikət/ "Connecticut," for example, consists of a string of nine phonemes.) This means that, theoretically (and in a moment we must add a drastic correction), the English language is able to provide shapes for the following number of symbols:

1 phoneme in length	40	40
2 phonemes in length	40 × 40	1,600
3 phonemes in length	40 × 40 × 40	64,000
4 phonemes in length	40 × 40 × 40 × 40	2,560,000
5 phonemes in length	40 × 40 × 40 × 40 × 40	102,400,000
6 phonemes in length	40 × 40 × 40 × 40 × 40 × 40	4,096,000,000

Total available symbol shapes 4,201,025,640

A symbolic system which provides, theoretically, for over four billion symbol shapes is enormously productive. No language needs more than a tiny fraction of this number.

However, although the above statistics are mathematically correct, they are linguistically wrong: they assume that symbol shapes can be built out of all possible sequences of phonemes, including, for English, such sequences as /pppppp/, /iiiiii/, and /fstgbš/. This is, of course, not so. Every language, English included, places strict limitations on the phoneme sequences that can be used for symbol shapes. In some languages these limitations are very strict indeed: all symbols must be built out of syllables which (writing "V" for vowel, "C" for consonant) have either the shape V or the shape CV. The only permissible symbol shapes are then such sequences as: V, CV, VCV, CVV, VCVV, CVCV, etc. English allows for a far greater variety of symbol shapes: they run all the way from C, for the /s/ meaning "plural" as in *hats,* to CCVCCC as in /glimps/ "glimpse," and CCCVCC as in /sprint/ "sprint." Yet English also as strict limitations. For example, symbol shapes may begin with a vowel: /it/ "it"; with one consonant: /rip/ "rip"; with two consonants: /trip/ "trip"; with three consonants: /strip/ "strip"; but never with *more* than three consonants. Furthermore, if a symbol shape begins with three consonants, the first must always be /s/, the second must be one of the set/p t k/, and the third, one of the set /l r y w/. Examples: CCC- sequences such as /spl-/ in "split," /str-/ in "straw," /spy-/ in "spew," /skw-/ in "squint." Other CCC- sequences, such as /ftr-/, /mbl-/, /ktv-/, are not permitted by the structural rules for English symbol shapes. The CC- sequences /tv- dv- ft- fs- zd- zn- gd- gn- kt- kn- mn-/ are all permitted in Russian, but none of them is permitted in English. Every language has its own particular rules for permitted sequences of phonemes.

Even considering such limitations, however, it is clear that the use of the structural principle provides each language with far more symbol shapes than its speakers will ever need. The number of permissible but unused symbol shapes in any language is enormous. English examples: such very simple shapes as *kib, keb, bep, dup;* such more complicated shapes as *splink, squog, blooth, gremp;* or, to quote Lewis Carroll, *brillig, slithy, tove, gyre, gimble, wabe.*

Signaling elements like those we have just been considering, those realized in sound as vowels and consonants, are often called *segmentals* because they occur as linearly arranged segments, like beads on a string. In addition, all languages seem to use two other types of signaling elements— often called *suprasegmentals* because, in a sense, they occur "on top of" the strings of phonemes. One of these is *stress,* which is realized in sound as acoustic prominence of various sorts. English, and perhaps all languages, use stress as part of the structure of sentences. For example, in answer to the question, "Who works here?", we reply, "*Joe* works here," with sentence stress on "Joe." In answer to "What does Joe do here?", we reply: "Joe *works* here," with sentence stress on "works." And in answer to "Where does Joe work?", we reply: "Joe works *here,*" with sentence stress on "here."

Stress is also used in English (but by no means in all languages—not, for example, in French) as one of the elements in the symbol shapes for words. It is stress that distinguishes, for example, the noun "*in*sert," with word stress on the first syllable, from the verb "in*sert,*" with word stress on the second syllable. It is also stress that distinguishes the phrase "a *black board*" with two word stresses, from the compound noun "a *black*board" with only one word stress.

These two uses of stress as a signaling element are, in one sense, highly economical. Without sentence stress, we would have to use strings of segmentals —saying, perhaps, something like "Joe-um works here," "Joe works-um here," "Joe works here-um"; and without word stress we would perhaps have to say something like "insert-en" for the noun and "insert-ev" for the verb. Of course, this latter solution would also have the advantage that we would no longer have to bother with stress as a signaling element. Every communication system that uses the structural principle must strike its own balance between these two possibilities. If we want shorter symbols, we must have a larger number of elements. And if we want fewer elements, we must have longer symbols.

The second type of suprasegmental signaling element is *pitch*, so-called because it is realized in sound by differences in the pitch of the voice. English, and perhaps all languages, use pitch as part of the structure of sentences; this use of pitch is customarily called *intonation*. If we say "Yes" with falling pitch (/yes↓/), this *affirmative intonation* signals agreement. But if we say "Yes?" with rising pitch (/yes↑/), this *interrogative intonation* signals the fact that we are asking our hearer for further information.

Pitch is also used in many languages, though not in English, as part of the structure of words; this use of pitch is customarily called *tone*. In *tone register languages* the pitch varies from one syllable to the next. For example, *BAba*, with high pitch on the first syllable and low pitch on the second syllable, may be a symbol with a totally different meaning from *baBA*, with low pitch on the first syllable and high pitch on the second syllable. Such languages may have two, three, or even four such pitch levels or *tone registers*. In *tone contour languages*, on the other hand, the pitch varies within the syllable. For example, the phoneme sequence /ma/ may be a totally different symbol depending on whether the tone contour accompanying it is high, low, rising, falling, rising-falling, falling-rising, up to—apparently—a maximum of nine different contours.

These two uses of pitch as a signaling element are again highly economical. Without sentence intonation, we would have to say something like "yes-ah" for /yes↓/, and perhaps "yes-oh" for /yes↑/. And, lacking tone, we in English have to use totally different sequences of segmentals for what can be signaled in Mandarin Chinese by the single sequence /ma/ accompanied by high level tone as the symbol for "mother," by high rising tone for "hemp," by low rising tone for "horse," and by low falling tone for "scold."

Meanings

In the simple communication systems which we first considered, every symbol was associated with a meaning, and every meaning constituted *an entire message*. With the one meaning of the barbershop language we can transmit only one message; with the two meanings of Paul Revere's language we can transmit only two different messages; even with the forty-odd meanings of the Morse code we can transmit only forty-odd different messages, each containing only one meaning. (We can, of course, transmit an unlimited *sequence* of messages; but that is quite another matter.) The design of all these communication systems is such that messages have no internal structure: they contain only a single meaning.

Human language is very different from this. Here, normally, even the smallest message has an internal structure: it consists of a *meaningful arrangement* of *meaningful elements*. The smallest normal human language message is the *sentence;* and every sentence quite obviouly consists of a set of meaningful elements in a meaningful arrangement. An illustration is provided by such a pair of sentences as "John loves Mary" and "Mary loves John." Both contain the same set of meaningful elements. They constitute different messages because these elements occur in different meaningful arrangements.

There are two apparent exceptions to the above statement that even the smallest human language messages consist not of just one meaningful element, but of several meaningful elements in a meaningful arrangement. First, we occasionally use a single symbol-and-meaning association which constitutes an entire message. For example, the symbol spelled "sh," associated with the meaning "quiet," constitutes an entire message meaning something like "Be quiet!"; and the symbol spelled "tsk-tsk," associated with the meaning "imagine that" (or something similar), constitutes an entire message meaning something like "Imagine that!" However, messages of this sort are customarily called *interjections;* and we can probably all agree that such interjections are not *normal* human language messages. Interestingly enough, their symbolic shapes are often also not normal. The element spelled "tsk," for example, occurs only in this one interjection.

Second, we often use substitute or elliptical sentences in which an entire message seems at first glance to contain only a single meaningful element, but a closer look shows that this is not the case. Such a substitute sentence as "Yes," in answer, let us say, to "Does John love Mary?" may seem to contain only the meaningful element "yes"; but it also contains the meaningful element /↓/, affirmative intonation. And such an elliptical sentence as "Mary?" in surprised reaction, let us say, to "John loves Mary," may seem to contain only the meaningful element, "Mary," but it also contains the meaningful element /↑/ or interrogative intonation.

The human language use of the structural principle not only in the formation of symbols, but also in the formation of messages, is fantastically productive. Let us take a language, like English, in which we can form sentences consisting of a verb in meaningful relation with a noun—sentences like "Fire burns," "Water boils," and "Smoke rises." Given this sentence formula plus 1000 verbs and 1000 nouns (and these numbers are of course very modest), we can, theoretically, form 1000×1000 or a million different sentences. The only limitations will be semantic ones. At the moment we have no use for such a sentence as "Fire boils"; but if we ever need it, it will be there, ready and waiting—and we will understand it immediately. Our ideas as to what arrangements of meaningful elements are semantically useful are constantly changing. A generation or two ago we would have understood the theoretical meanings of the sentences, "He split the atom," and "This is heavy water," but we would have considered them semantically useless. Today they are taught to us even before we reach college.

Let us take next a language, again like English, in which we can form sentences consisting of a verb in meaningful relation not just with one noun but with two nouns—sentences like "Boy loves girl," "The cat killed the rat," and "The dog bit the man." Given 1000 such verbs and again only 1000 nouns, we can now form, theoretically, not just a million sentences but $1000 \times 1000 \times 1000$ or a billion sentences.

Statistics are often meaningless; let us try to make these statistics meaningful. Take a talkative lady who says, on the average, one sentence of this type every two and a half seconds. This makes twenty-four sentences per minute— call it twenty-five, just to make the figuring easier. This makes 1500 sentences per hour. This makes 27,000 sentences in an eighteen-hour talking day. This makes 9,855,000 sentences in a 365-day year. Adding a quarter of a day to take care of leap year, this makes an average of 9,861,750 sentences per year. To make the figuring easier, let us have the lady talk just a bit faster and round this upwards to 10,000,000 sentences per year. In ten years our talkative lady will say 100,000,000 sentences. It will take her 100 years and a billion sentences of this type before she has to start repeating herself; and the most complicated sentence she will have said will be of the type, "The cat killed the rat." This is what we mean by "fantastic productivity."

But this is only the beginning. In English, and probably in all languages, we can add to such sentences many further types of meaningful elements: expressions of time—"always," "often," "sometimes," "last Monday"; expressions of place—"here," "there," "in Cleveland," "in Oshkosh"; expressions of manner—"fiercely," "passionately," "slowly," "with his teeth"; etc. The number of possible sentences has by this time become so large that it is futile to try to compile statistics. Presumably, however, the number of such additions comes to an end somewhere. That is to say, though we have accounted for an enormous number of sentences, this number is still limited. Furthermore, each of these sentences—even though there is an enormous number of them—is still quite simple in structure. We now need to consider two design features which can account for sentences of more complicated grammatical structure, and which at the same time will explain how it is possible for us, in any language, to use a limited number of grammatical rules to produce an unlimited number of sentences.

One type of process that can account for an unlimited number of anything is called, in mathematics, *recursion*. Recursion permits a system to feed upon itself over and over again, theoretically without end—like that cereal box with a picture of a boy holding a cereal box with a picture of a boy holding a cereal box, and so on and on. In human language, the principle of recursion takes two quite different forms: *coordination* and *subordination*.

A classic example of *coordination* is the following nursery rhyme:

(1) John Patch made the match,
and (2) John Clint made the flint,
and (3) John Puzzle made the muzzle,
and (4) John Crowder made the powder,
and. . . .

The coordinate clauses numbered (1), (2), (3), (4) contain all the elements of full sentences except final intonation—in this case, the affirmative intonation /↓/. Let us call each such clause an S′. And let us call the entire sentence, with its final intonation, an S. We can then diagram such a coordinate sentence as follows:

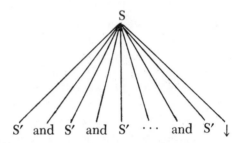

Coordination can obviously go on and on, with no theoretical limit to the number of clauses that can be grouped together by means of conjunctions and then terminated with an intonation. Depending on the nature of the clauses, parts of them may, optionally, be deleted. For example, if we join together the clauses, "John Patch made the match," "John Patch made the flint," "John Patch made the muzzle," and "John Patch made the powder," the resulting coordinate sentence is normally, "John Patch made the match, the flint, the muzzle, and the powder"—with deletion of all but the first occurrence of "John Patch made," and all but the last occurrence of "and."

When two or more clauses are joined together by means of coordination, we cannot say that any one of them is embedded inside any other one. They are simply joined together, are coordinate with each other, and constitute comparable parts of the whole. Quite different from this is the second recursive device used in all languages: *subordination*. Here we *can* say that a clause is embedded within a sentence, or within another clause, and is thus subordinate to it.

A classic example of *subordination* is again provided by a nursery tale:

(1) This is the cat.   This is the cat
(2) the cat killed the rat   that killed the rat
(3) the rat ate the malt   that ate the malt
(4) the malt lay in the house that lay in the house
(5) Jack built the house   that Jack built.

The full sentence to the right is the result of a succession of embeddings. Clause (5) is embedded in clause (4); the resulting complex clause is embedded in clause (3); the resulting complex clause is embedded in clause (2); and the resulting complex clause is embedded in the sentence (1). Or, to put matters the other way around, we have here the sentence (1), which contains clause (2), which contains clause (3), which contains clause (4), which contains clause (5). We can diagram such successive embeddings as follows:

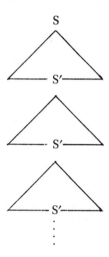

Obviously, there is again no theoretical limit to the number of clauses that can be embedded within clauses. Subordination is, therefore, a second device that we can use to go beyond the structure of simple sentences, and also a second device that permits us to construct an unlimited number of sentences.

Structures

At the beginning of the preceding section we noted that a sentence, the smallest normal human language message, always consists of a set of meaningful elements in a meaningful structure. We now need to ask: What are these meaningful structures like? In our present state of knowledge it is impossible to give a definitive answer to this question. But we can at least make some speculative suggestions. In doing so, we must make clear both the immense freedom which English, or any other language, grants us in the choice of some meaningful elements; and, at the same time, the strict bondage which it places upon us in the choice of other meaningful elements.

Consider such simple sentences as "The dog bites the man," "The dogs were biting the man," "The men had been bitten by the dogs," etc. One way of diagramming the meaningful elements of these sentences and the meaningful structures in which they occur is as follows:

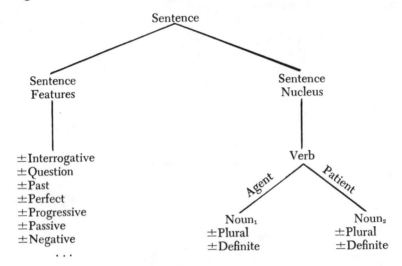

English grants us immense freedom in our choices for the items noted here as Verb, Noun₁, and Noun₂. Let us assume that for the item Verb we choose the meaningful element "bite," for Noun₁ the meaningful element "dog," and for Noun₂ the meaningful element "man." How should we now describe the meaningful relations among these three meaningful elements? Let us say that the relation of "dog" to "bite" is that of *agent*, the performer of the action of the verb; and that the relation of "man" to "bite" is that of *patient*, the undergoer of the action of the verb.

Having chosen "dog" for Noun₁ and "man" for Noun₂, English now *forces* us to add to each of them the *word feature* ±Plural, in either its plus or minus value. If we choose the value +Plural, the eventual results will be "dogs" and "men." Here English uses special signals to mark the value +Plural, namely the "−s" of "dogs" and the vowel change of "men" (changed from "man"). If on the other hand we choose the value −Plural, the eventual results will be "dog" and "man." Here English does not use any special signals to mark the value −Plural; this value is eventually signaled simply by the *absence* of any signal for its opposite, namely +Plural. This is a very economical symbolic device: instead of two signals, one for −Plural, one for +Plural, we need only one signal, for +Plural. Note, however, that this very economical device is possible only because the presence of ±Plural is *compulsory*. Only because English *forces* us to make every noun either +Plural or −Plural can we know that the absence of any signal for +Plural signals the value −Plural.

The word feature ±Definite behaves rather differently. First, in certain special styles (newspaper headlines, aphorisms) it can be omitted altogether: "Dog bites man," "Boy meets girl." In other styles, however, it is compulsory; and the signals for its plus and minus values then depend in part on the choice of −Plural vs. +Plural, as indicated in the following diagram:

	−Plural	+Plural
−Definite	a dog	dogs
+Definite	the dog	the dogs

The value +Definite is always signaled by the definite article "the." The value −Definite is signaled, in the singular, by the indefinite article "a"; but in the plural simply by the *absence* of the signal for its opposite, namely +Definite.

Having chosen a sentence nucleus of this type (Verb "bite" accompanied by Noun₁ "dog" as Agent, and Noun₂ "man" as Patient), we are now forced to include a number of *sentence features* (and the list of sentence features given here is surely incomplete). Choosing for ±Interrogative the value +Interrogative, we get "The dog bites the man?," with the interrogative intonation /↑/; and choosing the value −Interrogative, we get "The dog bites the man," with the affirmative intonation /↓/. Choosing the value +Question, we get "Does the dog bite the man?" which is usually also +Interrogative; choosing −Question, we get "The dog bites the man." Choosing +Perfect we get "The dog has bitten the man." Choosing +Progressive we get "The dog is biting the man." Choosing +Passive we get "The man is bitten by the dog." And choosing +Negative we get "The dog does not bite the man."

The fact that we can choose plus or minus values for these seven sentence features means that, with a single sentence nucleus of this type, we can produce 2^7 or 128 different sentences—all the way from "The dog bites the man," with minus values for all seven sentence features, to "Hadn't the man been being bitten by the dog?" with plus values for all seven sentence features. This design feature—the fact that any given sentence nucleus must be accompanied by various sentence features in plus or minus values—is another important source of the great productivity of language. Consider, for example, that, still using only 1000 verbs and 1000 nouns, our talkative lady can now say 128 billion sentences of this type. Talking time: 128 centuries.

In section 2 above, we used the term *phoneme* for those meaningless elements in language that are used to build symbols. What term should we now use for those meaningful elements that are used to build sentences—elements such as "bite," "dog," "man," word features, and sentence features? Curiously, there is among linguists no generally accepted term for such meaningful elements. Some linguists, however, use the term *sememe* (from Greek *sêma* "sign"). Using this term, we can now diagram the design of language as described thus far:

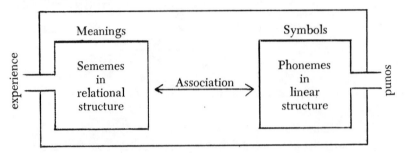

This diagram makes clear a very fundamental dilemma which faces us in trying to understand the design of language. Sememes, we assume, occur in *relational* structure. We make this assumption because it reflects the way we understand sentences. We understand a meaningful relation between "bite" and "dog," between "bite" and "man," between a noun and the word features ±Plural and ±Definite, and between a sentence nucleus and the various sentence features that accompany it. On the other hand, we assume that phonemes occur in *linear* structure. We make this assumption because it reflects the way we say and hear sentences. In the world outside of language, every spoken sentence is a linear stream of sound, running through the dimension of time; we therefore assume that this linear stream of sound reflects a linear sequence of phonemes, or more exactly, a linear sequence of phonemes with linear overlays of stress and pitch. The dilemma that now faces us is this: what sort of device should we assume in order to convert a set of sememes in relational structure into a set of phonemes in linear structure?

In theory, at least, we might assume some mechanism which converts the relational structure of sememes *directly* into a corresponding linear structure of sememes. For the English sentence, "The dog bit the man," this might then give something like this: "bite" *−Interrogative −Question +Past; Agent* "dog" *−Plural +Definite; Patient* "man" *−Plural +Definite*. We might then agree that any feature with a minus value can at this stage be dropped; and that all other sememes are then converted into strings of phonemes, ready for transmission via conversion into audible sound.

In actual fact, every language seems first to interpose a somewhat different structure—a structure customarily called *syntax* (from Greek *sýntaxis* "composition, ordering, organization"). The most striking aspect of this syntactic structure is the fact that, for the sentence nucleus, it is typically *bipartite*—giving the familiar subject vs. predicate structure that we know from traditional grammar. We can show this in the following "tree structure diagram" for the syntax of the sentence "The dog bit the man":

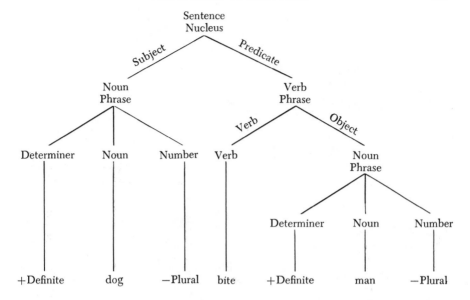

Here the noun phrase +*Definite* "dog" −*Plural* (later: "the dog") functions as the syntactic *subject* of the sentence nucleus; and the verb phrase "bite," +*Definite* "man" −*Plural* (later: "bite the man") functions as the syntactic *predicate* of the sentence nucleus.

In English, and many other languages, the requirement of this bipartite subject-predicate structure is so strict that, if there is no sememe available to function as subject, a *dummy element* must be introduced into the syntax. An example is such a sentence as "It rained." In terms of sememes (meaningful elements), this sentence consists only of the verb "rain" plus a set of sentence features. When this sentence is rearranged syntactically, however, the dummy subject "it" must be introduced; otherwise there would be no syntactic element to function as subject. As a result, we can no longer say that the syntactic structure consists of an arrangement of *sememes*—since a syntactic element like this "it," having no meaning, cannot be a sememe (a meaningful element). Linguists therefore customarily use another term for the elements arranged in syntactic structure: they call them *morphemes* (from Greek *morphē* "form"). The vast majority of morphemes represent sememes, but a few, like the "it" of "It rained," do not.

There are many other differences between the meaningful structure of sememes and, after conversion into syntax, the syntactic structure of morphemes. In the sentence, "The boy broke the window," the sememe "window" clearly bears to the sememe "break" the meaningful relation of *patient;* and it presumably bears this same relation also in the sentence, "The window broke." Syntactically, however, these two sentences are very different. In "The boy broke the window," the syntactic noun phrase, "the window," functions as the *object* of the verb phrase; whereas in "The window broke," it functions as the syntactic *subject* of the sentence nucleus.

Though the syntactic structure of morphemes is, in many respects, quite different from the meaningful structure of sememes, it is still not linear but *relational*. Linguists customarily try to express this relational structure visually by presenting syntax in terms of "tree structures," like that given above for the nucleus of the sentence, "The dog bit the man." The *nodes* and the ends of the *branches* of such trees indicate syntactic *categories:* sentence nucleus, noun phrase, verb phrase, noun, verb, determiner, number. The *branches* of such trees indicate the syntactic *functions* of these categories: the noun phrase of the sentence nucleus functions as its *subject;* the verb phrase of the sentence nucleus functions as its *predicate;* the verb of the verb phrase functions as its *verb* (since this is the only way verbs can function, no new term is needed); the noun phrase of the verb phrase functions as its *object;* etc.

We now again face the dilemma mentioned above: how should the *relational* structure of elements in syntax be converted into the *linear* structure of elements needed for the transmission of messages by way of sound, through the dimension of time? Linguistic theory assumes that this is accomplished, in each language, by its own particular set of *transformational rules*. In English, the above tree structure diagram of the sentence, "The dog bit the man," represents its syntactic *deep structure*. This is now converted by transformational rules into the proper syntactic *surface structure*, where morphemes occur in linear order (the symbol # indicates word boundaries):

+Definite # dog −Plural # bite +Past # +Definite # man −Plural

Phonological rules now convert this into a linear sequence of phonemes, interrupted by word boundaries:

/# ðə # dɔg # bit # ðə # mæn #/

This particular message, after the addition of stress and intonation, is now ready for transmission by way of sound.

If transformational and phonological rules are to operate successfully, the linear structure which they eventually produce must somehow contain signals for all of that aspect of language which we have labeled *meanings:* sememes in relational structure. In the sentence, "The dog bit the man," the meaningful elements "bite," "dog," "man" are obviously signaled by the phoneme sequences /bit/, /dog/, /mæn/; the two occurrences of +Definite are signaled by the phoneme sequence /ðə/; and the two occurrences of −Plural are signaled, negatively, by the absence of any signal for +Plural. The meaningful relations, *agent* and *patient*, later converted into the syntactic functions, *subject* and *object*, are signaled in quite a different way—by taking advantage of the fact that elements are now arranged in linear structure. In sentences with the linear surface structure order *noun phrase + verb + noun phrase,* putting a noun phrase *before* the verb signals, in English, the fact that it is functioning as the *subject;* and putting a noun phrase *after* the verb signals the fact that it is functioning as the *object.* Note, for example, the very different meanings of "The dog bit the man," and "The man bit the dog." As for the sentence features of this particular sentence, only two of them are signaled positively: —Interrogative is signaled by the final intonation /↓/, and +Past is signaled by the change of the phonemic shape of the verb from /bait/ "bite" to /bit/ "bit." The remaining sentence features (−Question, −Perfect, −Progressive, −Passive, −Negative) are signaled negatively, through the absence of any signals.

The above description of the nature of human language as a communication system can be summarized in the following diagram, which notes (1) the types of elements that occur in human language, and (2) the structural arrangements in which they occur:

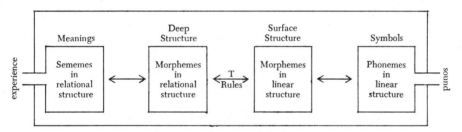

Let us return, in conclusion, to a statement we made earlier: that any communication system must be connected at two ends with the world outside the system. At one end, human language is connected with the world of human experience—all the things we talk about when we use language. At the other end, human language is connected with audible sound—the noises we make when we use language. These two external ends are our only points of entry when we try to study the nature of human language. We cannot observe directly what goes on between these external ends, within language itself. The best we can do is to note the correlation between experience and sound—and try, from this, to deduce something of the inner workings of this most enigmatic, ingenious, flexible, productive, and elegant of all human communication systems. Because we cannot observe language directly, we can know only a little about it. The above remarks are an attempt to convey some notion of the little we think we *do* know.

CHARLES FERGUSON

Language Problems of Variation and Repertoire

IN THE PAST DECADE we have had much evidence in all parts of the world of language problems, that is, of social problems in which language aspects are preeminent. Perennial problems, such as the use of Dutch vs. French in Belgium, have reached new levels of political divisiveness and bitterness. Problems long thought to have vanished or to be in the last stages of resolution have erupted anew, as with the sudden push for bilingual education in the United States and the resulting federal legislation and widespread experimentation. Language issues previously unmentioned in the presses of Europe and America have been major factors in destructive civil strife in Malaysia and Pakistan. Students of human language behavior, in spite of impressive advances in linguistic theory and the growth of professional institutions, are just beginning to acquire understanding and technical expertise to apply to these problems.

Most of the language problems which come to public attention represent differences in view as to which language or which variety of a particular language should be used on which occasions by which people. In such countries as Canada or Belgium where the use of two languages has had official sanction for a long time, the disputes seem to center on extensions or restrictions on the use of one language or the other in which its customary use on certain occasions or by certain people is questioned. Although the internal qualities of the language and its recognition or proposed status are the questions talked about, the underlying concerns almost never seem to be purely linguistic. Rather, they seem to grow out of socio-economic shifts such as those caused by population growth and migrations, or rapid industrialization, or new group identifications and political processes. With regard to the highly emotional issue of the existence and value of "Black English" which has become so prominent in American and Caribbean education problems, the forces which have brought the question to the surface are not purely linguistic but have to do with population movements and changing expectations. The explosive political issue in India, concerning the kind of writing system to be used in Punjabi-medium education, while tied to the facts of the linguistic structure of Punjabi, is more significantly related to the reli-

23

gious segmentation of the Punjabi-speaking community in India and Pakistan. What can linguistics or the other language sciences contribute to the understanding of these problems and of the historical processes which led to them? Traditional linguistics, despite all its vaunted precision and the explanatory power of its theories, seems at first sight to have little to say.

However, a promising possibility of help for analyzing and dealing with these problems lies in the increasing focus of sociolinguistic research on the phenomenon of *language variation* and the concept of *language repertoire*. These two terms themselves point to the new recognition of the complex, constantly shifting nature of human language behavior. There are strong traditions which encourage scholars and laymen alike to regard the language of an individual or a community as essentially uniform or at least to consider such uniformity desirable. How often scientists or philosophers, school teachers or workmen express the wish that words and ways of using them were clear, unambiguous, and stable. How confidently we ask simple questions like "How many languages does he speak?" or "How old is this language?" It is painful to realize that these are all false hopes and pseudoquestions since it is part of the very nature of language to be varied, and part of the nature of individuals and communities to command complex repertoires of language behavior.

Individual Repertoires

As soon as a child begins to speak he varies his mode of expression depending on the person he is talking to, the situation he is in, and the things he wants to say.[1] The different varieties of speech which he uses tend to be systematically patterned and, increasingly as he grows up, they conform to the patterns of variation apparent in the speech community around him.

A recent study of variation in three preschool children with normal language development has documented the interplay of individual and social patterns of variation. For example, all three children used whispering as a special mode of speech, but they differed in their use of it and in their individual patterns of development. Two of the children started to use whispering at about the same time that they started to talk and used it regularly at times when they were asked not to talk, when, for example, their parents were on the telephone. The third child did not begin whispering until he was four and a half and then he used it for telling secrets, a purpose for which the other two did not use it at all. Of the first two children, one also used whispering to mimic the third child, and the other used whispering to make requests of his parents, for a drink of water, say, when they were visiting someone. This child also tended to use whispering when talking to himself in a state of great concentration on a task, while the third child used a softened voice quality in this situation.

Even children with the most marginal verbal capacities develop varieties of speech which differ in pronunciation, grammar, selection of vocabulary, and associated nonverbal behavior. To take an extreme example, a five-year-old Mongoloid boy[2] who was studied recently was shown to have at least three distinct styles of speech. A typical victim of Down's Syndrome, the boy was extremely retarded in language development and many of his utterances were unintelligible even to his immediate family. Patient study by a linguistic analyst eventually showed that almost all of his speech was structured and meaningful. She was able to formulate the systematic deletions and distortions by which his own internalized grammar modified the English to which he was exposed. So far, so good; the child was behaving, though with considerable retardation, in the way we would expect any human child to behave. What is of interest here is that the child used one kind of pronunciation when he was trying to make himself understood to his mother and a considerably different pronunciation when he was "talking to himself." It is probably universal in human language to include different registers for ordinary conversation and for speech which is being produced carefully to clarify a previous utterance or to make certain a message is transmitted under adverse conditions. Certainly every individual and every speech community has patterned ways of speaking with extra clarity. What is impressive is that such differences of register begin so soon and are part of the repertoire even of seriously retarded children.

Children at very early ages may have complex repertoires of different registers, different dialects, or different languages which they use for different functions. As a child matures, typically his repertoire becomes more differentiated, although in the life history of an individual some varieties of speech may diminish in importance or disappear. At the risk of belaboring the obvious, let us look at the respective functions of two languages spoken by the child of an American anthropologist in Assam.[3]

The little boy was learning both Garo and English between the ages of sixteen months and three years. He became very fluent in both languages and spoke Garo with the local people and English with his parents and other native speakers of English. When the family left Assam, they spent about a month traveling across India. At first the boy tried to speak Garo with every Indian he met. Garo, however, is limited to about a quarter of a million people in Assam and is not known in the rest of India. By the end of the month, the boy had learned that his attempt was futile. The last time he ever used any substantial amount of Garo was on the plane leaving Bombay. In the words of his father:

He sat next to a Malayan youth who was racially of a generalized southern mongoloid type, so similar to many Garos that he could easily have passed for one. Stephen apparently took him for a Garo, recognizing the difference between him and the Indians that had failed to understand his language in the past weeks. A torrent of Garo tumbled forth as if all the pent-up speech of those weeks had been suddenly let loose. I was never again able to persuade him to use more than a sentence or two at a time. For a couple of months he would respond to Garo when I spoke to him, but he refused to use more than an occasional word. After this, he began failing to understand my speech, though it was frequently difficult to know just how much was really lack of understanding and how much was deliberate refusal to cooperate. Certainly at times he would inadvertently give some sign that he understood more than he meant to, but increasingly he seemed genuinely not to understand, and within six months of our departure, he was even having trouble with the simplest Garo words, such as those for the body parts, which he had known so intimately.

This boy had two very different languages in his repertoire, strongly specialized as to function, and when one set of functions disappeared, the language appropriate to them soon became inaccessible to him.

— important

Community Repertoires

Just as every individual has a repertoire of language varieties, so every society or social group has a language repertoire shared by its members, although individuals or subgroups will differ in the extent to which they control and make use of the entire repertoire. To take a familiar example, any American university community shares a set of norms and expectations about the structure and use of each of the varieties of English available to it for communicative interaction. The kind of English used by coaches in talking to players differs systematically from the kinds of English used in public lectures, dormitory rap sessions, and advanced seminars. Differences between freshmen and seniors, males and females, philosophy majors and chemical engineers in the way they use vocabulary, forms of address and the like are easy to document.

Studies carried out by a freshman seminar on *Language and Society* at Stanford have produced evidence, for example, that male seniors use less obscenity than male freshmen, but female seniors use more than female freshmen; nicknames referring to physical characteristics are common in addressing males, rare in addressing females; and majors from different departments differ in the forms they use to address and refer to faculty. Some of these differences represent fairly well-defined varieties or registers of English, while others differentiate within or cut across varieties.

University communities in other parts of the world may have greater language differences than are evident in monolingual American universities, but the principles of variation are essentially the same. In an Arab university the difference between the kind of Arabic used in a public lecture and that used in ordinary informal conversation among students is far greater than the corresponding difference in an American university, but the fact of difference is the same and in both places the shock of hearing an inappropriate speech variety in any given context is apparent. In an Ethiopian university, class lectures are almost entirely in English; informal conversation is predominantly in Amharic; and a number of other languages are used by special subgroups. Again, however, the principles of variation and repertoire are the same.

The level of societal organization which is the focus of most discussion of social, political, and economic problems is the nation, and the language problems which come to our attention are generally seen at the national level as well. Accordingly, it is useful to examine the kinds of variation and the differences in repertoire which are evident among nations.

A pair of examples which illustrate national differences in language situation are Jamaica[4] and Paraguay.[5] Each has a population of about 2,000,000 people and a very low percentage of secondary school graduates. Jamaica belongs to the English-speaking nations of the world, Paraguay to the Spanish-speaking ones, and this difference has something to do with the nature of the language problems in each although it is probably much less important than their intrinsic differences in language repertoire and pattern of variation. In Jamaica, the language used in all publication, except for some poetry and folk song, is recognizably the same as the Standard written English used throughout the British Commonwealth; and the mother tongue of all Jamaicans, no matter how far removed it may be in some instances, is recognizably sufficiently similar in vocabulary and grammar to be called English, or at least English-based.

In Paraguay, all formal publication, again except for some poetry and folk literature, is in a variety of Standard South American Spanish, essentially identical with that used in other countries. The mother tongue of most Paraguayans, however, is an Indian language, Guarani, which is radically different from Spanish in sounds, grammar and vocabulary, and the increasing influence of Spanish on its vocabulary and forms of expression does not change this essential difference.

Jamaican English varies greatly in details of pronunciation, grammar and vocabulary depending on the social status of the speakers and the social context in which the communication is taking place. Even on the university campus the range of variation seems greater than on an American campus, and in ordinary conversations around the island varieties of English can be heard which are not readily intelligible to English speakers from other parts of the world. Jamaica as a whole is called a *post-Creole* speech community because a *Creole* English is in the process of merging with the Standard. David DeCamp, one of the sociolinguists working in the Jamaican community, has asserted that there is a linguistic continuum on the island ranging from "bush talk" to Standard English, within which each Jamaican commands a span of varieties.

In Paraguay there cannot be a continuum in the same sense. Perhaps 40 percent of the population are bilingual in Spanish and Guarani, and for these speakers the functional allocation of Spanish and Guarani tends to be in the pattern of *diglossia:*[6] Spanish is used in writing and a number of other formal educational and urban contexts, while Guarani is used informally and in home and intimate contexts. Although both Spanish and Guarani have different registers neither one has the full range of varieties which the language of a fully monolingual nation would have. Switching between Spanish and Guarani in conversation—the use, that is, of elements from one language in the other—plays a similar role to that played by English variations in Jamaica. There remain, however, fundamental differences in the repertoires of the two countries: not only does Paraguay use two discrete languages while Jamaica uses one broad continuum, but in the Paraguay population there are monolingual speakers both of Spanish and of Guarani.

Patterns of Variation

Some societal patterns of language structure and use recur, at least in their major features, in many parts of the world and at different times. For example, the diglossic pattern of Spanish and Guarani in Paraguay can be documented for many times and places, often in the typical *classical* form in which the high and low varieties are similar enough in structure to be called the same language. The pattern is evident, for example, in the use of classical and colloquial Arabic for different functions in Arab countries, of literary and spoken Tamil in Southern India and other Tamil-speaking countries, of French and Creole in Haiti, of Standard German and Swiss dialect in Germanic Switzerland, and of Latin and the incipient Romance languages in the eighth to tenth centuries.

Even within well-known and widespread patterns, such as standard language with dialects, post-Creole continuum, or diglossia, it is astonishing how the twists of history can produce fascinating, unique configurations of language repertoires. For example, in sub-Saharan Africa, along with the many multilingual nations, there are a handful of basically monolingual countries—including Madagascar, Somalia, and Lesotho—whose inhabitants share a common mother tongue. Yet each of these has a unique pattern. In Somalia,[7] to take a single case, everyone speaks Somali, but the language most widely used for formal purposes, including writing, is Arabic. There is no doubt that Somalis are strongly attached to the beauty of their language. The role of traditional oral poetry is very great; in the changing socio-political scene in Somalia today the citified radio broadcasters even utilize the reactions and new coinages of nomadic poets to develop the terminology needed for new concepts of modernization and national development. Yet with all this love of their language and all these resources of linguistic creativity in the Somali speech community, the general consensus remains that Arabic is the appropriate language for education, government, and publication, while English and Italian are used as connecting links with western technology and the non-Arabic-speaking world. The functional allocation of Arabic in Somalia has no full counterpart in the other monolingual nations of sub-Saharan Africa although partial analogues are found in several other Muslim countries.

Again, a number of countries in the world have two official languages side by side (Belgium, Finland, Canada, Cameroun, South Africa) and thus share many sociolinguistic features; yet each is unique in the demography of its language use and in its citizens' attitudes toward language. For example, Finland is officially bilingual: its capital is called both Helsinki and Helsingfors, and its second city Turku and Åbo. Less than 10 percent of the people of Finland have Swedish as their mother tongue, but all speakers of Finnish study Swedish in school, and vice versa. Thus every citizen of Finland has in his repertoire both a mother tongue and the "other language," and, in addition, whatever languages his education may prescribe for contact with the rest of the world. The attitudes of the two speech communities in Finland and the attitudes of Swedish and Finnish speakers in other countries constitute a complex picture compounded of pride, suspicion, tolerance, ethnic and national identification, and varying notions of language cultivation.

If we acknowledge that every speech community has variation within it and that very different kinds of individual, social and national repertoires exist, in what sense can we speak of "problems of variation and repertoire"? As we said in the beginning, problems arise from differences in people's views as to which language or variety *should* be used on which occasions by which people. The problems arise not from the complexity and variety of patterns of language structure and use themselves, but from changes in those patterns and from people's expectations and commitments about potential changes. A West African accustomed from early childhood to the use of several different languages in different social settings, such as the market place, religious ceremonies, conversation with neighbors, and visits to relatives, will not see his repertoire as a problem until national goals of mass literacy, extensive political participation, technological education, or a nationally deployable civil service, begin to affect him.

Changes in Repertoire

Most of the changes we can see taking place in the distribution of language varieties are occurring without explicit recognition of the goals and problems involved. Some changes can be understood readily as soon as a framework of problems and responses is supplied; others remain mysterious and are intriguing challenges for the student of human language behavior. Two small examples will be suggestive.

Most of the Chinese living on Taiwan are speakers of Amoy Chinese, although, of course, Mandarin is the only official language of government and education, and there are a few hundred thousand speakers of aboriginal languages unrelated to Chinese. Since Amoy and Mandarin Chinese are not mutually intelligible, speakers of the Amoy mother tongue must learn varie-

ties of Mandarin Chinese to serve various important functions in their daily
communication. Amoy Chinese is not written as such, but there is a tradition
of writing texts in Mandarin Chinese, classical or modern, and then reading
them aloud in Amoy pronunciation. Differences in word order, idiom, and so
on make for difficulties but Mandarin and Amoy are sufficiently close in semantics and syntax that these texts pronounced in Amoy are intelligible to
Amoy listeners. As might be expected with such a specialized use of the
language, the variety of Amoy used in reading aloud is a special register,
characterized by its own features of pronunciation and vocabulary which
go back centuries and do not occur in spoken Amoy. So far, so good; just
another example of special registers. Nowadays, however, if the young
Amoy speaker wants to read a text aloud in this style to his grandparents,
he often finds he does not know the right pronunciation or the right word;
in short, the control of this register is declining in the community even
though it is still heard on the radio and in various other appropriate settings.
The explanation for this change in repertoire is not hard to find: the new
generation is attending school and learning to speak Mandarin itself and
to consider it the normal language for reading a written text aloud. Thus
the grandparents' register of oral literary Amoy is being replaced in their
grandchildren by the use of Mandarin, the second language corresponding
to a set of registers in the earlier "monolingual" Amoy speech community.

In the early days of radio broadcasting in America, radio announcers spoke
with a variety of accents representing their regional and social origins. For example, some announcers pronounced their *r*'s after vowels: "car," "guard";
others did not: "cah," "gahd."[8] As national networks became increasingly important, almost all announcers came to pronounce their *r*'s. This development
of network English pronunciation took place without any strong official
backing from government or educational systems and largely without public
awareness. William Labov has shown that the pronunciation of the postvocalic *r* is a sensitive indicator of regional provenience, socio-economic
status, and degree of formality in speaking, and that the change in network
pronunciation is but one instance of a set of broad shifts in American pronunciation which are altering individual and community repertoires in many
parts of the country. This particular part of the shift is probably related to
broad trends toward homogenization and standardization in some aspects
of American life.

The disappearance of the spoken literary Amoy register and the spread of
network English are both examples of language standardization, of an overriding norm replacing partly or completely regional, social or registral variations in language. Indeed, the reduction in linguistic diversification is a recog-
nizable trend in many parts of the world today. Regional dialects decline in
range of use, and in multilingual countries national languages spread at the
expense of local languages. Thus regional dialect variation in German has

apparently been diminishing rapidly, and Amharic is spreading throughout Ethiopia at the expense of other languages.

As we might expect from our earlier discussion of individual and community repertoires, however, there are also trends toward increased linguistic diversity. Languages are used for new purposes and variant forms achieve greater recognition. For example, regional and colonial accents are increasingly welcome on the BBC, and Norway now has two standard languages where several decades ago it had one. Trends toward standardization in language, like other aspects of modern socio-cultural systems, are matched by increasing differentiation as technology advances and economies become more complex. Shifts in individual and community repertoires signal social change and often serve as rallying points for groups suffering social tensions and conflict.

An examination of the processes at work in changes of language structure and use is doubtless fundamental to the linguist's understanding of human language behavior and its underlying principles, but their social dimensions have kept the linguist from studying them with his traditional tools. The growing emphasis in sociolinguistic research[9] on variation and repertoire has great ultimate promise for general theories of human language, but the progress is very slow. In the meantime, social problems in which language is a salient aspect seem to be intensifying. Let us hope that the problems will stimulate the research and that ways will be found of applying theoretical advances to the solution of some of the problems.

REFERENCES

1. T. Weeks, "Speech Registers in Young Children," *Child Development*, XLII (1971), 119-131.

2. A. Bodine, "A Phonological Analysis of the Speech of Two Mongoloid (Down's Syndrome) Children," Ph.D. dissertation (Ithaca, New York: Cornell University, 1971).

3. R. Burling, "Language Development of a Garo and English-Speaking Child," *Word*, XV (1959), 45-68.

4. D. DeCamp, "Toward a Generative Analysis of a Post-Creole Speech Continuum," *Pidginization and Creolization of Languages*, ed. Dell Hymes (Cambridge: Cambridge University Press, 1971).

5. J. Rubin, *National Bilingualism in Paraguay* (The Hague: Mouton, 1968).

6. C. Ferguson, "Diglossia," *Word*, XV (1959), 325-340.

7. B. W. Andrzejewski, "The Role of Broadcasting in the Adaptation of the Somali Language to Modern Needs," *Language Use and Social Change*, ed. W. Whitely (Oxford: Oxford University Press, 1971).

8. W. Labov, "Phonological correlates of Social Stratification," *Ethnography of Communication*, eds. J. Gumperz and D. Hymes (Washington, D.C.: American Anthropological Association, 1964).

9. A convenient introduction to current sociolinguistic research is the Penguin reader, ed., P. P. Giglioli, *Language and Social Context* (Middlesex, England: Penguin, 1972).

EINAR HAUGEN

The Curse of Babel

THERE IS, in Genesis, an intriguing tale about the origin of language diversity, well known as the "Tower of Babel" story, which will serve me as the text of my discourse. We are told, in the King James Version, that "the whole earth was of one language, and of one speech." But then pride fills the hearts of men, so that they are misled into trying to build "a city and a tower, whose top may reach unto heaven." The Lord Jehovah comes down to earth and decides to punish this presumption, perhaps worried that men might usurp His omnipotence, for "now nothing will be restrained from them, which they have imagined to do." In His infinite wisdom He proceeds to "confound their language, that they may not understand one another's speech." They are no longer able to cooperate in the building of their tower, and are "scattered abroad upon the face of all the earth."

Similar stories are known from other cultures, but among the Hebrews the story was associated with the name of Babylon, which, by a false etymology, was understood to derive from a verb *bālal* meaning "to confuse."[1] Babylon, as the capital of the Babylonian and Assyrian empires, was a big and sinful city in the eyes of the rural and severely religious Hebrews. The story not only explained why the towers of Babylon had crumbled, but more important, it answered the question thoughtful men and women must have asked everywhere: why is it that all men have languages, but all so different? In the multilingual Near East the natural answer was: the diversity was a curse laid upon men for their sinful pride.

Those of us who love languages and have devoted our lives to learning and teaching them, and who find in language a source of novel delights and subtle experience, find it hard to put ourselves in the right frame of mind to understand the conception of language diversity as a curse. Yet we need only find ourselves in a country, say Hungary, where every sign looks like an abracadabra, and speakers shrug their shoulders at our efforts to communicate, to sense some of the terror of isolation that underlies the Hebrew view. As linguists, however, we are entitled to offer one basic correction to the Hebrew tale: men were not scattered abroad because they could not understand one another's speech. They could not understand one another *because they were*

33

scattered; in the story cause and effect have been turned around. When men are separated by barriers of time and distance, their languages deviate in regular, if sometimes astonishing, ways.

The reason for this is clear: language is man's most distinctive and significant type of social behavior, and is, like all social behavior, learned anew by every child. The child not only can, he *must* learn whatever language is spoken around him. In learning it, however, he never learns it exactly like those from whom he heard it. His "creative imitation" (as we may call it) is not identical with its model, since it is not turned out in a factory, but is a piece of human craftsmanship. The gift of language is certainly innate and instinctive, but human speech differs from the music of birds precisely by being diverse and relatively idiosyncratic. What keeps it from being totally idiosyncratic is that each act of communication forces the communicators to monitor their expression by the response of those they are trying to reach. When one group ceases to communicate with another, the groups drift apart and develop their idiosyncrasies, which linguists call idiolects, and as these accumulate, they grow into dialects, and languages, and language families.

The historical and social parallel between linguistic and biological inheritance has often obscured the fundamental difference between them. Races and languages have been confounded to the detriment of both, leading to a type of linguistic racism which is the true curse of Babel. Linguists know better, but they are not without fault in having developed a terminology that speaks of "language families" and "mother tongues," the "generation of dialects" and the "descent of words." These are all metaphors that can be drastically misleading, for there is nothing at all in language that is identical with biological descent. *There are no genes in language,* aside from the universal human gift of tongues. When linguists say that English is "descended" from Germanic and Germanic from Indo-European, they are only saying that there has been an unbroken transmission of speech habits all the way back to that tribe of conquerors who issued from the Caucasus or wherever, some five or six thousand years ago, and succeeded in imposing their language on most of Europe, on much of western Asia, and eventually on America, Australia, and other parts of the world. At every step of the way there were children who learned the language of their elders in their own way, and there were adults who learned and unlearned their languages to meet the demands put upon them by social and political necessity. There are no genes; there is only learning .

That *learning* is the key to every language problem is so obvious as to be almost a truism. Its implications are being worked out in research that is reported on in this volume. But there is one condition of learning that I have observed over and over in various societies, without having heard of research upon it. This is the cross-fire of mutual criticism and correction within a close-knit social group. As children we have all felt the taunts that were directed at us when we deviated from the valid norms of speech. Children are cruel in applying laughter and ridicule to those who speak "differently." As they grow older, they become aware that linguistic deviation is an index to social distance. As adolescents they discover the difference between upper and lower class, the significance of belonging on this side or the other side of the tracks, and the speech mannerisms of the current peer-group hero as opposed to those of their obsolescing parents. As adults they have internalized these norms to the point that they register automatically, not that somebody's language is deviant, but that a speaker is "vulgar," or "stuck-up," or "foreign," and behave toward him according to these identifications. Wherever such identifications lead to antagonism or prejudice, to the exclusion of outsiders, or to the denigration of individuals, there I would find an example of the curse of Babel.

The gradual drifting apart of languages and dialects is a natural and inevitable consequence of the drifting apart of mankind. The Hebrew legend was surely right in assuming that all men were once of "one language and of one speech"; I cannot find any other hypothesis adequate to account for the basic similarities of all known natural languages. Insofar as mankind is *one* and language is man's chief distinction from the animals, polygenesis of language is hard to imagine. The further back we go in the known history of languages in the last four thousand years, the less difference we find among them. If we cannot yet find the ultimate point at which the so-called "families" or proto-languages diverged, this is presumably due to the enormous length of time that has passed. In this sense the tower of Babel is a profound symbol for man's ultimate unity and for his common descent as a talking animal. The tower is the hypothetical point at which all the converging threads of today's and yesterday's languages meet, one which we can probably never know, and which is therefore best expressed in symbolic terms.

In their efforts to remove God's curse, men have resorted to various policies, ranging from neighborly tolerance to rigid isolation, from eager acceptance of a new language to brutal suppression of its speakers. Out of this crucible of language contact has come a class of speakers who can manage more than one language, the multilinguals or polyglots. To simplify our expression we shall call them all "bilinguals" and define them as "users of more than one language." To use a language does not necessarily entail mastering all its skills or its entire range: often it is enough, for example, to understand it when spoken, or to read it when written. Even the students in our language classes are bilinguals after a fashion, though one is tempted to call most of them semilingual.

There is a vigorous flurry of interest these days in bilinguals and bilingualism in our country. Some of us would say: about time! This country has had bilingual problems since its inception and has always taken it for granted that with time they would go away. The present interest is triggered by many factors: militancy among the blacks, sensitivity to minority problems, and faith in the power of education to overcome internal discord. Linguists, sociologists, and educators have been mobilized to implement the congressional Bilingualism Act of 1968, which recognizes for the first time in American history that "the use of a child's mother tongue can have a beneficial effect upon his education." Black English and Chicano Spanish have emerged as valid and highly productive subjects of study by linguists. Ethnic groups are being urged to maintain their identity by teaching their native tongue to their children. Bilingual schools have been established in a number of communities where large blocs of non-English speakers live. Some degree of training in the native languages of these speakers has been introduced into the early grades in the hope of reducing the children's sense of alienation in an English-speaking world. To be sure, its goals go no further than to produce what is called "transitional bilingualism," a step on the way to integration into the English-speaking world. And it is hardly less discriminatory than earlier policies, since it does not provide for advanced training in these languages and does not give their communities any hope of continuing to exist as ethnic identities within our country. Above all, it is primarily designed as poor relief: the schools are set up in communities where the income averages at or below $3,000. There is no change in the official policy of "Anglo-Conformity," only a passing toleration of "linguistic pluralism." Nevertheless, even this is a great step forward and should be encouraged.

We are hardly unique in the world in having such problems. What is unique is that in our time a great many populations which speak minority languages are refusing to accept the status of second-class citizens in the countries they inhabit. Such a refusal could not arise as long as most peoples were locally bound as hewers of wood and drawers of water. We rarely hear of language problems arising in the Middle Ages or in the Czarist Empire; only when governments instituted universal school systems, which in Europe was in the eighteenth century, did language become an explosive issue. The schools brought into age-old local communities a force for linguistically homogenizing the population; they were a kind of mold imposed on the people by a previously tolerant or indifferent government. The school became an instrument for "mobilizing" the population, in Karl Deutsch's happy phrase,[2] so that it could participate in national life, opening opportunities and imposing responsibilities that had never before been imagined. But this mobilization also had the effect of plugging the entire population into a network of communication that was expected to function fast and efficiently, which it could not do unless one language rather than many was spoken. Translation is slow and costly, and interference between codes results in loss of information; the obvious solution was to insist on one government, one language.

To illustrate the resulting problems and to offer a parallel with our own situation let me take you with me to a remote corner of Sweden, the province of Norrbotten, at the top of the Gulf of Bothnia. Sweden, like the other

Scandinavian countries, is often viewed as a highly homogeneous society with a successful social policy that insures equality and prosperity for all. When Sweden has been touted to Americans as a model of the "middle way" between capitalism and communism, one deprecatory reply has been that, after all, Sweden is a small and homogeneous country, and has no problems of the magnitude of those facing America.

Norrbotten is a province a little bigger than Maine, with a population a little less than Alaska's and at the same latitude. It is located squarely on the Arctic Circle, a good 500 miles north of Stockholm, the capital. It is separated from Norway on the west by high barren mountains, from Finland on the east only by the Torne River. From sea to mountain there is virtually nothing but forest and tundra, with some agricultural valleys as one approaches the sea, and a few coastal towns, the largest being Luleå with 32,000 inhabitants. Inland is Sweden's most important mining town, Kiruna, the heart of her steel industry. In this remote district there exist within a population of a quarter of a million people no less than three kinds of bilingual problems. Each of these has called forth some of the same passions and concerns that such situations arouse elsewhere in the world. Each of them has also produced doctoral dissertations, on which I build the following account.

First are the Lapps. They speak dialects of the language used by Lapps in various parts of northern Sweden, Finland, Russia, and Norway. Lappish is a Finno-Ugric language, related to but mutually incomprehensible with Finnish. The Lapps constitute a very small proportion of the population of Norrbotten, possibly only 1.5 percent or something over 3,000 persons, a third of all the Lapps in Sweden. They are the aboriginal inhabitants, not only of this region, but of much of northern Norway and Sweden and all of Finland. They were a nomadic people of hunters and fishermen, who step by step were forced back from the more desirable lands, until they were left with territory that proved to be suitable only for reindeer herding. Even this occupation, traditional since the sixteenth century, is threatened today, and many Lapps have abandoned their native heath for occupations in urban centers and more southerly climes. As late as 1913 a nomad school system was devised by Sweden, in which the children were taught Swedish, with Lappish used chiefly for religious training. By now many have drifted off into urban areas and have slowly been climbing the ladder of Swedish life, a few succeeding to the extent of going to a university. The jobs most of them have found, however, have been service positions as kitchen maids, shop assistants, office clerks, nurses, or teachers; as railway workers, unskilled laborers, miners, or builder's workmen. The Lapps were dominated, gradually pushed northwards, and even partially assimilated by the Finns, who were their superiors, being cattle breeders and culturally dominant. They had not been fully Christianized until the eighteenth century, but in the second half of the nineteenth century many of them were the more thoroughly converted by a lay religious movement known as Laestadianism, which is ecstatic and primitive in its expression. Finnish became the language of this Christian revival, a sacred language with which most Lapps were familiar even if they did not speak it. In addition, although Finnish was not their own language, they felt at home with it because it was related.

We are told by Dr. Hansegård, a Swedish scholar with a Lappish wife, that

some of the Lapps are proud of their Lappish descent, others are ashamed of it and try to conceal it. Some of them value their Lappish mother tongue highly, others would care little or nothing if it should disappear—and there are many attitudes in between. . . . Some Lapps are firmly convinced of the superiority of Swedish in comparison with Lappish (and Finnish) as a means of communication, as a cultural instrument and as a social symbol.[3]

Lapps who have found nonagricultural occupations have taken over "maners, customs, views, opinions, values or other cultural elements from the Swedes."[4] Their Lappish language shows a growing number of Swedish loanwords, and even among themselves they switch from one language to the other, often without pause in the middle of a sentence. Fifty or sixty years ago Swedish was represented in the area only by a few civil servants, including clergymen and teachers, but today there has been a large influx of Swedes from other parts of the country. The residents are impressed on every hand by the usefulness of Swedish and the uselessness of their native tongue. "Some parents speak Swedish on purpose to their children, but often the fact that Swedish has become the language of the children seems to be due to the fact that Swedish is the language spoken by their playmates."[5]

While the Lapps mostly live in the backwoods and mountain areas, the Finns of Norrbotten occupy one large agricultural area, the west bank of the Torne River. When Finland was separated from Sweden in 1809 after the Russian defeat of the Swedish armies, the border was arbitrarily drawn at the Torne River, without regard to the fact that several thousand speakers of Finnish lived on the west bank of the river. Today it is estimated that 40,000 speakers of Finnish live there, in partial isolation from their kinsmen across the border on the other side of the river. Before the separation, the two areas were one continuous community, speaking the same dialect of Finnish and sharing all cultural conventions. Today, more than a century and a half later, there are marked differences. The Swedish community is more prosperous, more urbanized, and more modern. Their Finnish is a daily language, used for home purposes and out of touch with that of Finland, since they do not learn to read or write modern Finnish in their schools. In school they learn only Swedish, a situation that has existed since schools were instituted in the nineteenth century. The Swedish government feared that Finland's Russian masters would demand that it hand over the incredibly rich ore fields of Norrbotten on the plea that the inhabitants were Finnish. So they proceeded to enforce Swedish as the language of school and government, completing the process by 1920, and not until 1970 has it once again become possible to study Finnish as a subject in the lower grades. In 1945, 72 percent of the school beginners spoke only Finnish; twenty years later this was reduced to 14 percent. The proportion of bilinguals has grown from 21 percent to 57 percent, while the number of monolingual Swedes has multiplied from 7 percent to 29 percent.

The trend is unmistakable. A study by a Finnish research team[6] found that in spite of the obvious value of knowing both languages, there was marked discrimination against those who did. Only 22 percent of the Finnish-speaking children went on beyond grade school, compared to 46 percent of those who came from Swedish-speaking homes. The positions of social importance, the decision-making jobs, are nearly all in the hands of Swedish speakers. Bilingual Finnish speakers tend to be limited to agriculture and manual occupations. They feel themselves to be inadequate both in Finnish and in Swedish. In other parts of Sweden they claim to have suffered discrimination, and some have returned home rather than expose themselves by their inadequacy in Swedish. One interviewee complained that only by learning her Swedish lessons by rote could she manage to get through school. A few insisted that they were discriminated against and that Finns from the Torne valley were met with scorn and contempt. When speaking Finnish, they constantly borrowed Swedish words to fill gaps in vocabulary left by their lack of constant contact with modern Finnish life. Hansegård, who was a high school teacher in Kiruna for ten years, emphasizes that, even so, Finnish is the mother tongue of 70 percent of the population, and he insists that every consideration of minority rights calls for a new Swedish policy here.[7] He asks for the introduction of Finnish into the lower schools, not merely as a subject but also as a medium for at least some subjects, and that pupils be given the opportunity to continue studying it up to the point where they can make it a useful instrument for culture and contact. The Finns in Norrbotten are actually in a worse position culturally than the Lapps, for whom at least a degree of paternalistic interest has been shown.

From this account one would judge that at least the Swedes of Norrbotten should be at the top of the heap and happy with their linguistic lot. But in fact the language spoken by the old established Swedish population in the area is a dialect so remote from the standard Swedish which is taught at school that at first blush other Swedes are quite baffled. The indigenous population has for centuries been so isolated from the main body of modern, bourgeois, increasingly urbanized Sweden that they have developed a Swedish dialect that is virtually a language of its own.

The author of a dissertation on the language problem of Swedish school children, Tore Österberg, was himself a teacher in the community for many years. Here are some of the episodes he describes. A teacher in the seventh grade who was teaching a famous poem written in another Swedish dialect, made reference to the dialect spoken by her own pupils. The pupils "began tittering, crouched together on the benches, waved their arms defensively, and one or two made themselves comic. The class reaction, however, gradually became dumb, crushed and repressed. The pupils—especially the girls—blushed, stammered, and—what was worse—in many cases retreated into silence."[8] A ten-year-old boy who was asked to write an essay could not remember an essential word in standard Swedish and was too bashful to ask, so instead he wrote nothing at all. Österberg reports that school beginners are tense and stiff in their self-expression and bring to their work a fear instilled by their parents which makes them conceal their dialect as well as their descent from dialect speakers. Österberg performed the experiment of giving beginners reading materials written in their own dialect alongside materials in Standard Swedish. For four weeks they got intense instruction in the dialect, and for the rest of the year a gradual transition was made to Standard Swedish. He found, at the end of the year, that the experimental group could read better and assimilate more than the control group. He contends that consistent teaching along these lines would reduce the tension in the community between dialect and Standard Swedish and ease the transition from one to the other for those whose lives will be led outside the community.

In this microcosm of Norrbotten, I see remarkable parallels to our own language problems. The *Lapps*, like our Indians, are a people driven back from their original territory by invaders, and they have been assigned to areas so infertile that the invaders do not usually molest them. They have developed occupations so strenuous or so unprofitable that they are not threatened by entrepreneurs. The *Finns*, like our Spanish speakers in the Southwest, are an established population who found themselves on the wrong side of a border and are being gradually de-ethnicized, but meanwhile are playing the role of proletariat in their new nation. The *Swedish dialect* speakers are like our West Virginia mountaineers or our ghetto blacks, who are being forced into urban areas where they find themselves discriminated against unless they change their speech. It is a layer cake with Standard Swedish on top over successive layers of rejected minorities: dialect speakers, Finns, and Lapps.

Language is not a problem unless it is used as a basis for discrimination, but it has in fact been so used as far back as we have records. The trend in Sweden as in the United States is clearly toward a language shift on the part of the minorities as they are more fully integrated into the national life. But this is a process that promotes cultural dislocation and social rootlessness, that deprives the minorities not only of their group identity, but even of their human dignity. Because their language is not considered valid in the larger society, they are made to feel that they are not personally adequate.

There are several ways one can look at these situations. One can take the cold-blooded, even cynical point of view that such differences in language stand in the way of progress and should be eliminated by a firm and ruthless policy of assimilation: it impedes the efficiency of the national machine to have a multitude of codes which interfere with one another and slow up the process of organizing the people into a homogeneous work force. At the opposite extreme, one can wish to preserve forever such enclaves in the name of ethnic variety and the sacredness of mother tongues; local and even national romanticism has played on these chords for going on two centuries, with the result that many languages have come into being which might perhaps just as well have died.

And yet, who are we to call for linguistic genocide in the name of efficiency? Let us recall that although a language is a tool and an instrument of communication, that is not all it is. A language is also a part of one's personality, a form of behavior that has its roots in our earliest experience. Whether it is a so-called rural or ghetto dialect, or a peasant language, or a "primitive" idiom, it fulfills exactly the same needs and performs the same services in the daily lives of its speakers as does the most advanced language of culture. Every language, dialect, patois, or lingo is a structurally complete framework into which can be poured any subtlety of emotion or thought that its users are capable of experiencing. Whatever it lacks at any given time or place in the way of vocabulary and syntax can be supplied in very short order by borrowing and imitation from other languages. Any scorn for the language of others is scorn for those who use it, and as such is a form of social discrimination.

What are the solutions? The economic disadvantages of having more than one language in a country or in the world are so patent as to make an almost irresistible argument for homogenization to be used by administrators who are congenitally and professionally hostile to language minorities. Such people argue for (1) assimilation by force; (2) assimilation by precept; (3) assimilation by teaching. In any case, assimilation. Groups that refuse to assimilate must either be (1) repatriated or (2) segregated. Repatriation can be brutal and may be impossible. Segregation is contrary to the spirit of an open society. Yet it is the policy practiced by most religious communities and the ultimate justification for the existence of nations. Within a nation it is enforced by geographical separation, by economic necessity, by class differences, and by caste distinctions. There are two humanistic solutions which suggest themselves immediately to men of good will: (1) deliberately to inculcate and to promote by means of education a spirit in the general population of interest and understanding of minority peoples, and (2) to make sure that people who speak differently understand and are understood, if necessary by making them bilingual.

In principle this is the policy that Sweden is today trying to implement, at least for the Lapps. In the law that regulates educational policy in this area since 1962 we read:

As far as the schooling of the Lapps is concerned, they [the Lapps] have the right to an instruction which is in all respects equal, but which does not therefore have to be identical with that which the majority receives. By virtue of being a minority group they have certain peculiar instructional needs which society cannot overlook. They have the right to get in their schools an orientation concerning the development of their own culture and its status in the present, an orientation which does not merely aim to communicate knowledge, but also to awaken respect for and piety towards the heritage from earlier generations as well as a feeling of solidarity with their own people.[9]

The same spirit has led to the passage of a Massachusetts statute that provides for

. . . the teaching of academic subjects both in a child's native language and in English; for instruction in reading and writing the native language, and in understanding, speaking, reading, and writing English; and for inclusion of the history and culture associated with a child's native language as an integral part of the program.[10]

The first step in applying our best scientific knowledge to language problems is to realize that no man's speech is inferior, only different. Like Lappish, American Indian languages have not been used for atomic science, but their subtleties of expression for their aboriginal users are beyond our imagination. Like Finnish in Sweden, Chicano Spanish may be the idiom of a population lost in an alien land, but in its homeland it is a language of the highest literary and scientific cultivation. Just as Norrbotten Swedish sounds strange to Swedes, ghetto or backwoods English sounds quaint or baffling to speakers of Standard English; nevertheless, it follows internal laws of its own that permit its users to express anything they wish to say. Our problem is how to teach tolerance of difference and acceptance of a man for what he is, not for how he talks.

So, by a long and circuitous route, we are led back to bilingualism as the solution to the curse of Babel. Bilinguals are often unpopular, and may be looked on with distrust by monolingual neighbors, who suspect that their loyalties are divided. They are viewed as mentally handicapped by certain misguided psychologists who depend on I.Q. tests to assess human potentialities. Bilinguals do have problems of their own in keeping their languages apart. But in hundreds of situations in our world, bilingualism offers the only humane and ultimately hopeful way to bridge the communication gap and mitigate the curse of Babel.[11]

REFERENCES

1. S. Michelet, S. Mowinckel, and N. Messel, tr. *Det gamle testamente: Loven eller de fem mosebøker* (Oslo: Aschehoug, 1930), p. 20.

2. Karl W. Deutsch, *Nationalism and Social Communication* (Cambridge, Mass.: M.I.T. Press, 1953).

3. Nils Erik Hansegård, *Recent Finnish Loanwords in Jukkasjärvi Lappish* (Uppsala: Acta Universitatis Upsaliensis, 1967), p. 84.

4. *Ibid.*, p. 55.

5. *Ibid.*, p. 84.

6. Magdalena Jaakkola, "Språk och sociala möjligheter i svenska Tornedalen," *Studier kring gränsen i Tornedalen,* ed. E. Haavio-Mannila and K. Suolinna (Stockholm: Nordiska Rådet, 1971), pp. 110-128.

7. Nils Erik Hansegård, *Tvåspråkighet eller halvspråkighet?* (Stockholm: Aldus/Bonniers, 1968), p. 131.

8. Tore Österberg, *Bilingualism and the First School Language—an Educational Problem Illustrated by Results from a Swedish Dialect Area* (Umeå: 1961), p. 45.

9. Israel Ruong, *Samerna* (Stockholm: Aldus/Bonniers, 1969), p. 157.

10. Jeffrey W. Kobrick, "The Compelling Case for Bilingual Education," *Saturday Review,* April 29, 1972, pp. 54-58.

11. Einar Haugen, "The Stigmata of Bilingualism," *The Ecology of Language,* ed. Anwar S. Dil (California: Stanford University Press, 1972), pp. 307-324. The author is grateful to Professor Karl-Hampus Dahlstedt, Umeå, and School Inspector Gösta Anderson, Luleå, for assistance in securing data.

DELL HYMES

Speech and Language: On the Origins and Foundations of Inequality Among Speakers

I conceive of two sorts of inequality in the human species; one, which I call natural or physical, because it is established by nature and consists in the difference of ages, health, bodily strengths, and qualities of mind or soul; the other, which may be called moral or political inequality, because it depends upon a sort of convention and is established, or at least authorized, by the consent of men. The latter consists in the different privileges that some men enjoy to the prejudice of others, such as to be richer, more honored, more powerful than they, or even to make themselves obeyed by them.

Rousseau (1775)[1]

I use the second paragraph of Rousseau's second *Discourse* as an epigraph, and adapt its title, because I want to call attention to a link between his concerns and ours. Like him, we think knowledge of human nature essential and pursue it; like him, we think the present condition of mankind unjust, and seek to transform it. These two concerns, for example, provide the frame for Noam Chomsky's recent Russell lectures.[2] Unlike Chomsky, but like Rousseau, moreover, some linguists are beginning to attend to a conception of linguistic structure as interdependent with social circumstances, and as subject to human needs and evolutionary adaptation. And like Rousseau, our image of the linguistic world, the standard by which we judge the present situation, harks back to an earlier stage of human society. Here Rousseau has the advantage of us. He knew he did this, and specified the limitations of it (see the end of note *h* to the *Discourse*). We do it implicitly, falling back on a "Herderian" conception of the world as composed of individual language-and-culture units, for lack of another way of seeing the resources of language as an aspect of human groups, because we have not thought through new ways of seeing how linguistic resources do, in fact, come organized in the world. Thus we have no accepted way of joining our understanding of inequality with our understanding of the nature of language.

Chomsky's Russell lectures are a case in point. The first lecture, "On Interpreting the World," presents implications of a certain conception of

45

the nature of language and of the goals of linguistic research, leading to a humanistic, libertarian conception of man. The second lecture, "On Changing the World," is about injustice, its roots in inequality of power, and the failure of scholars and governments to deal with the true issues in these respects. There is little or no linguistics in the second lecture, just as there is little or nothing of social reality in the first. Such principled schizophrenia besets linguistics today; the scientific and social goals of its practitioners are commonly compartmentalized. Such an alienation from experience and social reality of one of "the many kinds of segmental scientists of man," against which Edward Sapir warned years ago,[3] does not mirror either the true nature of language or its relation to social life; rather, it reflects a certain ideological conception of that nature and that relation, one which diverts and divorces linguistics from the contribution, desperately needed, that it might make to the understanding of language as a human problem.

The heart of the matter is this. A dominant conception of the goals of "linguistic theory"[4] encourages one to think of language exclusively in terms of the vast potentiality of formal grammar, and to think of that potentiality exclusively in terms of its universality. But a perspective which treats language only as an attribute of Man leaves language as an attribute of men unintelligible. In actuality language is in large part what users have made of it. Navaho is what it is in part because it is a human language, and in part because it is the language of the Navaho. The generic potentiality of the human faculty for language is realized differently, as to direction and as to degree, in different human communities, and is useless except insofar as it is so realized. The thrust of Chomskian linguistics has been to depreciate the actuality of language under the guise of rejecting an outmoded philosophy of science. We need not now reject a modish philosophy of science, but we must be able to see beyond its ideological use and recognize that one cannot change a world if one's theory permits no purchase on it. Thus, one of the problems to be overcome with regard to language is the linguist's usual conception of it. A broader, differently based notion of the form in which we encounter and use language in the world, a notion which I shall call *ways of speaking*, is needed.

Let me subsume further consideration of how it is that linguistics is part of the problem, under the following consideration of some of the other dimensions of language and of some general sources of inequality with regard to it. In both sections I shall try to indicate the need for a conception of *ways of speaking*.

Some Dimensions of Language as a Human Problem

It is striking that we have no general perspective on language as a human problem, not even an integrated body of works in search of one. Salient problems, such as translation, multilingualism, literacy, and language development, have long attracted attention, but mostly as practical matters constituting "applications" of linguistics, rather than as proper, theoretically pertinent parts of it. There are notable exceptions, as in the work of Einar Haugen, but for about a generation most linguistic thought in the United States has seen in the role of language in human life only something to praise, not something to question and study. Perhaps this situation reflects a phase in the alternation of "high" and "low" evaluations of language to which the philosopher Urban called attention.[5] The skeptical period after the First World War did see leading American theorists of language devote themselves to language problems, such as those involving new vehicles for international communication (Jespersen, Sapir), the teaching of reading (Bloomfield), literacy (Swadesh), language as an instrument and hence a shaper of thought (Sapir, Whorf), and linguistic aspects of psychiatric and other interpersonal communication (Trager, Hockett, in the early 1950's). Perhaps this book is a sign that the climate of opinion is shifting once again toward a balanced recognition of language as "at one and the same time helping and retarding us," as Sapir put it in one context.[6]

In any case, it is unusual today to think of language as something to overcome, yet four broad dimensions of language can usefully be considered in just that way: diversity of language, medium of language (spoken, written), structure of language, and functioning of language. Of each we can ask,

(1) when, where, and how it came to be seen as a problem;

(2) from what vantage point it is seen as a problem (in relation to other vantage points from which it may not be so seen);

(3) in what ways the problem has been approached or overcome as a practical task and also as an intellectual, conceptual task;

(4) what its consequences for the study of language itself have been;

(5) what kinds of study, to which linguistics might contribute, are now needed.

I cannot do more than raise such questions here; limitations of knowledge would prevent my doing more, if limitations of space did not. To raise such questions may, I hope, help to stimulate the development of a general perspective.

Overcoming Diversity of Language. This problem may be the most familiar, and the historical solutions to it form an important part of the subject matter of linguistics itself: lingua francas, koinés, pidgins and creoles, standardized languages, diffusion and areal convergence, multilingual repertoires, and constructed auxiliary languages. The myths and lexicons of many cultures show a widespread and presumably ancient recognition of the diversity of language, although not uniformly in the mold of the Tower of Babel. The Busama of New Guinea and the Quileute of the present state of Washington believed that originally each person had a separate language, and that community of language was a subsequent development created by a culture hero or transformer. Thus it is an interesting question whether it is unity or diversity, within or between speech communities, that has seemed the thing requiring an intellectual explanation.

In Western civilization the dominant intellectual response to the existence of diversity has been to seek an original unity, either of historical or of psychological origin (sometimes of both). The dominant practical response has been to impose a novel unity in the form of the hegemony of one language or standard. The presence of the Tower of Babel story in the civilization's sacred book legitimated, and perhaps stimulated, efforts to relate languages in terms of an original unity and played a great part in the cumulative development of linguistic research. Indeed, some rather sophisticated work and criticism on this subject can be found from the Renaissance onward, and the dating of the origin of linguistic science with the comparative-historical work of the early nineteenth century reflects its institutionalization as much as or more than its intellectual originality.[7] The force of Christian and humanitarian concern to establish the monogenesis of man through the monogenesis of language was felt strongly well through the nineteenth century, from the dominance of the "ethnological question" in the first part through the controversies involving Max Müller, Darwin, Broca and others.[8] The special interest of Europeans in Indo-European origins became increasingly important in the latter part of the century, the idea of a common linguistic origin stimulating and legitimating studies of common cultural origins and developments. Humanitarian motives played a part as well—Matthew Arnold appealing to Indo-European brotherhood as a reason for the English to respect Celtic (Irish) culture and perhaps the Irish, and Sir Henry Maine making a similar appeal on behalf of the peoples of India. Sheer intellectual curiosity and satisfaction must always be assigned a large part in motivating work in comparative-historical linguistics, and humanistic concern has probably played a part in the major contemporary effort to establish empirically a common historical origin for languages, that of the late Morris Swadesh.[9]

The most salient effort to establish a conceptual unity of human languages today is, of course, linked with the views of Noam Chomsky. Concern for such a unity is itself old and continuous—the appearance of disinterest among part of a generation of U. S. linguists before and after the Second World War was a local aberration whose importance is primarily due to Chomsky's reaction against it. He has reached back to the seventeenth and eighteenth centuries for an ancestral tradition,[10] when he had only to take up the tradition in this country of Boas and Sapir, or the European tradition, partially transplanted to this country, of Trubetzkoy and Jakobson. In both of these traditions some significant things were being said about the universals of language in the 1930's and early 1940's. It is true, however, that the history of the tradition of general linguistics stretching back through the nineteenth century (and, Jakobson would argue, continuing straight back through the Enlightenment to origins in medieval speculative grammar), had been lost from sight in American linguistics, and a sense of it is only now being recovered. It is true, too, that since Herder and von Humboldt, the tradition does not much appeal to Chomsky, since its universalism is combined with an intense interest in typology, that is, in the characterization of specific languages as well as, and as an instrument of, the characterization of language.

Here we touch on the inescapable limitation of either kind of effort to conceive the unity of human language. Although one used to speak of the discovery of a genetic relationship as "reducing" the number of linguistic groups, both the language and the thought were badly misleading. Languages may disappear through the destruction of their speakers, but not through the publication of lingistic papers and maps. The newly related languages remain to be accounted for in their differences and developments as well as in terms of the portion (often quite small) of their makeup that shows their common origin. Likewise, the discovery of putative universals in linguistic structure does not erase the differences. Indeed, the more one emphasizes universals, in association with a self-developing, powerful faculty of language within persons themselves, the more mysterious actual languages become. Why are there more than one, or two, or three? If the internal faculty of language is so constraining, must not social, historical, adaptive forces have been even more constraining, to produce the specific plenitude of languages actually found? For Chinookan is not Sahaptin is not Klamath is not Takelma is not Coos is not Siuslaw is not Tsimshian is not Wintu is not Maidu is not Miwok is not Yokuts is not Costanoan . . . (is not Tonkawa, is not Zuni, is not Mixe, is not Zoque, is not any of the numerous Mayan languages, or affiliates of Mayan, if one extends the horizon). The many differences do not disappear, and the likenesses, indeed are far from all Chomskyan universals; some likenesses exist because of a genetic common origin (Penutian), some because of areal adaptations (Northwest Coast for some, California for others), some because of diffusion, some because of limited possibilities and implications (à la Greenberg). Franz Boas once argued against exclusive concentration on genetic classification, calling the full historical development of languages the true problem.[11] A similar point can be made today as against concentration on putative universals. Most of language begins where abstract universals leave off. In the tradition from Herder and von Humboldt through Boas and Sapir, languages are "concrete universals," and most of language as a human problem is bound up with the adjective of that term.

Both of these modes of overcoming diversity of language intellectually, genetic classification and the search for putative universals, locate their solutions in time. There is a past reference, a historical origin of languages

or an evolutionary origin of the faculty of language; and there is a present
and future reference, one which draws the moral of the unity that is found.
Neither speaks to the present and future in terms of the processes actually
shaping the place of language in human life, for the faculty of language
presumably remains constant and genetic diversification of languages is
literally a thing of the past. The major process of the present and foreseeable future is the adaptation of languages and varieties to one another
and their integration into special roles and complex speech communities.
The understanding of this process is the true problem that diversity of
language poses, both to mankind and to those who study mankind's languages.

The essence of the problem appears as communication, intelligibility.
Some are concerned with the problem at the level of the world as a whole,
and efforts to choose or shape a common language for the world continue.[12]
Some project this contemporary concern onto the past, speaking of a "stub-
born mystery" in the "profoundly startling, 'anti-economic' multiplicity of
languages spoken on this crowded planet."[13] Such a view is anachronistic,
however, for the diversity was not "anti-economic" when it came into being;
it was just as much a "naturally selected, maximalized efficiency of adjustment to local need and ecology" as the great variety of fauna and flora to
which Steiner refers in the phrase just quoted. Universal processes of change
inherent in language, its transmission and use, together with separation and
separate adaptation of communities over the course of many centuries
suffice to explain the diversity. Simply the accumulation of unshared changes
would in time make the languages of separate groups mutually unintelligible.
There is of course more to it than physical and temporal distance (as Steiner
insightfully suggests); there is social distance as well. Boundaries are
deliberately created and maintained, as well as given by default. Some
aspects of the structures of languages are likely due to this. If the surface
form of a means of communication is simplified greatly when there is need
to overcome barriers, as it is in the formation of pidgin languages, then
the surface form of means of communication may be complicated when
there is a desire to raise or maintain barriers.[14] This latter process may
have something to do with the fact that the surface structures of languages spoken in small, cheek-by-jowl communities so often are markedly
complex, and the surface structures of languages spoken over wide ranges
less so. (The observation would seem to apply at least to North American
Indian languages and Oceania).

In any case, the problem is one of more than languages; it is one of

speech communities. Here the inadequacy of dominant concepts and
methods in linguistics is most painfully apparent. The great triumph of
linguistic science in the nineteenth century, the comparative-historical
method, deals with speech communities as the source and result of genetic
diversification. The great triumph of linguistic science in the twentieth

century, structural method, deals with speech communities as equivalent to language.[15] Genetic diversification can hardly be said to occur any longer, and a speech community comprising a single language hardly exists. The study of complex speech communities must benefit mightily from the tools and results both of historical linguistics, for the unraveling and interpretation of change, and of structural linguistics, for the explicit analysis of linguistic form. But it cannot simply apply them, it must extend them and develop new tools.

The needs can be expressed in terms of what is *between* speech communities and what is *within* them. Despite their well-known differences as to psychology, both Bloomfield and Chomsky reduce the concept of speech community to that of a language.[16] This will not do. The boundaries between speech communities are thought of first of all as boundaries of communication, but communication, or mutual intelligibility as it is often phrased, is not solely a function of a certain objective degree of difference between two languages or some series of related languages. One and the same degree of "objective" linguistic differentiation may be taken to demarcate boundaries in one case, and may be depreciated in another, depending on the social and political circumstances.[17] And intelligibility itself is not only a complex function of features of linguistic form (phonological, lexical, syntactic), but also of norms of interaction and conduct in conversation, and of attitudes towards differences in all these respects. In Nigeria one linguist found that as soon as members of a certain community recognized a related hinterland dialect, they refused to understand it;[18] other communities are noted for the effort they make to understand despite great difference. Such considerations cut across language boundaries. One may be at a loss to understand fellow speakers of his own language if his assumptions as to appropriate topics, what follows what, and the functions of speech are different (as happens often enough in classrooms between teachers of one background and students of another); and many of us have had the experience of following a discussion in a language of which we have little grasp, when the topics, technical terminology, and norms of conduct are professionally shared.

To repeat, communication cannot be equated with a "common" language. A term such as "the English language" comprises all linguistic varieties that owe their basic resources to the historical tradition known as English. That "language" is no longer an exclusive possession of the English, or even of the English and the Americans—there are perhaps more users of English in the Third World, and they have their own rights to its resources and future. Many varieties of "English" are not mutually intelligible within Great Britain and the United States as well as elsewhere. In fact, it is an important clarification if we can agree to restrict the term "language" (and the term "dialect") to just this sort of meaning: identification of a historically derived set of resources whose social functioning—organization into used varieties, mutual intelligibility, etc.—is not given by the fact of historical derivation itself, but is problematic, needing to be determined, and calling for other concepts and terms.

We are in poorly explored territory here. Even with consideration restricted to groups which can communicate, there is a gamut from "I can make myself understood" at one end to "he talks the same language" at the other. Probably it is best to employ terms such as "field" and "network" for the larger spheres within which a person operates communicatively, and to reserve the term "community" for more integral units. Clearly the boundary (and the internal organization) of a speech community is not a question solely of degree of interaction among persons (as Bloomfield said, and others have continued to say), but a question equally of membership, of identity and identification. If interaction were enough, school children would speak the TV and teacher English they constantly hear. Some indeed can so speak, but do not necessarily choose to do so. A few years ago I was asked by teachers at Columbia Point why the children in the school did not show the influence of TV, or, more pointedly, of daily exposure to the talk of the teachers. A mother present made a telling observation: she had indeed heard children talk that way, but on the playground, playing school; when playing school stopped, that way of talking stopped too.

Community, in this sense, is a dynamic, complex, and sometimes subtle thing. There are latent or obsolescent speech communities on some Indian reservations in this country, brought into being now principally by the visit of a linguist or anthropologist who also can use the language and shows respect for the uses to which it can be put. There are emergent communities, such as New York City would appear to be, in the sense that they share norms for the evaluation of certain variables (such as postvocalic *r*), that have developed in this century. There are other communities whose stigmata are variable and signs of severe insecurity, like those of New York, or the community of *porteños* in Buenos Aires, comprised principally of immigrants concerned to maintain their distance and prestige vis-à-vis speakers from the provinces (who, ironically enough, have lived in the country much longer). There can be multiple membership, and there is much scope for false perception; authorities, both governmental and educational, are often ignorant of the existence of varieties of language and communication under their noses. An unsuspected variety of creolized English was discovered recently on an island off Australia by the chance of a tape recorder being left on in a room where two children were playing. When the linguist heard the tape and could not understand it, he came to realize what it was. That such a language was known by the children was entirely unknown to the school. Indians who have been beaten as children for using their Indian tongue or blacks who have been shamed for using "deep" Creole will not necessarily trot the language out for an idle inquirer. In general, when we recognize that this diversity of speech communities involves social as well as linguistic realities, we must face the fact that there are different vantage points from which diversity may be viewed. One person's obstacle may be someone else's source of identity. In the United States and Canada today one can find Indians seeking to learn the Indian language they did not acquire as children. Leveling of language seems neither inevitable nor desirable in the world today. It is common to mock efforts at preservation and revitalization of languages as outmoded romanticism, but the mockery may express a view of human nature and human needs whose shallowness bodes ill for us.

What is within a speech community in linguistic terms has begun to be understood better through recent work in sociolinguistics. Empirical and theoretical work has begun to provide a way of seeing the subject "steadily as a whole." It suggests that one think of a community (or any group, or person) in terms, not a single language, but of a *repertoire*. A repertoire comprises a set of *ways of speaking*. Ways of speaking, in turn, comprise speech styles, on the one hand, and contexts of discourse, on the other, together with the relations of appropriateness obtaining between styles and contexts. Membership in a speech community consists in sharing one or more of its ways of speaking—that is, not in knowledge of a speech style (or any other purely linguistic entity, such as a language) alone, but in terms of knowledge of appropriate use as well. There are rules of use without which rules of syntax are useless. Moreover, the linguistic features that enter into speech styles are not only the "referentially-based" features usually dealt with in linguistics today, but also the "stylistic" features that are complementary to them, and inseparable from them in communication. Just as social meaning is an integral part of the definition and demarcation of speech communities, so it is an integral part of the organization of linguistic features within them. (Cf. Bernstein's concepts of "restricted" and "elaborated" code, classical diglossia, liturgy.) The sphere adequate to the description of speech communities, of linguistic diversity as a human problem, can be said to be: *means of speech, and their meanings to those who use them.*[19]

No one has ever denied the facts of multilingualism and heterogeneity of speech community in the world, but little has been done to enable us to comprehend and deal with them. Until now a "Herderian" conception of a world of independent one-language-one-culture units, a conception appropriate enough, perhaps, to a world pristinely peopled by hunters and gatherers and small-scale horticulturalists, has been tacitly fallen back upon. There now begins to be work to characterize complex linguistic communities and to describe speech communities adequately. Such description must extend to the place of speech itself in the life of a community: whether it is a resource to be hoarded or something freely expended; whether it is essential or not to public roles; whether it is conceived as intrinsically good or dangerous; what its proper role in socialization and demonstration of competence is conceived to be, and so forth.[20] Through such work one can hope to provide adequate foundations for assessing diversity of language as both a human problem and a human resource.

"Diversity" could stand as the heading for all of the problems connected with speech and language, once our focus is enlarged from languages as such to speech communities—existing diversity as an obstacle, and sometimes diversity that it is desired to maintain or achieve. Nevertheless, it is worthwhile to comment separately on three topics that have been singled out for attention in their own right. These are problems connected with the media, the structures, and the functions of language.

Overcoming the Medium of Language. Not long ago one might have said that most of the world was attempting to overcome the spokenness of language through programs of literacy, while some of the advanced sectors of civilization—the advertising and communications industries, and the university—were hailing the imminent transcendence of language in graphic form. McLuhan is less prominent now, but these twin poles of spoken and written language remain very much with us. A good deal has been said about speaking and writing, about oral and literate cultures,[21] and I have no new generalization to add, but I do have a bit of skepticism to advance. We really know very little as to the role of the medium of language. Technological determinism is not generally popular, for good reason, so it is puzzling to find it avidly welcomed in the sphere of communication. There is no more reason to regard it as gospel there than elsewhere. Certainly, it is impossible to generalize validly about "oral" vs. "literate" cultures as uniform types. Popular social science does seem to thrive on three-stage evolutionary sequences—David Riesman, Margaret Mead, Charles Reich have all, like McLuhan, employed them—but if dogmatic Marxism is not to be allowed such schemes, again for good reason, it really seems a little unfair to tolerate it in dogmatic McLuhanism.

In such theses, nevertheless, lies the threat and fascination of media. Is use of one medium rather than another more than transfer of a constant underlying competence in language; is the medium in which language is used itself constitutive of the meaning or reality expressed, and hence perhaps of the language itself? No doubt the evolutionary adaptation of communication through the oral channel has shaped some aspects of human language (e.g., the range in number of phonological units and distinctive features). Modern linguists have commonly treated writing as merely a derivative of speech. Their attitude was due, in part, to the need to overcome the massive dominance of written forms of language as symbols of cultural dominance, a struggle that continues. (It is no accident that many of the languages of the world have been "reduced to writing," not by natives, but by outsiders, that is, by missionaries, anthropologists and other linguists, and that the efforts of the outsiders toward an accurate orthography for representing the spoken form of a language are often deeply resented. Haitian Creole is a case in point.) Even in the period in which any interest in writing was heterodoxy in U.S. linguistics, more realistic scholars, such as Dwight Bolinger and Josef Vachek, defended the obvious fact of writing's relative autonomy. It seems fair to say that the issue is now a matter of indifference, especially to the Chomskyan school, who denigrate concern with the "external realization" of language as of little or no theoretical interest. Their own work often enough depends on examples possible only in written communication, and commonly ignores features inseparable from spoken communication (try characterizing narrative discourse without reference to intonation and voice quality). We are left, as we so often are, with sweeping claims, on the one hand, and on the other hand, with indifference on the part of those who could contribute precision to the study of the matter.

As a general principle, one may assume that difference of means will condition differences in what is accomplished; that would seem to hold for the comparative study of symbolic forms as a whole, including those of speech and writing. That speech and writing are not simply interchangeable, and have been developed historically in ways at least partly autonomous, is obvious. There is little hard knowledge, however, as to the degree of autonomy and the consequences of it.

One thing we do know is that a given society may define the role of any one medium quite differently from another society, as to scope and as to purpose. I have elaborated this theme with regard to speaking elsewhere. Here, let me illustrate it briefly with regard to writing.[22] For one thing, new writing systems continue to be independently invented—one was devised in 1904 by Silas John Edwards, a Western Apache shaman and leader of a nativistic religious movement. The sole purpose of the writing system is to record the sixty-two prayers Silas John received in his vision and to provide for their ritual performance. Competence in the system has been restricted to a small number of specialists. Discovery and study of this system by Keith Basso has shown that existing schemes for the analysis of writing systems fail to characterize it adequately, and probably fail as well for many other systems, having been devised with evolutionary, *a priori* aims, rather than with the aim of understanding individual systems in their own terms. The development of an *ethnography of writing*, such as Basso is undertaking, is long overdue.[23] Here belongs also study of the many surrogate codes found round the world—drum-language, whistle-talk, horn-language, and the like—for their relation to speech is analytically the same as that of writing,[24] and they go together with the various modalities of graphic communication (handwriting, handprinting, typing, typographic printing, etc.) and the various modalities of oral communication (chanting, singing, declamation, whispering, etc.) in a general account of the relations between linguistic means and ends.

As to ends, the Hanunoo of the Philippines are literate—they have a system of writing derivative of the Indian Devanagari—but they use it exclusively for love-letters, just as the Buan of New Guinea use their writing. In central Oregon the town of Madras has many signs, but the nearby Indian reservation, Warm Springs, has almost none, and those only where strangers impinge—the residents of Warm Springs do not need the information signs give.[25] Recently Vista workers tried to help prepare Warm Springs children for school by asking Indian parents to read to them in preschool years. U.S. schools tend to presuppose that sort of preparation, and middle-class families provide it, showing attention and affection by reading bed-time stories and the like; but Warm Springs parents show attention and affection in quite other ways, had no need of reading to do so, and the effort got nowhere. The general question of the consequences of literacy has been forcefully raised for contemporary European society by Richard Hoggart in a seminal book.[26]

In general, many generalizations about the consequences of writing and the properties of speaking make necessities out of possibilities. Writing, for example, *can* preserve information, but need not be used to do so (recall IBM's shredder, Auden's "Better Burn This"), and we ought to beware of a possible ethnocentrism in this regard. Classical Indian civilization committed vital texts to memory, through careful training in sutras, for fear of the perishability of material things. Classical Chinese calligraphy, the cuneiform of Assyrian merchants, and the style of hand taught to generations of Reed students by Lloyd J. Reynolds, are rather different kinds of things. Television may have great impact, but one cannot tell from what is on the screen alone. In any given household, does the set run on unattended? Is the picture even on? Is silence enforced when a favorite program or the news comes on? Or is a program treated as a resource for family interaction?

We have had a great deal more study of means than of meanings. There appear to be many more books on the alphabet than on the role of writing as actually observed in a community; many more pronouncements on speech than ethnographies of speaking; many more debates about television and content-analyses of programs than first-hand accounts of what happens in the rooms in which sets are turned on. The perspective broached above with regard to speech communities applies here, since media are a constituent of the organization of ways of speaking (i.e., ways of communication). We need particularly to know the meanings of media relative to one another within the context of given roles, settings, and purposes, for the etiquette of these things enters into whatever constitutive role a medium may have, including the opportunity or lack of it that persons and groups may have to use the medium. In England a typed letter is not acceptable in some contexts in which it would be taken for granted in the United States; the family

Christmas letter in the United States is a genre that can be socially located; subgroups in the United States differ dramatically in their assumptions as to what should be photographed and by whom.[27] At Warm Springs reservation last August, at the burial of a young boy killed in a car accident, his team-mates from the Madras High School spoke haltingly in their turn beside the grave and presented the parents with a photograph of the boy in athletic uniform, "as we would like to remember him"—a shocking thing, which the parents stoically let pass—for the last sight of the dead person, which bears the greatest emotional distress, had already been endured in the church before coming to the cemetery. When the rites were complete, Baptist and Longhouse, when all the men, then all the women, had filed past the gravesite, taking each in turn a handful of dirt from a shovel held out by the uncle of the boy, and dropping it on the half-visible coffin within the site, when the burial mound had been raised over the coffin, the old women's singing ended, and the many flowers and the toy deer fixed round the mound, then, as people began to leave, the bereaved parents were stood at one end of the mound, facing the other, where their friends gathered to photograph them across it. That picture, of the manifestation of solidarity and concern on the part of so many, evident in the flowers, might be welcome.

The several media, of course, may occur together in several mixes and hierarchies, in relation to each other and in relation to modalities such as touch. Communities seem to differ as to whether tactile or vocal acts, or both together, are the indispensable or ultimate components of rituals of curing, for example. In some parts of Africa, languages are evaluated partly in terms of their greeting systems, and the Haya of northern Tanzania, who are acquiring Swahili, find it less satisfying than their own language, for in a Haya greeting one touches as well as talks.[28]

Finally, the use of media and modalities needs to be related to the norms by which a community takes responsibility for performance and interpretation of kinds of communication. My stress here obviously is on the qualitative basis of assessing media as a human problem. Statistics on radios and newspapers and the like barely scratch the surface. I think it entirely possible that a medium may have a constitutive effect in one community and not in another, due to its qualitative role, its social meaning and function, even though frequencies of occurrence may be the same in both. We have to do here with the question of identities and identifications, mentioned earlier with regard to varieties of language in schools. We need, in short, a great deal of ethnography.

Overcoming the Structure of Language. Concern to overcome the structure of language seems to have centered around the function of naming, either to achieve a uniform relation between language and meaning as a semantic ideal, or to avoid it as a spiritual desert or death. Early in the development of Indo-European studies, when modern languages were thought degenerate

in form, the great pioneer of reconstruction, Franz Bopp, sought to infer an
original Indo-European structure in which meanings and morphemes went
hand in hand, reflecting perhaps an original, necessary relationship. Others
have sought to realize a semantic ideal in the present, by constructing an
artificial language, or by reconstructing an existing one to convey the universal meanings required by science and philosophy. One thinks especially of
the late seventeenth century (Dalgarno, Bishop Wilkes, Leibniz) and the
early twentieth century (Russell, the early Wittgenstein, Carnap, Bergmann
and others). Still others have thought that the ideal relationship between
meaning and form might be glimpsed in the future, once linguists had
worked through the diverse structures of existing languages to the higher
level of structure beyond them. Such was Whorf's vision.[29]

At an opposite extreme would be a philosopher like Brice Parain, who
despairs of the adequacy of language, and of course adherents of the Zen
tradition that regards language's inveterate distinguishing of things as a
trap to be transcended. Intermediate would be the conscious defense of
other modes of meaning than that envisioned in the "semantic ideal," in particular, the defenses of poetry and of religious language.[30] And here would
belong conceptions of literary and religious use of language as necessarily
in defiance of other, conventional modes of use. Much of philosophy and
some of linguistics seem to have found their way back to an open-ended
conception of the modes of meaning in language, and are experiencing great
surges of interest in poetics and rhetoric.

Such work is of the greatest importance, but it does leave the general
question of the adequacy of language, or of a particular language, in
abeyance. It would seem that the structures of languages have never been
wholly satisfactory to their users, for they have never let them rest. Shifts in
the obligatory grammatical categories of languages over time, like the shift
from aspect to tense in Indo-European, bespeak shifts in what was deemed
essential to convey. Conscious reports of such concerns may have appeared
first in classical Greece, when Plato complained that the processual character of Greek verbs favored his philosophical opponents, although, at the
time, devices such as the suffix -itos for forming abstract nouns were growing
in productivity. When in the fourth century A.D. Marius Victorinus tried to
translate Plotinus from Greek into Latin, there was no adequate abstract
terminology in his contemporary Latin, and his clumsy efforts to coin one
met with little acceptance, thus inhibiting the spread of the Neo-Platonic
philosophy in that period. Some centuries later "theologisms" had evolved
in Latin which quite matched the terms of the Greek fathers in precision
and maneuverability.[31] In the early modern period, English writers
lamented the inadequacies of English and set out to remedy them.[32] At
Warm Springs, some fifteen years ago, a speaker of Wasco (a Chinookan
language), acknowledging Wasco's lack of a term for a contemporary object, said that when he was a boy, if one of the old men had come out of

his house and seen such a thing, he would have coined a word for it, "just like that" (with a sharp gesture). There are no such old men anymore to coin words or shape experience into the discourse of myth.[33] Such fates are common, though not much attended to by linguists. The official preference is to stress the potentiality of a language and to ignore the circumstances and consequences of its limitations. Yet every language is an instrument shaped by its history and patterns of use, such that for a given speaker and setting it can do some things well, some clumsily, and others not intelligibly at all. The cost, as between expressing things easily and concisely, and expressing them with difficulty and at great length, is a real cost, commonly operative, and a constraint on the theoretical potentiality of language in daily life. Here is the irreducible element of truth in what is known as the "Whorf hypothesis": means condition what can be done with them, and in the case of languages, the meanings that can be created and conveyed. The Chomskyan image of human creativity in language is a partial truth whose partiality can be dangerous if it leads us to think of any constraints on linguistic communication either as nugatory or as wholly negative. As to the force of such constraints, the testimony of writers and the comparative history of literary languages should, perhaps, suffice here.[34] As to their positive side, we seem to need to repeat the development of thought discerned by Cassirer in Goethe, Herder and W. von Humboldt:

To them, the Spinozistic thesis, that definition is limitation, is valid only where it applies to external limitation, such as the form given to an object by a force not its own. But within the free sphere of one's personality such checking heightens personality; it truly acquires form only by forming itself. . . . Every universal in the sphere of culture, whether discovered in language, art, religion, or philosophy, is as individual as it is universal. For in this sphere we perceive the universal only within the actuality of the particular; only in it can the cultural universal find its actualization, its realization as a cultural universal.[35]

We need, of course, ethnography to discover the specific forms which the realization of universality takes in particular communities, and, where the question is one of speech, we need ethnographies of speaking.

Whorf himself led in describing the organization of linguistic features pertinent to cultural values and world views as cutting across the usual sectors of linguistic description, and as involving "concatenations that run across . . . departmental lines" (that is, the lines of the usual rubrics of linguistic, ethnographic or sociological description that divide the study of a culture and language as a whole).[36] Whorf referred to the required organization of features as a *fashion of speaking*, and one can see in his notion an anticipation, though not developed by him, of the sociolinguistic concept of *ways of speaking*. The crucial difference is that to the notion of speech styles, the sociolinguistic approach adds the notion of contexts of situation and patterns relating style and context to each other.

Here, as before, the great interest is not merely in diversity or uniformity, but in the possibility that such differences shape or constitute worlds. Do semantic-syntactic structures do so? Sapir and Whorf thought that for the naive speaker they did, although contrastive study of language structures was a way to overcome the effect. What Chomsky describes as the seemingly untrammeled "creative aspect" of language use was treated by Sapir as true, but not true in the same way for speakers of different languages. Each language has a formal completeness (i.e., it shares fully in the generic potentiality of human language), but does so in terms of an orientation, a "form-feeling" of its own, so as to constitute quite a unique frame of reference toward being in the world. A monolingual's sense of unlimited adequacy is founded on universality, not of form or meaning, but of function, and that very sense, being unreflecting, may confine him all the more. The particular strengths of a given language are inseparable from its limitations. This is what Sapir (preceding and giving the lead to Whorf) called

a kind of relativity that is generally hidden from us by our naive acceptance of fixed habits of speech as guides to an objective understanding of the nature of experience. This is the relativity of concepts, or, as it might be called, the relativity of the form of thought. . . . It is the appreciation of the relativity of the form of thought which results from linguistic study that is perhaps the most liberalizing thing about it. What fetters the mind and benumbs the spirit is ever the dogged acceptance of absolutes.[37]

I think this is as fair a statement of the evidence and parameters of the situation today as it was a half-century ago when Sapir wrote it. I cite Sapir here partly because I think that linguistics in the United States, having worked its way through a decade or so of superficial positivism, shows signs of having worked its way through another decade or so of superficial rationalism, and a readiness to pick up the thread of the complexly adequate approach that began to emerge in the years just before the Second World War in the work of men like Sapir, Firth, Trubetzkoy and Jakobson.

To return to relativity: the type associated with Sapir and Whorf in any case is underlain by a more fundamental kind. The consequences of the relativity of the structure of language depend upon the relativity of the function of language. Take, for example, the common case of multilingualism. Inference as to the shaping effect of some one language on thought and the world must be qualified immediately in terms of the place of the speaker's languages in his biography and mode of life. Moreover, communities differ in the roles they assign to language itself in socialization, acquisition of cultural knowledge, and performance. Community differences extend to the role of languages in naming the worlds they help to shape or constitute. In central Oregon, for example, English speakers typically go up a level in taxonomy when asked to name a plant for which they lack a term: "some kind of bush"; Sahaptin speakers analogize: "sort of an A," or "between an A and a B" (A and B being specific plants); Wasco speakers demur: "No, no name for that," in keeping with a cultural preference for precision and certainty of reference.[38]

This second type of linguistic relativity, concerned with the functions of languages, has more than a critical, cautionary import. As a sociolinguistic approach, it calls attention to the organization of linguistic features in social interaction, and current work has begun to show that description of *fashions of speaking* can reveal basic cultural values and orientations. The worlds so revealed are not the ontological and epistemological worlds of physical relationships, of concern to Whorf, but the worlds of social relationships. What are disclosed are not orientations toward space, time, vibratory phenomena and the like, but orientations towards persons, roles, statuses, rights and duties, deference and demeanor.[39] Such an approach obviously requires an ethnographic base.[40]

Overcoming the Function of Language. Diversity is a rubric under which the phenomena of language as a human problem can be grasped; the questions which underlie our concern with diversity can be summed up in the term, *function.* What differences do language diversities make through their role in human lives? Some of these differences have been touched upon, and I want to take space for only general consideration here. Linguists have mostly taken the functions of language for granted, but it is necessary to investigate them. Such investigation is indeed going on, but mostly not in linguistics. It is a striking fact that problems of overcoming some of the ordinary functioning of language in modern life attract increased attention from philosophers, writers, and sociological analysts of the condition of communication in society, while many linguists proceed as if mankind became more unified each time they used the word "universal"; freer and more capable of solving its problems each time they invoked linguistic competence and creativity. (This is what I mean by superficial rationalism.)

Serious analysis of the functioning of language is to be found in England and the continent much more than in the United States. Let me merely mention here Merleau-Ponty on the "prose of the world," Heidegger on speaking as "showing," Brice Parain (already cited) on the inadequacy of language, Barthes on *l'ecriture,* LeFebvre on *discours,* Sartre on precoded interpretations of events such as the Hungarian uprising, and Ricoeur on hermeneutics, and state briefly the significance of two approaches, those of Bernstein and of Habermas.

Bernstein's work has a significance apart from how one assesses his particular studies, which have been considerably shaped by the exigencies of support for practical concerns. His theoretical views, which precede these studies, are rooted in a belief that the role of language in constituting social reality is crucial to any general sociological theory, and that that role has not yet been understood because it has been approached in terms of an unexamined concept of language. For Bernstein, linguistic features affect the transmission and transformation of social realities through their organization into what he calls *codes;* that is, through selective organization of linguistic features into styles of speech, not through the agency of a "language" (e.g., "English") as such. He is noted for his twin notions of *restricted* and *elaborated* codes, and this dichotomy has not always done the texture of his thought good service, for the two notions have had to subsume a series of dimensions that ought analytically to be separated, since they cut across speech communities in different ways. (See an analysis in my paper cited second in references 20.) Nevertheless, one dimension essential to his views is particularly essential to understanding language as a human problem in the contemporary world. It is the dimension of contrast between restricted speech styles that are predominantly particularistic or context-specific, and elaborated speech styles that are predominantly universalistic or context-free.

The point is not that some groups have only one of these styles, and other groups only the other. The potentialities of both are universally present and to some extent employed. Bernstein's point is rather that certain types of communication and social control, especially in families, may lead to the predominant use of one style or the other. Nor is the point that one of these styles is "good," the other "bad." Each has its necessary place. The restricted style, in which understandings can be taken for granted, is essential to efficient communication in some circumstances, and to meaningful personal life in others. A life in which all meanings had to be made explicit, in which there was never anyone to whom one could say, "you know what I mean," with assurance, would be intolerable. Many life choices, not least among academics, are made for the sake or lack of "someone to talk to" in this sense. The elaborated style can be quite out of place, and even destructive, in many circumstances. But, and this is an element of Bernstein's views that has been largely overlooked, the universalistic meanings of the elaborated style are essential if one is to be able to talk about means of communication themselves, the ways in which meanings come organized in a community in the service of particular interests and cultural hegemony, and so to gain the objective knowledge necessary for the transformation of social relationships.[41]

Habermas develops a contrast somewhat like Bernstein's, in terms of uses of language or kinds of communication: those appropriate to contexts of symbolic interaction, on the one hand, and to the purposes of technological and bureaucratic rationality, on the other. It is Habermas' view that whereas the "free market" concept was the dominant rationalization of the capitalist order in the nineteenth century, that of "technological progress" serves that role today, and that one of the great threats to human life in modern society is the invasion of spheres of symbolic interaction by the technological, bureaucratic communicative style. Value preferences and special social interests masquerade in the language of instrumental necessity; personal and expressive dimensions of meaning become illicit over a greater and greater range of activity. Official social science in its positivistic interpretaton of its task actually aids in the maintenance and establishment of technological control, unlike those trends in social science concerned with understanding sociocultural life-worlds and with extending intersubjective understanding with what may loosely be called a "hermeneutic" orientation, and those trends concerned with analyzing received modes of authority in the interest of emancipating men from them. In his recent work Habermas has given special attention to the limitations of a Chomskyan conception of competence and to the positive contributions of a psychoanalytic perspective.[42]

Habermas might be said to give a reinterpretation of the Marxian categories of analysis in communicative, partly linguistic terms. He conceives of the forces at work in society in terms, not of classes or of superstructure and base, but of kinds of cognitive interests (technological-bureaucratic, symbolic interactive, and emancipatory) and their interplay. Such a reinterpretation may not be adequate sociologically (for non-Marxists any more than for Marxists), but it offers a mediation among sociological analysis, cultural criticism, and the study of the actual organization of linguistic means in contemporary life that is unparalleled. If his particular formulation does not prove adequate to overcoming the compartmentalization of professional work and social concern among linguists, then the solution must nevertheless be found along the lines that Habermas (building in part on Bernstein) has opened up. Clearly I think that Bernstein and Habermas, by focusing upon the functional organization of linguistic resources in society, stimulate the ethnographic work that is a necessary foundation for understanding language as a human problem.

Thinking About Linguistic Inequality

Occasionally linguists have been so carried away by ideological certitude as to state that all languages are equally complex. This is of course not so. It is known that languages differ in sheer number of lexical elements by an order of magnitude of about two to one as between world languages and local languages. They differ in number and in proportion of abstract, superordinate terms. They differ in elaboration of expressive and stylistic devices—lexical, grammatical and phonological. Languages differ in number of phoneme-like units, in complexity of morphophonemics, in complexity of word-structure (both phonological and morphological), in degree of utilization of morphophonemically permitted morpheme-shapes, etc.

The usual view is that such things are distinctions without a difference, that all languages are equally adapted to the needs of those who use them. Leaving aside that such equality might be an equality of imperfect adaptations, speech communities round the world simply do not find this to be the case. They are found to prefer one language for a purpose as against another, to acquire some languages and give up others because of their suitability for certain purposes. No Third World government can afford to assume the equality of the languages within its domain.

The usual answer to this objection is that all languages are potentially equal. In fact this is so in one vital respect; all languages are indeed capable of adaptive growth, and it is a victory of anthropologically oriented linguistic work, particularly, to have established this point. The difficulty with the usual answer is twofold. First, given that each language constitutes an already formed starting point, it is not at all clear that expansion of resources, however far, would result in languages being interchangeable, let alone identical. Limiting consideration to world languages, we find that many who command more than one prefer one to another for one or more purposes, and that this is often enough a function of the resources of the languages themselves. The other difficulty is that the realization of potentiality entails costs. The Chomskyan image of the child ideally acquiring mastery of language by an immanent unfolding misleads us here. It has an element of truth to which the world should hearken, but it omits the costs, and the constitutive role of social factors. Most of the languages of the world will *not* be developed, as was Anglo-Saxon, into world languages over the course of centuries. (It is speculated that Japanese may be the last language to join that particular club.)

I regret to differ from admired colleagues on this general issue, but it seems necessary, if linguistic work is to make its contribution to solution of human problems, not to blink realities. How could languages be other than different, if languages have any role at all in human life? To a great extent, languages, as I have said, are what has been made of them. There is an element of truth in the thesis of potentiality and an element of truth in the thesis of equivalent adaptation across communities; but both theses fall short of contemporary reality, where languages are not in fact found unmolested, as it were, one to a community, each working out its own destiny in an autonomous community. Not to take the step to that reality is to fall back on the "Herderian" image, a falling back that is all too common. If that image were a reality, then the analysis of linguistic inequality would perhaps be only an academic exercise for scholars who take pleasure in languages the way one may take pleasure in kinds of music. Given our world, however, analysis of linguistic inequality is of great practical import.

What, then, are the sources and consequences of linguistic inequality? The kinds of diversity already discussed contribute, of course; but the plain fact is that having hardly raised the question we have no clear notion. A Parsonian set of categories can serve as an initial guide.

First, languages differ in their makeup as adaptive resources; the linguistic resources of speech communities differ in what can be done with them, as has been indicated. A generation ago some kinds of difference were regarded with a spirit of relativistic tolerance, as the special virtues of the languages that had them, and so one got at least some account of their lexical and grammatical strengths. The present temper, however, treats mention of differences as grounds for suspicion of prejudice, if not racism, so that poor Whorf, who believed fervently in the universal grounding of language, and extolled the superiority of Hopi, has become, like Machiavelli, a perjorative symbol for unpleasant facts to which he called attention. Until this temper changes, we are not likely to learn much about this fundamental aspect of language.

Second, linguistic resources differ as an aspect of persons and personalities. In addition to the variability inevitable on genetic grounds, there is the variability due to social patterning. Conceptions of male and female roles, or of specialized roles, including that of leadership, may differ markedly among speech communities so that eloquence or other verbal skills may be necessary for normal adult roles in one society (commonly for men, not women), and essential to no important role at all in another. The requirements of a speaking role may be simple, or subtle and difficult as they are in the special bind of a traditional Quaker minister who had to speak out of spiritual silence and, desirably, after periods of doubting his calling.[43] Differences in verbal skills desired, of course, feed back upon the ways in which the linguistic resources of a community are elaborated.

Third, linguistic resources differ according to the institutions of a community. So far as I know, comparative analysis of institutions has not much considered the ways in which they do and do not require or foster particular developments of verbal skill and resource, or at least has not phrased its findings as contributions to the understanding of language. There are indeed some analyses of the development of the verbal style and resources of particular sciences, of science as a social movement, and of religious and political movements. My impression is, however, that one finds case studies, but not coordinated efforts toward a comparative analysis and a theory.

Fourth, linguistic resources differ according to the values and beliefs of a community. Infants' vocalizations, for example, may be postulated as a special language, one with serious consequences, such that special interpreters are required, so that a child's wishes can be known and its soul kept from returning to whence it came. The shaping of linguistic resources by religious concerns appears to be attracting a surge of interest.[44] A community's values and beliefs may implicitly identify spontaneous speech as a danger to the cultural order, as among the traditional Ashanti, or they may treat speaking and especially elaborate speaking, as a badge of inferiority, both between persons and among the orders of a social hierarchy, as is the case with the Wolof of Senegal. The normal condition of a community may be constant chatter on the one hand, or pervasive quiet on the other, according to how speech is valued.

Such a guide to differences does not in itself go beyond a "Herderian" perspective of discrete speech communities, each part of the cultural plenitude of the world. Such description bears on inequality, however, when speech communities are viewed in a larger context. Differences by themselves would constitute inequality only in the sense of lack of equivalence, not in the sense of inadequacy. But just as the resources of a speech community must be described as speech styles in relation to contexts of situation, so must they also be assessed in relation to their contexts when the perspective is that of human problems. The essential thing seems to me to be to assess the situation of a speech community in terms of the relation between its abilities and its opportunities. Every speech community is to some degree caught up in a changing relationship with a larger context, in which opportunities for the meaningful use of traditionally fostered abilities may be declining, and novel opportunities (or requirements) for which members have not been traditionally prepared may be impinging. The term *competence* should be employed within just such a perspective. It should not be used as a synonym for ideal grammatical knowledge as by Chomsky, or extended to a speech community collectively as by De Camp, or extended to ideal communicative knowledge as by Habermas, or done away with as Labov would seem to prefer; rather, *competence* should retain its normal sense of the actual ability of a person. Just such a term is needed to assess the processes at work in actual speech communities, and their consequences for persons. *Competence* as a term for ideal knowledge may overcome inequality conceptually for linguists, but only as a term for the abilities of persons, assessed in relations to contexts of use, can it help to overcome inequality practically for the members of speech communities.

Conclusion

To sum up: from one standpoint the history of human society can be seen as a history of diversity of language, of diversity as a problem—both diversity of languages as such, and diversity as to their media, structures, and functions. From another standpoint, that same diversity has been a resource and an opportunity—for scholars to understand the potentialities of human language, and for speakers to develop the potentialities of their forms of life and of their identities.

From antiquity it has been the mark of a true science of man, of greatness in a science of man, to attempt to comprehend the known diversity of cultures and history. Herodotus did so in a narrative of his age's great conflict between East and West, incorporating the ethnology of his world. The Enlightenment, while recognizing a debt to antiquity, was conscious also of the superiority and the challenge of a new horizon provided by its knowledge of manners and customs from the New World, and from remoter Africa and Asia; the Victorian evolutionists, while recognizing an Enlightenment precedent, were conscious of a superiority and the challenge of a new horizon provided by the recent recognition of the great prehistoric antiquity of man. In this century there has been no new horizon of data in space or time that has vivified the whole (unless one counts primate studies and finds of fossil man as such), but a principle of methodological relativism has been gradually established that is of equal importance. Now we are at a juncture where only the future of man offers the challenge of a new horizon to a science of man; the choices for its future appear to be irrelevance, the service of domination, or the service of liberation through universalization. That is, the sciences of man have developed in the matrix of a certain relationship between one part of the world and the rest; a relationship defined in terms, not of aspirations, but of activities. Anthropology, for instance, is fairly described as the study of colored people by whites.[45] That matrix has changed irreversibly. A science of man limited to certain societies or interests was always implicitly a contradiction in terms; increasingly, it has become an impossibility or a monstrosity. Knowledge about people is a resource, like control of oil and of armies. Nations cannot accept permanent inferiority in this regard. For the social scientists, the problem is complicated by the relations not only between his own country and others, but by the relations between the governments of other countries and their own peoples; for usually any knowledge that he can gain that is worth the having entails entering into a relationship of mutuality and trust with the people he is studying. Thus universalization of the science of man must mean extension not only to all countries of participation, but to all communities. The proper role of the scientist, and the goal of his efforts, should not be "extractive," but mediative. It should be to help communities be ethnographers of their own situations, to relate their knowledge usefully to general knowledge, not merely to test and document. Such a role could be the safeguard of both the intellectual and the ethical purposes of the science itself.

The study of language has had a checkered career in the history just sketched. It first became a self-conscious activity, and to a great extent has developed since, as an instrument of exclusion and domination. The analysis of Sanskrit in ancient India, of classical songs and writings in ancient China, of Greek and then Latin in the ancient Mediterranean, of nascent national languages in the Renaissance (e.g., Nebrija's grammar of Castilian), were all in the interest of cultural hegemony. It is only in our own century, through the decisive work of Boas, Sapir and other anthropologically oriented linguists (as components of the general triumph of "methodological relativism" in the human sciences) that every form of human speech has gained the "right," as it were, to contribute on equal footing to the general theory of human language.

The present situation of linguistics in the United States is quite mixed, where it is not obscure. Chomskyan theory holds out the liberation of mankind as an aspiration, but its practice can contribute only conceptually at best, if it does not in fact stand as an obstacle to the kind of work that is actually needed. This paper has argued for the study of speech communities as actual communities of speakers. In this way we can go beyond a liberal humanism which merely recognizes the abstract potentiality of all languages, to a humanism which can deal with concrete situations, with the inequalities that actually obtain, and help to transform them through knowledge of the ways in which language is actually organized as a human problem and resource.

REFERENCES

1. Jean-Jacques Rousseau, *Discourse on the Origin and Foundations of Inequality Among Men* (1756), trans. Roger D. and Judith R. Masters, *The First and Second Discourses,* ed. Roger D. Masters (New York: St. Martin's Press, 1964).

2. Noam Chomsky, *Problems of Knowledge and Freedom* (New York: Pantheon Books, 1971).

3. Edward Sapir, "Psychiatric and Cultural Pitfalls in the Business of Getting a Living" (1939), *Selected Writings of Edward Sapir,* ed. D. G. Mandelbaum (Berkeley and Los Angeles: University of California Press, 1949), p. 578.

4. "Linguistic Theory" ought to refer to a general theory of language, or at least a general theory of the aspects of language dealt with by linguists, but it has been appropriated recently for just those aspects of language dealt with in transformational generative grammar—another instance of Chomsky's skill as a polemicist. Hence the quotation marks.

5. W. M. Urban, *Language and Reality: The Philosophy of Language and the Principles of Symbolism* (London: George Allen, 1939), p. 23.

6. Edward Sapir, "Language," *Encyclopedia of Social Sciences,* IX (New York: Macmillan, 1933), pp. 155-169, cited from Mandelbaum, ed., *Selected Writings of Edward Sapir,* p. 11.

7. G. J. Metcalf, "The Development of Comparative Linguists in the Seventeenth and Eighteenth Centuries: Precursors to Sir William Jones," and P. Diderichsen, "The Foundation of Comparative Linguistics: Revolution or Continuation?" *Studies in the History of Linguistics,* ed. Hymes (Bloomington: Indiana University Press, forthcoming).

8. Discussed in Hymes, "Lexicostatistics and Glottochronology in the Nineteenth Century" (with notes toward a general history), *Proceedings of the Conference on Genetic Lexicostatistics* (tentative title), ed. I. Dyen (The Hague: Mouton, forthcoming).

9. M. Swadesh, *Origin and Diversification of Languages* (Chicago: Aldine, 1971).

10. N. Chomsky, *Cartesian Linguistics* (New York: Harper and Row, 1966).

11. F. Boas, "The Classification of American Languages," *American Anthropologist,* XXII (1920), 367-376.

12. "The Problem of Linguistic Communication in the Modern World," *La Monda Lingvo-Problemo,* III, No. 9 (1971), 129-176.

13. G. Steiner, *Extraterritorial* (New York: Atheneum, 1971), p. 70.

14. Hymes, "Introduction to Part III," *Pidginization and Creolization of Languages*, ed. Hymes (London and New York: Cambridge University Press, 1971), p. 73.

15. There are noble exceptions—Schuchardt in the seventeenth century, for one, and the Prague School and J. R. Firth in the twentieth century, but the main thrust of successive developments has been as described. Transformational grammar is included under structural method here because it shares the same assumptions when contrasted to a functional approach; cf. the contrast drawn in Hymes, "Why Linguistics Needs the Sociologist," *Social Research*, XXXIV, No. 4 (1967), 632-647.

16. L. Bloomfield, *Language* (New York: Holt, Rinehart & Winston, 1933), Ch. 3, and N. Chomsky, *Aspects of the Theory of Syntax* (Cambridge: M.I.T. Press, 1965), p. 3.

17. Assumptions as to the bases of mutual intelligibility, and as to relations among linguistic boundaries, ethnic boundaries, and communication are analyzed in Hymes, "Linguistic Problems in Defining the Concept of 'Tribe,'" *Essays on the Problem of Tribe*, ed. J. Helm (Seattle: University of Washington Press for the American Ethnological Society, 1968).

18. H. Wolff, "Intelligibility and Inter-Ethnic Attitudes," *Anthropological Linguistics*, I, No. 3 (1959) 34-41.

19. This conception is dealt with in more detail in my "Introduction" to *Language in Society*, I, No. 1 (1972) 1-14; and "The Scope of Sociolinguistics," *Report of the 23rd Annual Round Table Meeting on Linguistics and Language Study; Sociolinguistics*, ed. R. W. Shuy (Washington, D.C.: Georgetown University Press).

20. On complex linguistic communities, see C. A. Ferguson, "National Sociolinguistic Profiles," *Sociolinguistics*, ed. W. Bright (The Hague: Mouton, 1966). On comparative study of the role of speaking, see Hymes, "Two Types of Linguistic Relativity," *ibid.*; and "Models of the Interaction of Language and Social Life," *Directions in Sociolinguistics: The Ethnography of Communication*, eds. J. Gumperz and D. Hymes (New York: Holt, Rinehart and Winston, 1972), pp. 35-71. The work of John Gumperz and William Labov has been of special importance to the understanding of the problems dealt with in this and the preceding note.

21. D. Wade, "The Limits of the Electronic Media," *T.L.S. Essays and Reviews*, V (May 1972) 515-516.

22. See works cited in reference 20 and, on writing, "Toward Ethnographies of Communication," *The Ethnography of Communication*, eds. J. Gumperz and D. Hymes (Washington, D.C.: American Anthropological Association, 1965), pp. 24-25.

23. K. Basso and N. Anderson, "The Painted Symbols of Silas John: A Western Apache Writing System," *Science*, CLXXIX (forthcoming in 1973).

24. T. Stern, "Drum and Whistle Languages: An Analysis of Speech Surrogates," *American Anthropologist*, LIX (1957) 487-506.

25. These observations are from the work of Susan Philips, to be presented in an article in *Foundations of Language Development*, eds. E. and E. Lenneberg, sponsored by UNESCO.

26. R. Hoggart, *The Uses of Literacy* (London: Chatto and Windus, 1957); note the introduction to the French edition, *Working Papers in Cultural Studies*, trans. J. C. Passeron (Birmingham: Centre for Contemporary Cultural Studies, University of Birmingham, 1971), pp. 120-131.

27. The ethnography of taking pictures in U.S. society is being studied by Richard Chalfen of Temple University; see Sol Worth, *Through Navaho Eyes* (Bloomington: Indiana University Press, 1972).

28. I owe this information to Sheila Seitel.

29. B. L. Whorf, "Language, Mind and Reality," 1942; cited from *Language, Thought, and Reality: Selected Writings of Benjamin Lee Whorf,* ed. J. B. Carroll (Cambridge: The Technology Press, 1956), pp. 246-270.

30. B. Parain, *Petite Métaphysique de la Parole* (Paris: Gallimard, 1969), translated as *A Metaphysics of Language* (Garden City, N.Y.: Doubleday, Anchor Books, 1971); K. Burke, "Semantic and Poetic Meaning," *The Philosophy of Literary Form* (Baton Rouge: Louisiana State University Press, 1941); E. L. Mascall, *Words and Images* London: Darton, Longman and Todd, 1968); I. T. Ramsey, *Religious Language* (New York: Macmillan, 1957).

31. From a comment by G. E. von Grunebaum, in *Language in Culture,* ed. H. Hoijer (Chicago: University of Chicago Press, 1954), pp. 228-229.

32. R. F. Jones, *The Triumph of the English Language* (Stanford: Stanford University Press, 1953); cf. F. Brunot, "La Propagation du francais en France jusqu'à la fin de l'Ancien Régime," *Histoire de la Langue Francaise des Origines à 1900,* VII, 2nd ed. (Paris: Colin, 1947); and E. A. Blackall, *The Emergence of German as a Literary Language* (Cambridge: Cambridge University Press, 1959).

33. E. Sapir, *Wishram Texts* (Leiden: E. J. Brill, 1909), p. 48, lines 1-2.

34. E.g., Eliot's "one has only learnt to get the better of words/For the thing one no longer has to say, or the way in which/One is no longer disposed to say it." *Four Quartets* (New York: Harcourt Brace, 1943), p. 16. The general question of the "Herderian" standpoint and of the mixed standing of linguistic resources as determinants is reviewed in Hymes, "Linguistic Aspects of Comparative Political Research," *The Methodology of Comparative Research,* eds. R. T. Holt and J. E. Turner (New York: The Free Press, 1970), pp. 295-341.

35. E. Cassirer, *The Logic of the Humanities* (New Haven: Yale University Press, 1961), pp. 24-25.

36. B. L. Whorf, *The Relation of Language to Habitual Thought and Behavior* (1941), cited from Carroll, *Selected Writings of B. L. Whorf,* pp. 158-159.

37. E. Sapir, *The Grammarian and His Language* (1924), cited from Mandelbaum, *Selected Writings of E. Sapir,* pp. 153, 157.

38. From work of David French. On the general issue, see my papers cited in reference 20.

39. H. M. Hogan, "An Ethnography of Communication among the Ashanti," *Penn-Texas Working Papers in Sociolinguistics,* I (Austin: University of Texas, Department of Anthropology, 1971); R. Darnell, "Prolegomena to Typologies of Speech Use," *Texas Working Papers in Sociolinguistics* (Austin: University of Texas, Department of Anthropology, 1972); and papers by J. T. Irvine, E. O. Keenan and J. F. Sherzer in *The Ethnography of Speaking,* eds. R. Bauman and J. F. Sherzer (London and New York: Cambridge University Press, forthcoming).

40. M. Cole, J. Gay, J. A. Glick, D. W. Sharp, *The Cultural Context of Learning and Thinking* (New York: Basic Books, 1971) is an excellent demonstration of the

necessity of ethnography for assessment of linguistic and cognitive abilities, even though, unfortunately, the authors do not disclose the linguistic characteristics of the material on which their work rests.

41. B. Bernstein, "A Critique of the Concept 'Compensatory Education,'" *Functions of Language in the Classroom,* eds. C. Cazden, V. John-Steiner, and D. Hymes (New York: Teachers College Press, 1972).

42. J. Habermas, *Knowledge and Human Interests* (Boston: Beacon Press, 1971); cf. T. Schroyer, "A Reconceptualization of Critical Theory," *Radical Sociology,* eds. J. D. Colfax and J. L. Roach (New York: Basic Books, 1971); Schroyer, "Toward a Critical Theory for Advanced Industrial Society," *Recent Sociology No. 2,* ed. H. P. Dreitzel (New York: Macmillan, 1970); and Habermas, "Toward a Theory of Communicative Competence," *ibid.*

43. R. Bauman, "Speaking in the Light: The Role of the Quaker Minister," *The Ethnography of Speaking,* eds. Bauman and Sherzer.

44. Papers on language and religion from a working group at the 1972 Georgetown Round Table Conference; it is expected that these papers will be published under the editorship of W. Samarin.

45. W. S. Willis, Jr., "Skeletons in the Anthropological Closet," *Reinventing Anthropology,* ed. D. Hymes (New York: Pantheon, 1973). This discussion draws on my introduction to the book.

KARL V. TEETER

Linguistics and Anthropology

LINGUISTICS AND anthropology today have a peculiar relationship, simultaneously intimate and estranged.[1] If anthropology is the study of man, then linguistics is concerned with a fundamental element of man's existence, language. Language is what basically differentiates man from other animals in thought and communication, and linguistics is properly a subdivision of anthropology on a par with, for example, archaeology. Yet linguistic theory and method have developed largely without regard to the broader field. At the same time, linguistics has become peripheral in the training of anthropologists, and we have ended up with a situation where anthropological attitudes toward the field alternate between distrust and uncritical admiration. There is a basis for the distrust, for linguists have also narrowed their concerns during the modern period, and have had little indeed to say about the sociocultural roots of language. In this paper I shall say something about the background of the two fields, illustrate the uncritical admiration to which I have referred, and speculate on the source of misunderstandings. I shall mention an area, that of field research, in which the present-day linguist has much to learn from the anthropologist, and conclude with an examination of prospects for the integration of mutual interests, taking as paradigm recent work done on the *ethnography of speaking* which bids fair to establish a new and genuine linguistic anthropology.

In the first part of this century the integral relationship of linguistics and anthropology was taken for granted, and realized in the work of such figures as Franz Boas, A. L. Kroeber, Edward Sapir, Leonard Bloomfield, and Clyde Kluckhohn. Among problems in which the fields shared an interest, two were particularly important at the outset: the elucidation of human universals and the classification of peoples. In both, linguistic data figured prominently because linguistic categories are psychologically deep and, at the same time, linguistic data is relatively accessible. However, although focus on such problems provided a framework for inquiry, scholars soon lost their way, for it became obvious that they did not have enough descriptive data on either languages or cultures to validate any such broad-gauged investigation. As a result, the initial problems still have not been cogently treated;

indeed, they have been lost from sight, primarily because of two movements, relativism in anthropology and behaviorism in linguistics.

I have sketched the course of these two movements and their effects on linguistics elsewhere;[2] here it will suffice to summarize their effects. Relativism led anthropologists to shift their concerns to differences among cultures, and to defer questions of universals. A commitment to behaviorism allowed linguists to concentrate on relatively tractable problems, and to avoid precisely those most clearly linked to culture, for those were the ones that would have required analysis of troublesome entities like "mind." And so it came about that anthropologists described cultures, linguists languages, and the relationship between the fields lost its rationale for practitioners of both disciplines. Not surprisingly, given the social organization of academia, the split was now formalized by the establishment of separate university departments devoted to linguistics (whereas previously the subject had been an adjunct to anthropology or language departments).

This was the situation when, in the 1950's, some anthropologists began to rediscover linguistics (although I have to report that recognition in the opposite direction still lags). At this point, linguists had achieved fine-grained and well-validated analyses of tractable areas of language structure, and certain scholars who had cheerfully accepted academic compartmentalization began to wonder whether anthropology could not apply what linguists had learned.[3] At the same time, both linguists and anthropologists in America began to learn of European work which suggested new techniques and applications.[4] Anthropologists, however, were not properly prepared to assimilate the new insights (recall that linguistic training in the field had declined); furthermore, the techniques they borrowed derived from narrowly linguistic concerns whose space and application to other areas of culture was naturally open to question. This was the beginning of the attitude of uncritical admiration to which I have alluded, and I must admit that matters are not entirely straight yet.

Two celebrated examples of the techniques which anthropology borrowed from linguistics are the use of *etic-emic* distinctions and of componential and distinctive feature analysis. In both cases there has been something akin to a cultural lag, with anthropologists just beginning to apply a given body of techniques at the point when linguists were incorporating them into a wider framework. Let me elaborate somewhat on each of these techniques.

Etic and *emic* are fragments of the words *phonetic* and *phonemic*. The importance of this distinction for language was made clear in a brilliant 1925 paper by Edward Sapir, which shows step by step how two putative languages with exactly the same sounds may differ fundamentally in the uses to which they put these sounds.[5] Sapir's work sparked fruitful research in the phonemic analysis of languages, especially in the 1930's and 1940's: Since then phonemic analysis has continued to be one of an interrelated set of operations performed on data, and its principles have been generalized beyond the study of sounds.

The *phonemic principle* can be illustrated as follows. English uses both an *aspirated* p^h (a p followed by a puff of breath) and a plain p sound, but it uses them in totally predictable places: for example, we always use p^h to begin a word ("pin"), but p after an s at the beginning of a word ("spin"). So the distinction in English is purely *phonetic*, and we can construct one phoneme /p/ to refer to both varieties of sound. In Thai, on the other hand, *paj* means "go" while *p^haj* means "danger," so the same phonetic distinction functions unpredictably, that is, *phonemically*.

Consistent with this, an *etic* entity is one defined independently of a cultural system, whereas an *emic* unit can be defined only according to distinctions within a bounded system. The relevance of this concept to the structure of culture is easy to see, but how, in fact, to apply it is something else again. It is a commonplace that different cultures treat the same *etic* phenomena in different ways, but there are many realms of culture. The pattern of sound distinctions is obviously crucial in language, but where is its analogue in culture? Clearly, there is not just one, and blind application of the phonemic principle may simply lead to terminological proliferation without concomitant conceptual simplification. This has, in fact, happened in anthropology. We have been offered many sorts of units, from *behavioremes* to *gustemes* (dealing with taste). All may be valid, but how do they help us? I would answer: Without a frame of reference, very little.

A second advance in linguistics was the discovery that the phoneme and comparable units in grammar are analyzable, a discovery which owed much of the work of Roman Jakobson and Zellig S. Harris,[6] and has served as the basis of valuable research, especially in the 1940's and 1950's. This corrected an excess of past phonemic analysis, for it had been generally assumed that these hard-won and significant units were like atoms, mutually unrelatable building blocks. The new distinctive feature analysis can be illustrated by another example from phonology: English p is the same as b in that it is articulated by the lips and in various other features; in fact b differs from p solely in that it is voiced (there is a humming of the vocal cords). Thus p and, in general, the sounds represented by English phonemes, can be characterized by answers to a series of yes-no questions: labial? yes; voiced? no (or yes for b). Each phoneme is then represented in terms of its simultaneous components.

This leads to a truly important insight for the study of language. Such components or features are *phonetically* defined. Yet if one derives a feature system based on the differential *phonemic* function of these components in the structure of words and sentences, this phonemic system is rather similar to the phonetic one. For example, English s and z are closely related phonetically, differing only in that z is voiced. They are also closely related in that they function similarly to form the English plural: s in *cats* and z in dogs. This kind of analogy suggests that, although languages may be free to use different sound structures, they are constrained to use their phonetic resources relatively efficiently. Again, however, culture as a whole is more complex than language, and one would not expect this particular insight of linguistics to have simple analogues in culture. In fact, to my knowledge, none have been found.

The *logic* of componential analysis (note its resemblance to binary computer logic, which grew contemporaneously) is, however, easily adaptable, and has been widely used in anthropology, with results which are most impressive in rather tightly structured semantic subsystems of culture, in the analysis of kinship terms, for example, where its use was pioneered in America by Floyd G. Lounsbury.[7] Earlier, Claude Lévi-Strauss in France had published a basic book on kinship and social structure, integrating and extending a structural linguistic approach. Lévi-Strauss is particularly ambitious, for he evidently aims to account for all cultural data by constructing various kinds of feature systems. Unfortunately, the definition of variables and their *etic* grounding is far less straightforward for most cultural data than it is in the case of linguistic structure and, correspondingly, Lévi-Straussian analysis often looks circular and *ad hoc,* or at least odd, as it does when he exhaustively trichotomizes the universe of cultural treatment of food into *raw* versus *cooked* versus *rotted.*[8] Such devices should have their validity tested by considerations of how well they fit into a general theory of culture, and are not by themselves much help in anthropology; it is not obvious that there is a principled basis for the choice of some features and not others as distinctive.

There are similar limitations to other attempts to apply *etic-emic* and componential analysis in anthropology; in studies, for example, of folk taxonomies. A very common scientific dilemma arises: as long as one deals with a narrow and tightly structured subsystem, features can be concretely defined; but when one attempts to generalize, one does so only at the expense of content, and hence of cogency.

A third area in which linguistic techniques have been borrowed into anthropology is newer, and involves transformational theory as developed primarily by Noam Chomsky in the 1950's and 1960's.[9] I shall forego detailed discussion of this area since to date the applications known to me are highly programmatic. The general point, however, can be made again that, just as anthropologists are beginning to experiment with transformational techniques, linguists are generally recognizing that they require revision, and are, at the same time, incorporating them into linguistic theory as an essential device, as was previously done with phonemics and distinctive feature analysis.

It is no wonder, given what has been said so far, that currently there tends to be more suspicion than cooperation between linguistics and anthropology. The reflective anthropologist may well think of the linguist as a boy crying "wolf!", for every time applications of linguistic techniques in anthropology start to look interesting, the linguists themselves abandon the trail and set out after some new will-o'-the-wisp. The linguist, on the other hand, is apt to view the anthropologist as naive and too quick to mistake technical advances for substantive conclusions.

Another example of misunderstanding grows out of the ongoing work of language classification. Here linguistics operates, especially in the case of less well-studied languages, simultaneously at several stages. Classification is a means to reconstruct protolanguages (earlier forms of contemporary languages) and their historical development. But classification and historical study, though related, are separate tasks, so that for any group of languages at a given stage of research, there coexist preliminary and often contradictory classificatory hypotheses based on mere external similarities; hypotheses, in various stages, on detailed subgroupings, and history based on postulations about historical entities and their interactions. The anthropologist wants immediately usable correlations, and is apt to seize on the wider of these hypotheses without regard to their tentativeness or their relation to historical work, and to give them more weight than they are fit to bear. An excellent case in point is the reception of Edward Sapir's 1929 classification of North American Indian languages, in which he offered two stages of his work at once: a grouping of twenty-three units based on evidence, and an educated guess on a reduction to six families which future evidence might validate.[10] Despite his caution that the latter scheme was still far from demonstrable (this is still the case), it was the one used in textbooks and in further speculation, to the virtual exclusion of the narrower, more fully validated classification. Such a fact is discouraging to those, linguists or anthropologists, seeking to work out actual linguistic relationships in detail.

But the situation described does not result solely from the naïveté of anthropologists and the parochialism of linguists. It reflects a real difference in the nature of the data handled by anthropologists when they are doing linguistics and when they are engaged in other pursuits such as the study of human culture, society, physique, or artifacts. Whether he is analyzing grammar or tracing history, the linguist deals with data that reflect system more directly than data in any other field of anthropology, simply because speech is a direct practical means of dealing with the world whose everyday utility would be defeated by intellectual reflection. People just do not have the time for extensive conscious reworking of the way they express themselves. To find a place for new discoveries and inventions, a culture must often tolerate profound changes; speech, however, accommodates them more easily, often by simply extending existing resources. The introduction of the tomato into the Mediterranean from the New World, for example, has extensively affected the cuisine and agriculture of circum-Mediterranean countries, necessitating deep cultural adaptations; linguistically, however, it was easily taken in stride. Italian *pomidoro* "golden apple" barely touches the grammar of the Italian language.

This is not to deny the role of reflection on speech—to do so would be to deny poetic art. The point is that poetry increases the resources of a language without deeply affecting the structure of everyday speech; language, in comparison with other cultural phenomena, is affected very little by secondary elaboration. Linguistic changes are slow and systematic and, in fortunate cases, can be reconstructed in detail undreamed of in a field like the history of agriculture. They are, however, only the tip of an unconscious iceberg which is immense and internally complex.

This point was cogently made by the father of American anthropology, Franz Boas, as long ago as 1911:

The essential difference between linguistic phenomena and other ethnological phenomena is, that the linguistic classifications never rise into consciousness, while in other ethnological phenomena, although the same unconscious origin prevails, these often rise into consciousness, and thus give rise to secondary reasoning and to re-interpretations.[11]

The mature Sapir echoes his teacher's words, citing language as "the symbolic guide to culture" and linguistics, therefore, as having "strategic importance for the methodology of social science."[12] One thing which language and the rest of culture do share, and which crucially influences their nature, is their mode of transmission. They are not "learned by experience," nor are they innate. Rather, language and culture are communicated, passed on by example and by word of mouth; hence, even to exist, they must be to some degree communicable, or symbolic. Furthermore, insofar as communication takes place by means of language, language is basic to culture. Both language and culture are, to be sure, uniquely human, and so innate to man. But their realization is, at one remove, linguistic.

Leonard Bloomfield, a founding father of American structural linguistics, has been charged with responsibility for the divorce of linguistic and anthropological (ethnological) concerns, and the charge has a certain credence, considering Bloomfield's concentration on descriptive methodology in linguistics. Yet Bloomfield also understood well the crucial relationship of linguistics and anthropology:

The science of language, dealing with the most basic and simplest of human social institutions, is a human (or mental or, as they used to say, moral) science. It is most closely related to ethnology, but precedes ethnology and all other human sciences in the order of growing complexity, for linguistics starts at their foot, immediately after psychology, the connecting link between the natural sciences and the human.[13]

The lesson here is that linguists and anthropologists must recognize their obvious and natural relationship if it is to be maximally fruitful. There is no reason to assume that a model or a method which is revealing for specific data in one field will even be applicable in the other. As Hymes points out, in cases where techniques inspired by linguistics have led to real results in anthropology, it has been "where the basic principles and goals of linguistic method have been understood, and the effort has been to work out the implications of those principles for the foundations of work in another area."[14] The fate of work that has been successful has not been "tied to the fate of a particular formulation of linguistic method."[15]

I have referred above to two linguistically influenced approaches in current anthropology which have indeed been successful: *structural anthropology* and *ethnoscience*. I shall characterize them very briefly here.[16] *Structural anthropology* is indissolubly associated with the name and work of Claude Lévi-Strauss and is, like the other Lévi-Strauss work mentioned, based on structural analyses of ethnographic phenomena in terms of distinctive feature systems, often rather abstract and often difficult to validate.

Ethnoscience is the name given by its practitioners to a system of ethnographic description in which the main emphasis is on how members of a culture classify their universe, and which utilizes *etic-emic* and other methods to make these matters precise. Much of the research in this area is rather narrow first-level description in which cross-cultural significance does not play a major role, but recently a very ambitious and not entirely successful attempt has been made to establish the universality and evolutionary order of the acquisition of color vocabulary.[17]

Anthropologists, then, can profit from what linguists do, in just the manner specified by Boas, Sapir, and Bloomfield. Perhaps in the future anthropologists and linguists will be able to return with more sophistication to a joint inquiry into the basic problems of culture which Boas posed. In the meantime, linguists also have much to learn from anthropologists, and to this matter I now turn.

The modern history of linguistics reveals a steady growth away from concern with the sociocultural context of language toward problems which were relatively easy to solve, or at least to delineate. If the trend in anthropology has been centrifugal, and threw linguistics apart, linguistics has, for the most part, gloried in the situation centripetally. The linguistic center has been an idealized homogenized speaker-hearer for each language, who speaks always in the same style and to the same purpose. Insofar as real people are like this, at least descriptive linguistics is autonomous. But for purposes of achieving any relevant notions about language as a means by which man communicates, limitation to a perspective of this sort is intolerable. Among its other defects, it fragments linguistics itself, for historical linguistics deals with the description of change, and a static grammar, strictly speaking, cannot change. There are several ways in which linguistics, in this situation, needs the cultural anthropologist. I shall speak of one very specific one and then conclude by discussing a joint enterprise, barely begun, by means of which the linguist can solve these particular problems and the anthropologist can solve some of his.

One specific situation in which linguists need anthropologists is the current desuetude of field methods in linguistic study, a dangerous thing if it continues, for theoretical predictions in linguistics can only be validated by an examination of what people in fact say. This inattention to field methods, I believe, grows out of an extension of the historical process sketched at the beginning of this paper to explain the rift between linguistics and anthropology. From the beginning of this rift, in the 1920's and 1930's, the autonomy of linguistics progressed as it came under the influence of psychological behaviorism and philosophical positivism.[18] Eventually this resulted in a narrowing of the linguist's conception of his task to that of "stating the facts," and, since even facts need to be warranted somehow, linguists of the 1940's and 1950's came to place an undue burden on their field techniques, virtually substituting them for theory.

By the late 1950's, linguists were sharply and justly criticized for what amounted to a requirement for the use of mechanical discovery procedures, to a demand that theoretical understanding flow automatically from raw data. Linguists have gradually accepted the critique and resumed their search, with considerable progress, for explicit theoretical formulations.

But along with this process, "field methods" and "discovery procedures" seem to have been confounded, and whereas twenty years ago, linguistics was centered on field methods, today even discussions of subtle syntactic problems are often carried on in the total absence of validated facts. The discussions are like a game, the principles of which anybody can learn. A person begins by asserting, "In my dialect, I say such-and-such," and then an analysis is proposed that turns out elegantly to account for just the deviant data which has been supplied. To be sure, the problems of such a method are minimized when the analytical principles under discussion have fairly wide application and when the language analyzed is native to the analyst, and both are typically the case. Just as analysis becomes more sophisticated, however, the point may begin to hang on more and more suspicious data, and all too frequently it does. The argument has even been heard that linguistic facts are so subtle as to render them impenetrable by any but a native-speaker linguist, which brings us uncomfortably close to the old half truth that experience is unique and translation therefore impossible. There is surely no question of the desirability of linguist and native speaker being the same, and some interesting programs in training speakers to describe their languages are underway. In the meantime there are a few thousand languages to study as best we can.

To shorten what could be a much longer story, then, one simple practical way in which linguistics now needs anthropology is to reaffirm the importance of direct study of the materials used to formulate theories and build descriptions. Validation should be as direct as possible; this has traditionally been the ideal throughout anthropology, and when a living language is the object, sound field study is vital, irrespective of whether the linguist is a native speaker or not. Self-deception as to the "real data" is all too easy.

So much for the mutual desiderata of cooperation. There is now a growing area in which linguists and anthropologists can work truly and equally to mutual profit, and I conclude this paper by sketching the main lines of this inquiry. The approach is new enough not to have a stable name. Dell Hymes has suggested *anthropology of communication*, but the two parts of the new linguistic anthropology which is developing are more modestly referred to as *sociolinguistics* and the *ethnography of speaking*.[19] The crux of the problem, as I mentioned above, is the dilemma of an autonomous linguistics which studies static systems. The difficulty arises when such systems are applied in sociocultural contexts. What people actually say is complex and even contradictory, and not to be accounted for on the basis of such systems alone. This has been an embarrassment to linguists, but one which they have sloughed off by drawing a distinction between what they call a speaker's *competence* and his actual *performance*, strongly implying that it is really competence alone that matters and is systematic (and perhaps static). But one can scarcely evaluate such claims without studying language in use, and it is in this direction that sociolinguistics and the ethnography of speaking are leading, a direction which will, in short, put linguistics back into anthropology.

There is no question that people *know* their language, in a deep sense. Every normal child has internalized a basic grammar of rules based on what he has really heard in his actual speech community; furthermore, such grammars are relatively uniform and quite regular in their output. It is just this situation which has allowed the independent development of linguistics and which accounts for its success. It also accounts for the fact, which every decent ethnographer must regard with envy, that one can pick a native speaker nearly at random, and construct a pretty good basic grammar for his speech community from the data he supplies.

The trouble is that if we aspire to an explanatory view of language, or even to a comprehensive description, we cannot stop here. Unquestionably, people talk the way they do in part because of the deep internalized knowledge of their language on which the linguist relies for his basic grammar. If he faces at all the problem of accounting for speech variation and linguistic change in the face of this uniform grammar, he tends to see them as due to randomness and slippage in the use and transmission of the grammar. But as soon as we look at actual speech communities we see that variation in speech is first, universal; second, highly patterned; and third, closely correlated to cultural and subcultural situations. That is to say, people not only know their language, they know how to use it. People talk the way they do not solely because they possess an abstract systematic *knowledge* of their language. They also have a *command* of the language. And by now research in the ethnography of speaking—the scientific description of the use and understanding of language in a culture—has clearly established that command is as patterned as knowledge.

So the study of language may still begin with what Bloomfield called the fundamental assumption of linguistics: that within a speech community some utterances are the same, though all differ as pure phenomena. Nobody says quite the same thing twice, but they are taken to do so. People share knowledge and grammar and speakers of the same language talk much the same way. Yet it is equally true that, no matter how limited the speech community, and even given a shared grammar, nobody always talks in exactly the same way. We can even adumbrate some of the reasons why this is the case. First of all, certain ways of talking serve as badges of membership in regional or social groups. Speech is not confined to cognitive communication. One's speech has distinctive characteristics depending on whether one is speaking within a group or outside of it, to a subgroup or to an individual, to those perceived as superior, or as inferior. All of these factors affect the output of a person's grammar in patterned and linguistically characterizable ways. Secondly, within a given group people talk in different ways in different situations. Some modes of speaking—swearwords, for example—call attention to one's feelings. Others, like "your congressman" used in direct address, cater to an audience. Still others place the form itself of an utterance in relief—"something there is that doesn't love a wall." The first group of factors have to do with *dialect*, the second with *style* and the functions of speech.

Not only do such observations have the potential to place the description of language variation on a scientific basis, but they also provide the material for a principled explanation of the process of linguistic change. In speech people adapt to their interlocutors and to their self-images, and as situations change, so do situationally determined modes of speaking. What has at one time been colorful speech, for example, may become banal. In the course of transmission, such speech may lose its special mark as an aspect of command and become instead a part of general knowledge of the language, for each new member of a speech community constructs his own grammar on the basis of what he hears. Labov has even demonstrated linguistic changes in progress, something previous linguists have tried to read out of existence, showing correlations between socioeconomic status and modes of pronunciation.[20]

There have been many vicissitudes in the status of linguistics relative to anthropology—some of which I have discussed here—and there will, no doubt, be more. The approach known as the ethnography of speaking, however, once more squarely unites the two fields in an inquiry essential to both, and gives us new hope of studying seriously what Einar Haugen has called the *ecology of language*.[21]

REFERENCES

1. In preparing this paper I have benefited immensely from the work of Dell Hymes, who has been the most cogent, prolific, and persistent writer on those interests shared by linguistics and anthropology.

2. Karl V. Teeter, "Descriptive Linguistics in America: Triviality vs. Irrelevance," *Word*, XX (1964), 197-206.

3. Here pride of place must be granted to Kenneth L. Pike, Ward H. Goodenough, and Floyd G. Lounsbury. See, for example, Pike, *Language in Relation to a Unified Theory of the Structure of Human Behavior* (The Hague: Mouton, 1967; preliminary edition published in three parts in 1954, 1955, and 1960); Goodenough, "Cultural Anthropology and Linguistics," *Monograph Series on Language and Linguistics*, IX (Washington, D.C.: Georgetown University Press, 1957), pp. 167-173; Lounsbury, "Similarity and Contiguity Relations in Language and in Culture," *Monograph Series*, X, pp. 123-128. Other scholars as well, of course, had never divided their linguistic work from anthropology, most notably students of Edward Sapir such as Mary R. Haas, Stanley Newman, and Morris Swadesh.

4. American scholars benefited from the presence here of Roman Jakobson and André Martinet after the Second World War. The anthropologist Claude Lévi-Strauss was also influential; see his "L'analyse structurale en linguistique et anthropologie," *Word*, I (1945), 33-53.

5. Edward Sapir, "Sound Patterns in Language," *Language*, I (1925), 37-51.

6. See, for example, many of the papers reprinted in Jakobson, *Selected Writings I: Phonological Studies* (The Hague: Mouton, 1962) and relevant portions of Harris, *Methods in Structural Linguistics* (Chicago: University of Chicago Press, 1951).

7. Lounsbury, "A Semantic Analysis of the Pawnee Kinship Usage," *Language*, XXXII (1958), 158-194; Lévi-Strauss, *Les structures élémentaires de la parenté* (Paris: Presses universitaires de France, 1949, rev. ed. 1967).

8. Lévi-Strauss, "Le triangle culinaire," *L'Arc*, XXVI (1965), 19-29. In fairness, I should also refer the reader to his major book *Le cru et le cuit, Mythologiques I* (Paris: Plon, 1964), in which more than meets the eye is done with this classification.

9. The canonical texts are Noam Chomsky, *Syntactic Structures* (The Hague: Mouton, 1957), and *Aspects of the Theory of Syntax* (Cambridge: M.I.T. Press, 1965).

10. Sapir, "Central and North American Indian Languages," *Encyclopedia Britannica*[14], V (1929), 138-141.

11. Boas, "Introduction," *Handbook of American Indian Languages* (1911), as reprinted in Bison Book 301 (Lincoln: University of Nebraska Press, 1966).

12. Sapir, "The Status of Linguistics as a Science," *Language*, V (1929), 207-214, esp. pp. 210, 213.

13. Bloomfield, "Why a Linguistic Society?," *Language*, I (1925), 1-5, esp. p. 1.

14. Dell Hymes, "Linguistic Models in Archaeology," *Archéologie et calculateurs* (Paris: Éditions du Centre National de la Recherche Scientifique, 1970), pp. 91-120, esp. p. 94.

15. Hymes, "Linguistic Method in Ethnography," *Method and Theory in Linguistics,* ed. Paul L. Garvin (The Hague: Mouton, 1970), pp. 249-325, esp. p. 295. This paper gives a comprehensive picture of the subject with a very helpful bibliography.

16. A convenient introduction to the former is Lévi-Strauss, *Anthropologie structurale* (Paris: Plon, 1958); translated into English by Claire Jacobson and Brooke Grundfest Schoepf as *Structural Anthropology* (New York: Basic Books, 1963, and available in paperback as well). No such comprehensive and accessible survey is available for ethnoscience, but an excellent summary is William C. Sturtevant, "Studies in Ethnoscience," *Transcultural Studies in Cognition,* eds. A. Kimball Romney and Roy Goodwin D'Andrade, published as a supplement to *American Anthropologist,* LXVI, No. 3 (June 1964).

17. Brent Berlin and Paul Kay, *Basic Color Terms: Their Universality and Evolution* (Berkeley and Los Angeles: University of California Press, 1969).

18. This is further discussed in my paper cited in fn. 2.

19. Basic documents are Hymes, "The Ethnography of Speaking," *Anthropology and Human Behavior,* eds. T. Gladwin and William C. Sturtevant (Washington: The Anthropological Society of Washington, 1962), pp. 12-53; "Introduction: Toward Ethnographies of Communication," *The Ethnography of Communication,* eds. John J. Gumperz and Dell Hymes, pp. 1-34, published as a supplement to *American Anthropologist,* LXVI, No. 6 (December 1964); "The Anthropology of Communication," *Human Communication Theory,* ed. Frank X. Dance (New York: Holt, Rinehart, and Winston, 1967), pp. 1-39; "Sociolinguistics and the Ethnography of Speaking," *Social Anthropology and Language,* ed. Edwin Ardener (London: Tavistock, 1971), pp. 47-93; William Labov, "The Study of Language in Its Social Context," *Studium Generale,* XXIII (1970), 30-87.

20. Labov, "The Study of Language in Its Social Context."

21. A. S. Dil, ed., *The Ecology of Language: Essays by Einar Haugen* (Stanford: Stanford University Press, 1972).

CALVERT WATKINS

Language and Its History

IN THE YEAR 1812 a young German named Franz Bopp—he was twenty-one at the time—traveled to Paris to read Oriental languages. He stayed for four years, serenely unconcerned with the Napoleonic wars; his biographer Windischmann wrote,

In these labors he did not let himself be disturbed by the storms of the times; with every change in things he stayed peacefully in Paris, always cheerful and hard at work, and doubly happy to be visited by German friends.[1]

The appearance, in 1816, of his book *On the Conjugation System of Sanskrit, Compared with That of the Greek, Latin, Persian, and Germanic Languages,* marks the birth of the comparative method. Bopp was not the first to discover that Sanskrit was related to these other languages, the family we now term Indo-European (the English orientalist Sir William Jones made that discovery in 1786), but he was the first to establish comparison on a systematic basis as an autonomous science to explain the forms of one language by those of another.

The comparative method is not very complicated. Certain languages have similarities which are so numerous and so precise that they cannot be attributed to chance, to contact (borrowing), or to linguistic universals. The comparatist's hypothesis is that these resemblances among languages must be the result of their development from a common original language no longer spoken. The similarities are said to be *genetic* in character, and the languages are spoken of as *related*.

The same method is perfectly applicable to domains other than that of language. Though the term "comparative law" in jurisprudence normally refers to purely typological comparisons, it can also refer to genetic comparisons. A historian of Roman law, Leopold Wenger, has written that

Any comparison of legal institutions [in different societies], when it is able to establish identities or similarities, must attempt to give account for the causes of such phenomena. Three primary possibilities come to mind: reception [borrowing], common provenience [inheritance], independent but similar creation of legal institutions [universality].[2]

Such a statement could be found in any linguistics textbook.

85

It is doubtless the model of linguistics which has been extended to other disciplines, and the method has been more successful in language than in other areas of culture. For comparison is a discovery procedure, not a discipline. It establishes the similarities and equations which presuppose a common origin. But the critical part comes afterward: as Antoine Meillet has stated of these similarities, "It remains to interpret them in a systematic manner. That is the object of comparative historical linguistics."[3]

Wherever the comparative method is carried to a successful conclusion, it leads to the restoration of an original, "initial" language. That is to say, it leads to the postulation of the grammar and lexicon of a protolanguage: in the case of our own family, Proto- or Common Indo-European. This is what we mean by the term *reconstruction*. In spite of all the cautionary hedges that we may put up, a reconstruction *is* a real model, constructed to the best of our ability, of how we think certain people talked at a remote period before recorded history. It remains true, as Mary Haas has put it, that a reconstructed protolanguage is "a glorious artifact, one which is far more precious than anything an archaeologist can ever hope to unearth."[4]

We must not forget, of course, that the reconstruction, the postulated grammar which is arbitrarily considered the initial point in the historical linguistic process, is an artifact reflecting the contemporary state of intellectual development. As such, it is subject to change, just as all intellectual artifacts or scientific propositions are. Linguists are for some reason continually surprised, indeed shocked, by this. The great Irish philologist Osborn Bergin once remarked wryly that no language had changed so much in the last fifty years as Indo-European. One tends to forget that in the quarter century between the first printing of a reconstructed Indo-European word and 1878, when Saussure's *Mémoire* appeared, the face of Indo-European changed more profoundly than during almost a century from that day to this.

This mutability applies also to the model of the kinship relations obtaining among a set of languages, the configuration of the family tree, which may also be modified—like any scientific proposition—by new data. The Hittite language, dating from the second millennium B.C. and deciphered only during the First World War, differs in many respects from the traditionally reconstructed Indo-European. Certain scholars, who have a following even today, decided that Hittite was only laterally related to Indo-European, and that the two should constitute a new family called *Indo-Hittite*. But this means accepting the traditional—indeed rather old-fashioned—reconstruction of Indo-European as an immutable natural entity, which it is not. As Benveniste has said, "we must integrate Hittite into an Indo-European whose definition and internal relations will be transformed by this new contribution."[5]

A grammar of Indo-European must take account of certain realities.

Naturally, the first is that in dealing with an unattested reconstructed language, we must operate by inference and not by direct observation of speech or written texts. Consequently, a description of a reconstructed language is necessarily far from complete. One must have no illusions on this matter: even after 150 years of steady progress in the comparative method and in the establishment of Indo-European grammar, we are still incapable of reconstructing a single well-made Indo-European sentence of the most trivial complexity. Reconstructing sentences is, of course, not our aim, but to a lesser degree the same indeterminacy is to be found in most parts of Indo-European grammar.

The second reality is that the grammar of a reconstructed language cannot be *synchronic*. It cannot describe a whole linguistic system as it existed at any point in time. We can establish the relative chronology of individual reconstructed features of, for example, the grammar, but it is beyond our powers to associate the reconstructed features of the grammar with each other so as to form a picture of a total linguistic system as it might have existed at a specific time in prehistory. Indo-European, or any other reconstructed language, can refer only to sets of separate linguistic states in a temporal continuum, sequences which cannot with certainty be coordinated with one another.

The third reality is the most important. The reconstruction of Indo-European, the establishment, that is, of the grammar of that language to the best of our ability, is not our fundamental object, as it would be if we were writing a descriptive grammar of a known language. Rather, our ultimate aim is to write the linguistic history of known languages. We are seeking a historical explanation for the grammar of languages accessible to us by observation or from written texts. Reconstruction is only a tool, a means to the end of understanding linguistic history.

Even if we were, by some miracle, handed a complete grammar of Common Indo-European as spoken somewhere in, say, 4000 B.C. (the date is meaningless), the work of the Indo-Europeanist would scarcely be done. In fact, it would be barely begun. For his task would be, then as before, to relate the facts vouchsafed him to the facts of attested languages: to construct hypotheses, and to demonstrate precisely how it is possible, within a linguistic tradition or traditions, for a language to pass from one system at one point in time to another system at a later point. The position of the specialist in Romance languages offers a clear analogue.

But we are, in fact, not vouchsafed this Indo-European grammar, and must operate by inference from the attested languages to restore a common prototype, a prototype which serves only as a means to establish the history of these same attested languages. Thus historical linguistics and comparative grammar necessarily have a dialectic relationship.

Comparison is not, as Meillet thought, the only effective tool for illuminating linguistic history. Purely internal comparison, termed *internal reconstruction*, in which the examination of synchronically alternating forms leads to historical statements, can be equally effective. We can explain the Latin *aes* "bronze," genitive *aeris*, and its adjectival derivative *aēnus* "brazen" on the basis of these forms alone. We can reconstruct the earlier form of the stem as the two syllable *aës-* with the adjectival suffix, *-nus*, and assume a set of phonological changes which are actually historical events: the earlier *aës* changed to *aes;* the earlier *aës-is* changed to the genitive *aeris*, and the earlier *aës-nus* changed to the three-syllable *aēnus*. An external comparison with the Sanskrit *ayas* "copper, bronze" would also tell us that a still earlier form of the word was *ayes-*, whence *aës-;* but it is the Latin evidence alone which discriminates the two vowels of the reconstruction, and the phonological changes we postulate are relevant only to the prehistory of Latin.

As Jerzy Kuryłowicz has stated: "Comparison is not an end in itself. It is one of the techniques which historical linguistics has at its disposal and which it makes use of for as long as it can be applied in a useful fashion."[6] As an alternative to the technique of straight comparison, the historical linguist may, and often must, formulate a hypothesis or reconstruction about a state of affairs in the parent or common language, and then control his hypothesis by reconstructing forward in time until he reaches historically attested documentation for the various languages of the family he is studying. The correctness of a hypothesis is proved precisely by its ability to predict—generate if you will—the correct output. Such a technique contrasts notably with the earlier view that the method of comparative historical linguistics was essentially retrospective, a working backwards in time. But *prospective reconstruction* is the only way we can hope to recover the internal dynamics of the process of change itself.

The term *prospective method* was used by Ferdinand de Saussure in a very different sense, to refer to the direct observation of *diachronic* change in a language by studying texts written at successive periods, a century or so apart. This exercise is valuable, but only in a limited way, for it reveals the results, the output of individual changes, but not the process of change. Only a dynamic, prospective model of the changes themselves can give a satisfactory account of the process; and the nature of such a model is still at issue. A historical sequence of texts is a series of outputs of successive *synchronic* grammars—grammars, in other words, which were complete at a particular point in time. The problem of the linguistic historian, however, is to determine how one grammar actually changes into a succeeding one.

It is to Ferdinand de Saussure that linguistics owes the concept of opposition between diachrony and synchrony in language, between the diachronic and the synchronic study of language. For Saussure there was an antinomy between the two, both as objects of study, and as branches of study. He contrasted language as a synchronic state at a particular point in time, with language undergoing change as a diachronic process. He made a corresponding distinction between two kinds of linguistics:

Synchronic linguistics will be concerned with the logical and psychological relations that bind together coexisting terms and form a system, as they are perceived by the same collective consciousness.

Diachronic linguistics, on the contrary, will study the relations that bind together successive terms not perceived by the same collective consciousness, and which are substituted for each other without forming a system.[7]

A cornerstone of this antinomy was Saussure's assumption that only synchrony could constitute a system. He correlated this with his even more famous antinomy, placing a synchronic state of a language on the plane of *langue* ("language" and to some extent "competence"), and diachrony or language change on the plane of *parole* ("speech" and to some extent "performance"). Since for him the notion of system or "structure" (though Saussure never used the latter term) was a feature of *langue* but not of *parole*, his view[8] of diachronic linguistics as lacking system or "structure" was inevitable. For Saussure, following the nineteenth century view, saw language change as blind, fortuitous, isolated, and involuntary—something which could be studied only from outside the system it disrupted. He considered language change equivalent to a deterioration which obliged speakers at a later synchronic stage to reorder as best they could various *disiecta membra* to form a new synchronic system.

Yet with Saussure (as with his most illustrious pupil Antoine Meillet) one must balance his programmatic statements with his actual practice as a linguist. As we might expect, his rarely read doctoral dissertation of 1881, *On the Use of the Genitive Absolute in Sanskrit,* is the model of a rigorously synchronic study. It is concerned with the pure description of a feature of Sanskrit grammar of the classical period and accomplishes its task with rare precision. The work contains not a whisper of the diachronic, nor of the comparative.

It is instructive, however, to contrast this study with Saussure's first and greatest publication, the *Mémoire sur le système primitif des voyelles en indo-européen,* which appeared in 1878 when Saussure was twenty-one. This contribution to Indo-European linguistics was destined to revolutionize the field, and to lay the foundation on which our notions of Indo-European grammar still rest today. The work is directed toward a problem which today would be regarded as diachronic or historical, namely the reconstruction of the Indo-European vowel system. The young Saussure, however, had already developed and refined the *classical structural* technique of linguistic analysis to a degree of perfection rarely equaled since. And in the *Mémoire* Saussure moves effortlessly and at will between the diachronic and the synchronic. The character of his demonstration and the relentless logic of his proof[9] is wholly structural, as he proceeds systematically over what he called a "series of problems of phonology and morphology, some of which still await their solution, and most of which have not even been stated."[10] The result, however, is a set of rigorously synchronic statements—cast in the form of synchronically ordered rules, be it noted—about the protolanguage Indo-European. For Saussure, his task as historian was to free the ancient vowel system from "the modern humus which various accidents had heaped upon it."[11] Once so freed, the original system could be and was described as a synchronic fact.

The theoretical basis for the antinomy between synchrony and diachrony posed in the *Cours de linguistique*, published in 1916, three years after Saussure's death, was happily dispelled by Roman Jakobson in 1929, with the publication of his *Remarks on the Phonological Evolution of Russian Compared to That of the Other Slavic Languages*.[12] As Jakobson eloquently showed, language change is neither blind, nor fortuitous, nor isolated, nor involuntary. On the one hand, any destructive process or "deterioration" is followed by a creative reaction; on the other, the very existence of change—a necessary consequence of the fact that language must be learned anew by each succeeding generation—entails evolutive, teleological developments. The notion of *conspiracy* in current generative phonology, whereby unconnected rules in a grammar are said to *conspire* to produce a common effect, is only a manifestation (not always recognized) of this principle. Jakobson took the Saussurian image of synchronic language as a chess game in which the position of every piece on the board enters into a relation with every other piece, and brilliantly extended it to the diachronic plane. He saw the loss of a piece (or, with regard to language, a historical event) as provoking a series of displacements among other pieces to re-establish balance. He stated that

the theory of a historical process is only possible on the condition that the entity undergoing change be considered as a structure governed by internal laws, and not as a fortuitous agglomerate. . . . A theory of the diachrony of language is possible only if viewed as a problem of the changes of structure and the structure of changes.[13]

In his *Remarks* Jakobson went on to demonstrate in elegant fashion the correctness of his view of linguistic change on the level of phonology. He showed the systemic character of sound change and counterchange, and the complex interplay of a great variety of implicational relations of the type "if *a*, then *b*" and "if *c*, then not *d*," whose very existence had not hitherto been suspected, and whose consequences have not to this day been fully explored.

It was understandable and indeed predictable that phonology, dealing with the sounds of language, would be the first aspect of linguistics submitted to the notion of structure in diachrony, just as the regularity of sound changes, the "exceptionlessness of sound laws," had become the rallying cry of the Neogrammarian movement in the 1870's. It is necessary to assert, however, that sound change is by no means the whole of language change, and that other aspects of grammar also have internal dynamics which profoundly influence the direction of changes within them. Indeed, we have yet to see a theory of diachronic linguistics which gives a full principled account of these dynamics and of their operation.

Consider an illustration. On the evidence of forms like the Sanskrit *syāt* we can confidently reconstruct the Indo-European third person singular, optative mood, of the verb "to be," as *siēt*. In Classical Latin the third person singular form is *sit*, this time in the subjunctive mood. *Siēt* becomes *sit* as the result of four successive changes: (1) final voiceless stops become voiced; -*p* -*t* -*k* go to -*b* -*d* -*g*, thus *siēt* changes to *siēd*, a form which happens to be documented in an inscription of the sixth century B.C. *Secondary* endings originally used in past tense and non-indicative moods (the third person singular was -*d*) were eliminated in favor of *primary* endings originally used only in the present indicative (the third person singular was -*t*). Thus *siēd* changed back to *siēt*. (3) Long vowels were shortened before certain final consonants, including -*t* but not -*s*; thus *siēt* changed to *siet*. (4) The anomaly (occurring here only in Latin) of alternating forms of the modal suffix in this verb, -*iē*- in the singular but -*ī*- in the plural (the Latin plural is *sīmus*), was eliminated, and the short form -*ī*- used in the singular as well as in the plural. Thus the second person singular *siēs* was replaced by *sīs*, and the third person singular *siet* became *sit*, the Classical Latin form.

Diagrammatically, and in chronological order, here are the four successive changes:

(1) *siēt* goes to *siēd*
(2) *siēd* is replaced by *siēt*
(3) *siēt* goes to *siet*
(4) *siet* is replaced by *sit*.

Only (1) and (3) are straight sound changes. (2) and (4) are basically morphological changes or replacements. They illustrate the elimination or realignment of morphological or morphophonemic categories, which have a profound effect on the phonetic shape of the forms which implement such categories. Equally profound is the change of the function of the form, *siēt*. In Indo-European, the form was in the optative mood, a modal category opposed both to the indicative and to the subjunctive; whereas in Latin, by the time of the first sound change in our series, the only modal category opposed to the indicative was the new "subjunctive" which used the old optative forms. (The old subjunctive had been utilized to form the future tense which Indo-European lacked.) It must be granted that beside these sweeping changes, the role of straightforward sound change, of changes in phonological rules, is rather small. Of course, the understanding of sound change remains an indispensable part of historical linguistics, but the importance of morphological change, of change in grammatical categories, has been consistently underestimated. Generative grammar, both synchronic and diachronic, has failed as well to appreciate this aspect of the nature of language and language change.

A profitable area of observation for the linguist concerned with the internal dynamics of linguistic history is observable change. Recent investigations of "sound change in progress" by W. Labov[14] involve very detailed observation of phonological variation within a speech community, and correlation of the variants (which may be phonetically minute) with styles of speech, or with social groups determined, for example, by class or age. The approach is certainly promising, although clearly it can only be used by trained linguists. Indeed, to assure effective coverage of a speech community of any size, it probably requires a considerable team of linguistic observers.

A more serious drawback, however, is the implicit assumption of the study that sound change, phonetic or phonological, is the only kind of language change, which it is not. Other vast areas of language change, in lexicon and grammar, whose effects on the fabric of the language are far more immediately observable than straight sound change, should show up in the same sort of investigation. A little over a hundred years ago, for example, cookbooks might give directions on how to "seethe" an egg; it is certain that between then and now there was a period when both "seethe" and "boil" were available as competing variants, with the choice governed by a variety of doubtless quite subtle factors. This period was followed ultimately by the total elimination of "seethe" in this context. Nothing theoretical would lead us to suppose that similar variants could not be observed in a fine-grained synchronic investigation, and correlations with speech style and social class might indicate the direction of future change.

It is to be hoped that in the future such studies will encompass a far greater range of observation than those of the present, which are essentially confined to phonology or to relatively surface-level morphological features. There is no principled reason why, for example, changes in whole systems of grammatical categories should not be equally observable. It would be of great theoretical interest if we could observe the precise mechanism by which a language loses a case system in its nouns, as did the Romance languages, or reduces or gives up entirely the opposition of grammatical genders, as did English, and Armenian in its prehistoric period.

In such synchronic investigations of language change in progress, what is of greatest theoretical interest is not the fact of change but the manner of change. We need much more precise information than we have about the interplay of competing variants, alternate styles, and linguistic inter-action among the social groups differing, sometimes widely, in class, age, occupation, and cultural allegiance, which make up a speech community of any complexity. Such investigations, founded squarely on the nature of language as a social fact, would shed much light on the social factors in linguistic change.

A more traditional area of observable linguistic history within lin-guistic synchrony deals with the distinction between productive and nonproductive forms within a language at a particular time. *Productive* forms, or features, or rules, are those which can be freely extended to new words, or utilized to form new derivatives, while *nonproductive* ones cannot. As Jakobson has put it, productive forms are those which have a future. The English past suffix "-ed" ("televise" : "televised") is pro-ductive, while the past with vowel change ("take" : "took") is not. Pro-ductivity is frequently a sign of relative lateness. It follows that a catalogue of the "irregularities," the nonproductive forms of a language, is at the same time a catalogue of the most archaic features of that language and those which are most valuable as tokens of its past. As Meillet has said, "We reconstruct on the basis of the exceptions, not of the rules."[15] There is a real difference between the descriptive linguist, who looks first for the synchronic rules of greatest generality, and the historical linguist, for whom the synchronic rules of least generality are the most valuable as evidence.

The cases considered so far—language change in progress and the relative productivity of linguistic features—presume the presence of the linguist as an observer of "history in progress," of diachrony in synchrony. Scarcely a human society is to be found, however, where the speakers themselves are not fully aware of differences in speech habits between generations; the age correlate makes the appellation "old-fashioned" an obvious one. In fact, the notion that a language—as spoken by a human society, however small—forms a totally unified whole, a synchronic system at a particular point in time, is in fact an illusion, as has long been known. William Dwight Whitney recognized this when he wrote in 1867, "There are words, or meanings of words, no longer in familiar use, antiquated or obsolescent, which yet may not be denied a place in the present English tongue."[16] The speaker has active or passive control (linguistic competence) over a great range of equivalent features of grammar and lexicon of variable age; a great deal of discourse, particularly of affective content, plays on these different registers. Within a single synchronic state of a language, there can be genuinely old features in, for example, the speech habits of certain members of the older generations, or in non-standard dialects. But it is also possible for younger members of the so-ciety to mimic these older speech habits, and the reverse. *Homo loquens* is the original *homo ludens.*

The attitude of the speaker or listener, his perception and identification of these different registers, will frequently be more positive toward features which are mimicked than toward genuine vestigial remains of earlier speech habits in those to whom they are native. For example, most of us find it easier to recognize the stage-Irish dialect than many real Irish dialects. People are sensitive to what they have been culturally trained to recognize.

Such imitation or mimicry of older features of speech, which I will term *pseudo-archaism*, deserves more investigation than it habitually receives. For the descriptive linguist, the mimicked archaism is the only *real* archaism. A linguistic feature is archaic as a synchronic fact only if the speech community regards it as one. It is here that we find the psychological and cultural realities of the notion of linguistic archaism. Older speakers and speakers of dialect do not consider their speech archaic; to them, and thus to the descriptive linguist, it is still current. Speakers only consider their speech archaic if they are deliberately engaging in imitation or pseudo-archaism. The attitude of the speaker is the same toward what he perceives or imitates as archaic, whether he is basing his view on earlier texts, on the habits of older speakers, or on pure convention. For the descriptive linguist, pseudo-archaism is only one of the many styles, registers, or dialects that co-exist as components in the linguistic competence of individual members of a speech community. It is the duty of the linguist to record this as a fact of the language to be entered in an adequate description.

Yet for the historical linguist the pseudo-archaism is equally important. To him, or to the philologist or the scientific antiquarian, a diachronic vestige such as an old text, or a synchronic vestige such as a linguistic feature found only in speakers over seventy, is a primary piece of linguistic evidence, while mimicked older speech is, in some ways, rather an annoyance, something not to be trusted as evidence and apt to misguide. Nevertheless, although it does not, by definition, reflect a normal linguistic feature of the time it is observed and thus cannot be utilized, for example, in dating a text, it does, by definition, serve as an index of speech forms anterior to the time when it is observed. A speaker's intuition about the archaic is, by and large, correct. Pseudo-archaism in vocabulary or in grammar (phonology, morphology, or syntax) cannot give a valid total picture of the language at a given anterior period; in fact different pseudo-archaisms in a grammar may and usually do reflect linguistic features of widely differing ages. But it is rare that a pseudo-archaism does not directly or indirectly reflect a real fact about the language at an earlier—and sometimes considerably earlier—period. One may draw the wrong conclusion in a particular instance, but the general inference is virtually always right.

The formal mechanism of pseudo-archaism, at least in phonology, consists in reversing a change: applying it backwards, so that the normal output (current usage) becomes the input, and vice-versa. Prehistoric Latin underwent a sound change (termed *rhotacism*) of the form $s \rightarrow r$ between vowels, with earlier r's in the same position remaining intact. When Cicero wished to clothe the laws he proposed in his philosophical treatise *De legibus* with an aura of venerability appropriate to the legal style, he replaced certain intervocalic r's by s's, thus applying the change backwards: $s \leftarrow r$. In so doing, he may have wrongly changed some instances of r to s where the r had always been r and never s (it is still debatable whether he in fact did so). But despite the uncertainty with regard to particular words, one can correctly restore a general phonological rule regarding a historical change $s \rightarrow r$ between vowels on the basis of Cicero's conscious pseudo-archaism. As it happens, we know from other sources that the sound change took place between three and four hundred years before Cicero's time.

The rhotacism rule $s \rightarrow r$ in Latin illustrates the cultural role played by pseudo-archaism, and its cultural transmission. We can infer from scattered notices throughout Latinity that every educated Roman was aware of this change. It was part of Latin metalinguistic "folklore," and we find references to it as part of a continuous tradition down at least to the eighth century A.D., when it passed into the humanistic tradition through the writings of the lexicographer and antiquarian Paul the Deacon.

One should not make the mistake of equating the reversal of a *diachronic* phonological rule to create a pseudo-archaism (such as the reversal of the Latin rule $s \rightarrow r$ to $s \leftarrow r$), with the probable or possible simultaneous *synchronic* existence in the grammar of normal language of the same rule applied to different words. The psychological processes are different. The pseudo-archaism is clearly on a fully conscious level and reflects an awareness or preserved memory of the historical change as a historical event.

To take an example from English, we are told by Chomsky and Halle[17] that the group of sound changes known collectively as the Great Vowel Shift, which took place in the fifteenth century, are incorporated in essentially similar form as a set of synchronic rules in contemporary standard English, in such cases as "sūth" (pronounced "sooth") $\rightarrow$ "south." Yet no ordinary speaker of English can reverse these rules to produce an archaic-sounding form: from "mouse," for example, he would get "moose." Where contemporary variants still exist in their original form, when, in Anglo-Irish, "tea," for example, is pronounced to rhyme with day, they are quite correctly perceived by speakers as regional or social rather than archaic.

There is another aspect of the pseudo-archaism which has gone largely unnoticed by the linguist. Certain language changes are remembered, become part of the folklore, or perhaps of the mythology, of a language, while others, once they have occurred, are soon forgotten. The rhotacism rule was remembered throughout Latinity. But the elimination of secondary endings in the subjunctive and certain past tenses in favor of primary endings (the third person singular *-d* became *-t*), which occurred at more or less the same time as the rhotacism change, was wholly forgotten. No trace of it whatsoever survives in the grammatical and glossatorial literary tradition which so faithfully preserved the memory of the rhotacism rule. Why should this be so? Consider the statement of Meillet:

For someone who proposes to study the Romance languages, the features of Latin which have disappeared without trace are of little importance. What is useful to him are the elements which have served to constitute the new forms taken by Latin.[18]

We may guess either that the language—the collectivity of its speakers, that is—in some sense "flees" what it perceives consciously as old, old-fashioned, or archaic; or else that the language moves by extrapolation in the direction indicated by what it preserves. The forward movement of language in time synchronically is *ex post facto*. Its anterior history may be of relevance or it may not. We have yet to determine whether the consciousness of the past of a language on the part of its speakers at a given point in time has any profound consequences on the direction of its future evolution.

It is tempting to suggest that this awareness of the past history in the present structure is a potent factor in explaining why, as Edward Sapir noted, languages have a "cut" to their jib.[19] Languages can maintain a characteristic personality for extraordinarily long periods. Irish is the oldest vernacular language of Western Europe, and this language, whose recorded history goes back some fourteen centuries, is a seamless garment. There have been changes, to be sure, and profound ones, but the essential uniqueness of the language, what differentiates it from other languages, has remained surprisingly intact over this whole period. It is a problem for the future to determine why this should be so.

REFERENCES

1. Karl Windischmann, preface to Bopp, *Ueber das Conjugations-system der Sanskritsprache* (Frankfurt: Andreäische Buchhandlung, 1816), p. iii. Here and elsewhere below quotations from French or German originals have been silently translated by me.

2. Leopold Wenger, *Die Quellen des römischen Rechts* (Oesterreichische Akademie der Wissenschaften. Denkschriften 2. Wien: Holzhausen, 1953), p. 10.

3. Antoine Meillet, *La méthode comparative en linguistique historique* (Paris: Champion, 1925, 1954), p. 7.

4. Mary R. Haas, *The Prehistory of Languages* (The Hague: Mouton, 1969), p. 34.

5. Emile Benveniste, *Problèmes de linguistique générale* (Paris: Gallimard, 1966), p. 107.

6. Jerzy Kuryłowicz, *L'accentuation des langues indo-européennes*, 2nd. ed. (Wrocław: Polska Akademia Nauk, Prace Jezykoznawcze 17, 1958), p. 12.

7. Ferdinand de Saussure, *Cours de linguistique générale*, 4th ed. (Paris: Payot, 1949), p. 140.

8. *Ibid.*, p. 138.

9. The reader may grasp Saussure's own appreciation of this aspect of scholarship from the following excerpt from the draft of a letter to an unknown addressee (one suspects Meillet): "Je veux malgré cela résumer quel est pour moi l'exact état des preuves, car ce que je déteste chez tous les Germains comme Pedersen, c'est la manière subreptice d'amener la preuve, et de ne jamais la formuler, comme si la profondeur de leurs reflexions les dispensait de mettre à nu leur opération logique. Il y a là, en même temps, une impertinence sur le temps que ces messieurs croient devoir être consacré à chacun de leurs travaux qui dépasse toute limite et m'a toujours révolté."

10. Ferdinand de Saussure, *Mémoire sur le système primitif des voyelles dans les langues indo-européennes* (1878; reprinted Hildesheim: Georg Olms, 1968), p. 1.

11. *Ibid.*, p. 50.

12. Roman Jakobson, *Selected Writings I* (The Hague: Mouton, 1962), pp. 7-116.

13. *Ibid.*, pp. 109-110. Readers will recognize the rhetorical figure used by Jakobson thirty years later in his "Grammar of Poetry and Poetry of Grammar."

14. William Labov, "The Study of Language in Its Social Context," *Studium Generale,* XXIII (1970), 30-87.

15. Antoine Meillet, "Caractère secondaire du type thématique indo-européen," *Bulletin de la Société de Linguistique,* XXXII (1931), 194-202.

16. William Dwight Whitney, *Language and the Study of Language* (1867; abridged reprint in *Whitney on Language,* ed. Michael Silverstein [Cambridge, Mass.: M.I.T. Press, 1971]), p. 13.

17. Noam Chomsky and Morris Halle, *The Sound Pattern of English* (New York: Harper and Row, 1968), *passim.*

18. Antoine Meillet, *La méthode comparative,* p. 15.

19. Edward Sapir, *Language* (New York: Harcourt Brace, 1921), p. 127.

THE LEARNING OF LANGUAGE

ERIC H. LENNEBERG

The Neurology of Language

WE HAVE BUT a vague idea of what we mean by *knowing a language*. In practical terms, it is an individual's ability to follow verbal directions, to answer yes/no questions, and to acquire new skills under the sole impact of verbal instructions given in a natural language such as English; it is the ability to paraphrase sentences and to comment on their meaning or grammaticality. The question to be asked here is, how might the biologist approach the problem of language knowledge; that is, how might he even begin to relate language knowledge to brain function, and how might he explain its biological development? The most important point of departure is that language knowledge, like any other type of knowledge, may be taken as a peculiar family of physiological processes or, in other words, of *cerebral activity states*. If we make this our central theme, then it may be possible to tie together a number of different clinical facts and to relate them to some theoretical aspects of developmental biology.

Aphasiology

If one reads the current publications on aphasia from both sides of the Atlantic, one quickly discovers that there are major disagreements with respect to both facts and interpretation. This is true of descriptions of the function and structure of the brain, of physiological facts, of language itself; it is true even of the claims as to what older authors are supposed to have said or believed. Take, for example, basic views on the general nature of brain function. In this country, there is a tendency to take the computer analogy very literally, engendering a picture of the brain as a collection of more or less independent apparatus connected to one another by cables. Personally, I find it hard to reconcile myself with the view that the sensory projection areas in the cerebral cortex should be the localities where percepts are received; that cortical association areas should be the workshops in which percepts are glued together; that Broca's area (a cortical region of the left frontal lobe) should be the machine that is responsible for the spoken word; and that Wernicke's area (a cortical region of the

101

left temporal lobe) should convert the raw sounds into perceived speech. There are neurologists whose discussions sound as if cortical loci were "offices" in which decisions are made about specific behavior and where that behavior is programmed and executed. If the communication lines between the "offices" are disrupted, the respective types of behavior are thought to run off independently from one another but are postulated to be otherwise undisturbed. In formulations of this sort, the layman has a hard time separating anatomical facts from highly speculative and sometimes wholly uncorroborated assumptions.

It is true that the brain shows a high degree of anatomical topographical differentiation and specialization that is unparalleled in any other organ. Most of the anatomical facts are beyond dispute today; but not so the "meaning" and function of the structural detail that we can discriminate in the gross or under the microscope. The best example of this is the cerebellum, whose anatomy has been fully worked out but whose function still presents more unsolved than solved problems. When it comes to the cerebral fiber tracts, especially the transcortical ones, there is still disagreement on many basic questions such as, in certain cases, even the direction of flow of impulses. It is very far from clear whether the principal interaction between cortical areas proceeds horizontally across the cortex, or vertically through subcortical relays. At present there is evidence for both, and we must remember that one possibility does not exclude the other. The diagrams that some "neurolinguists" draw, showing cortical centers for various types of language behavior interconnected by directional arrows, are fairly speculative. Moreover, there are logical difficulties in postulating brain centers that are exclusively in charge of specific types of behavior and that operate more or less independently as suborgans. No brain centers comparable in independence to those postulated for language in man have ever been demonstrated in other mammalian cortex. Functional autonomy of brain centers is also unlikely because all nervous tissue is forever active, and the anatomical connectivity of the cortex and the brain as a whole is such that a change in activity in one part of the brain is likely to influence activity in all those parts of the brain to which it is connected.

This consideration, which has been particularly stressed by clinical neurologists in Germany,[1] leads, however, to explanations of brain function that are quite different from those of the "behavioral-centers-and-connections" model. Instead of hypothesizing that a lesion has the effect of simply knocking out a particular neuronal component and its correlated specific function, leaving other componentry and their functions intact, this point of view would put it that a lesion deforms the normal pattern of interaction among a whole composition of activities; it does not merely eliminate one capacity from a roster of capacities, but deforms or alters physiological function on a broader base. This would be reflected in be-

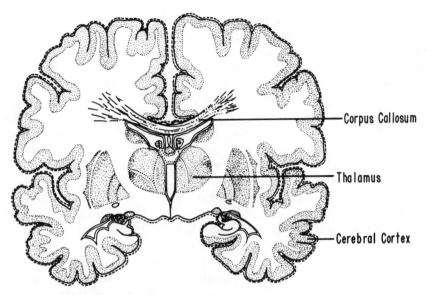

Schematic frontal section of the human brain, showing the corpus callosum which connects the cortices of the two hemispheres, and the position of the thalamus deep in the brain. The outer border of the diagram represents the cerebral cortex. Most parts of the cortex are connected to the thalamus by subcortical fibers.

havioral disturbances that could not be pinpointed or characterized in terms of the traditionally accepted psychological processes (arithmetic ability, writing, speaking, pattern perception, etc.), but would be likely to cause aberrations in the performance of a whole variety of tasks, usually affecting some a bit more than others, depending on the location and nature of the lesion.

It would seem as if this sort of controversy might easily be settled by empirical investigation of what *actually* happens to patients with brain lesions. Unfortunately, this is not so; in fact, we find neurologists of equal standing and with the same kind of practical experience reporting almost shockingly different findings, including conflicting clinico-pathological correlations. In the United States, Geschwind[2] has argued most persuasively that the lesioned patient's behavior is quite predictable and that it is therefore possible to construct a detailed typology of aphasic symptoms. He has stressed that it is at least theoretically possible to account for every aspect of behavioral deficit by the specific location of one or more lesions. To emphasize the importance of postulated centers and their anatomical connections, he speaks of constellations of symptoms as *disconnection syndromes*.

It is, however, important to realize that the elicitation of clinical symptoms and their theoretical interpretation is beset with practical problems.

What types of test are to be used? Do patients form sufficiently homogeneous populations for test results to be evaluated by sample statistics? May test results be expressed as numbers and then used for arithmetic operations? Are naturalistic observations preferable to formal testing, or should one use a combination of these techniques? There is controversy over every one of these questions and many more. It is therefore not so surprising that we often find neurologists unwilling to accept the typologies proposed by others. For example, Bay,[3] an aphasiologist of the highest repute in Europe, has argued just as persuasively as Geschwind that any kind of subclassification of the aphasic syndrome is dangerous, and that the fine detail of a particular patient's disabilities, though of theoretical interest, is of no localizing value in the clinic. A position somewhere between those of Geschwind and Bay is that of Luria,[4] who has probably studied more patients with traumatic aphasia than anyone else in the world.

The early aphasiologists did not bother much about the science of linguistics. The medical men simply assumed that the nature of language was something intuitively obvious, and the symptoms they described reflected their naive approach to language. They thought they could discern productive or receptive interference with speech sounds, with words (sometimes subclassified by the traditional parts of speech), with intonation patterns, and with sentences. Some neurologists attributed each of these symptoms to lesions in specific loci, almost as if nature had studied Latin grammar before designing man's brain.

Gradually, modern linguistics has begun to exert an influence upon aphasiology, so that now symptoms are often interpreted in terms of particular schools of thought in modern linguistics. But the field of linguistics itself has many divergent points of view, so the increase in sophistication in the analysis of language aberration has brought along a further source of differences in opinion and interpretation of facts. Modern grammarians, particularly those of the Chomsky school, have brought to light a great number of regularities in the way sentences are normally understood and constructed, most of which had not been described before and of which no native speaker had been aware. Students of aphasia have been rightly fascinated by these endeavors, but they have frequently failed to see that only certain aspects of grammatical theory are relevant to aphasia or to the study of the brain mechanisms of language. Generative grammar proposes, for example, certain orders in the application of specified rules of grammar. It might be tempting to see whether these orders correspond to any psychobiological order. Do they reflect physiological events that occur in the course of sentence production or sentence interpretation? Or do they reflect psychological levels of complexity? Unfortunately, from a biological or even a psychological point of view, the linguists' conceptual armamentarium is a somewhat mixed collection. Take, for instance, the rules* discussed by Chomsky.[5] These were not intended as physiological or even psychological rules; yet some of them may, perhaps, suggest the existence of some biological process, whereas others are biologically entirely uninterpretable. Branching rules, for example, and their order of application could not conceivably have any physiological correlate whatever. On the other hand, there is, perhaps, some plausibility to the suggestion that the transformations that map deep structure onto surface structure have at least a very rough psychological counterpart—namely, the changes that take place when an idea or a sentiment is crystallized into a verbal utterance. But even here, we are actually distorting the exact meaning of the grammatical theoretical constructs, and reference to syntactic transformation in the context of psychology or physiology is justifiable only as a metaphor.

Apart from the various factions of transformational grammarians, there are several other types of linguistic theory, each one likely to suggest different kinds of observations and tests on the patient. As long as there is such an appalling lack of agreement on theories that relate language to brain function and anatomy, the diversification of linguistic inquiries is likely to prove an *embarras de choix* to aphasiology, rather than an aid. We have said enough to indicate the many sources of divergent points of view, biases, and articles of faith that turn aphasiology into the confusing and often contradictory field that it is.

The traditional source material for aphasiology has been the symptomatology of neocortical lesions in adult patients. Other types of evidence have become available during the last thirty years and will be discussed in the next section. Since it is not my purpose here to evaluate the many different classificatory schemes and their respective theoretical positions, I shall confine myself to a brief discussion of three major types of interference with language performance that are beyond controversy (leaving out disturbances of articulation and many minor clinical syndromes). The three types may be called (1) *interference with production;* (2) *interference with language knowledge;* and (3) *interference with word finding.*

(1) The only interference with production to be discussed here is called Broca's aphasia. The patient can usually read, can often write using the left (unparalyzed) hand, and can answer questions appropriately by nodding his head or by giving short answers. He gives every evidence that he understands language well and that he knows what he wants to say, but he has great difficulty controlling the motor coordination of the speech muscles (although they are not paralyzed; he can eat and drink without

---

* Categorical rules, context-free and context-sensitive rewriting rules, branching rules, projection rules, phonological and syntactic redundancy rules, selectional rules, context-free and context-sensitive subcategorization rules, transformational rules, rules of agreement, and others.

difficulty). The production of every word seems to require inordinate concentration and effort. There are long pauses between words, and every sound comes out slowly and belaboredly. Apparently, the strain of speaking is so great that the patient confines himself to the barest minimum of words, resulting in a so-called telegraphic style. Some patients learn to say some few words with relatively greater ease, and make no attempts or seem unable to say any other words. Those who manage to write seem to have no unusual difficulty remembering words. This clinical picture is associated with a high degree of probability of a left-sided frontal lobe lesion usually involving Broca's area.

(2) Interference with language knowledge is more difficult to characterize, since its manifestations are much more varied. I am using the phrase (it is not part of the standard aphasiological terminology) to cover a multiplicity of symptoms and combinations of symptoms that either (a) constitute variations on a fairly unified theme, or (b) represent varying degrees of severity of one disease process, or (c) are, in fact, quite independent syndromes. The important points are that in all cases some cognitive aspect of language capacity is affected and that this kind of trouble can occur in complete dissociation from the control of oral speech production. In other words, a patient is sometimes unable to comprehend what is said to him (though his hearing is unimpaired) or to read or write; he has, however, no difficulty in the motor coordination of the muscles involved in speaking. In fact, some patients become markedly voluble, sometimes to the point of producing an incessant and uninterruptable flow of talk. When this occurs, the utterances are usually filled with neologisms; the phonology may undergo some remarkably consistent alterations; the grammatical structure becomes less varied; and phrases and sentences appear to be constructed in strange ways. Usually one can only guess at what the patient is trying to say, and in severe cases, it is not even certain that the patient is using his verbal output to communicate anything whatever. When the disorder is less extensive, the patient may answer a question by responding to or even repeating some of the words contained in the question, but he will at once go off on a tangent, so that his answer turns into discourse of an inappropriate and at least partially illogical nature. Most of his words and phrases are quite intelligible, and only occasionally some jargon or paraphrasic composition may occur. When asked to give the name of an object, a table, for instance, he may start with a well-pronounced neologism such as "blago"; this may sound strange to the patient himself, and he may try again, saying "blagel," and then, through a number of further approximations, finally reach the correct phoneme-pattern. It is noteworthy that a large percentage of patients with abnormally functioning language knowledge seem to be quite unaware of their own difficulties. Some of them are cheerful and always ready to engage in conversation, and if they complain about the communicative process at all,

they blame their interlocutor for the breakdown. This condition is called *anosognosia* and is a clear indication that aspects of cognition other than language are often affected by the disease. This complex of symptoms is associated with left-sided parieto-temporal lesions.

(3) A rather common interference with language is a pronounced difficulty in finding words. This is a vastly exaggerated "tip-of-the-tongue" phenomenon that may become so severe that the patient's speech is completely impaired. One can easily demonstrate that he understands everything that is said to him by phrasing questions in such a way that he can nod yes or no and by giving commands that he can follow. He has no difficulty with motor coordination, because he can repeat words fluently and easily, and one can show that he differs from both the first and second types of patients described above by asking him a question that calls for words, phrases, or sentences in response. If he is blocked in his answer, one can suggest a number of possible answers to him and he will readily choose the correct one and repeat it accurately and naturally. This phenomenon, called *anomia,* may appear with any left-sided cortical lesion, as long as the destruction does not impinge on any of the primary projection areas. If the lesion is focal, it is small; disseminated loss of cells throughout the cortex, however, may produce a similar effect, as, for instance, in the early stages of the presenile dementias.[6] Although this description is sufficient to rough out the general dimensions of aphasic symptomatology, it certainly does not do justice to the many variations and oddities that can be seen in the clinic.[7]

The controversy over the problem of *cerebral localization* is frequently misrepresented or misunderstood. Every serious student of the brain is impressed, even overawed, by the anatomy of the brain, and it is the firm credo of virtually every neurobiologist that tissue differentiation of this degree must have correlates in the realm of physiological function. Consequently, it is a sound and practically universal assumption that localized tissue destruction must, without exception, leave a specific effect upon the normal pattern of *physiological* activities. There are, however, serious problems in the way of our ability to identify these effects, and there is outright disagreement over whether such effects are necessarily demonstrable in purely *behavioral* studies. There is evidence that the organism is capable of internal physiological compensations and readjustments that make detection of behavioral deficits very difficult. There is also a problem of what to look for when we search for behavioral alterations. As far back as 1909, K. Brodmann, the eminent neuro-anatomist responsible for the histological maps of the human cortex that are still in use today, wrote:

Just as untenable as is the notion of an . . . "association layer" is the assumption of special "psychic centers of higher order." Especially recently, we had only too many theories which just like phrenology wanted to localize in certain circum-scribed parts of the cortex such complicated mental activities as memory, volition, fantasy, intelligence, or spatial qualities such as a sense for shapes or space. . . .

These mental capacities are notions which connote extremely complicated complexes of elementary functions. What has been said above of the presentations for which such physiological cortical processes lie at the bottom of these complex functions is still more valid of such universal "capacities." One cannot think of them arising in any other way as through an infinitely manifold and complex work-ing together of numerous elementary processes, in other words simultaneous func-tions of numerous cortical parts, probably the whole cortex, perhaps even includ-ing subcortical parts.[8]

A. R. Luria, the dean of clinical neuropsychology, has repeatedly em-phasized the dangers of regarding specific areas in the cortex as the places in which specific psychological processes, including perception, take place:

From the standpoint of modern psychology, the localization of such processes as visual or auditory perception in circumscribed sensory areas of the cerebral cor-tex, like the localization of voluntary movement and activity in circumscribed areas of the motor cortex, appears . . . more improbable than the localization of respiration or of the patellar reflex in a single, isolated area of the brain.[9]

Again, there is no controversy whatever that *some* correlation exists be-tween site and nature of lesion and type of language interference. The disagreements concern the degree of localizability of *specific* language and cognitive disabilities.

Further, there is rather sharp disagreement over interpretation of facts. It is because of this that neurologists find it difficult to persuade their dis-senting colleagues simply by exhibiting a deceased patient's lesioned brain, together with an account of his behavioral failures. The temporal correlation between the period of tissue destruction and the periods of observed deficits presents certain problems, as does the *extent* to which the patient was actually examined and observed. Even the exact deter-mination of the lesion in the specimen presents problems. Usually the brain is simply cut into slices by hand, each slice about one inch in thick-ness, and an attempt is made to reconstruct the lesion, along with its patho-physiology. Often small blocks of tissue are then prepared for micro-scopic examination. Under the circumstances, it is possible to miss lesions elsewhere in the brain, and there is always a considerable margin for doubt concerning the secondary or tertiary physiological consequences of destroyed tissues. Acute clinical syndromes are not, however, the only source of data for theories on brain mechanisms of language. Let us try to place these observations in a more general context.

Evidence for Brain Correlates of Language

The most common conditions producing the types of aphasia that are discussed in the literature are stroke, trauma, and surgical lesions. All three have a very important common denominator: the sudden and catastrophic incapacitation of a large amount of brain tissue that always includes (1) the cerebral cortex (whose thickness is but a few millimeters!), (2) the vascular bed (the entire system of blood vessels which extends its arterial tree into regions that go far beyond a circumscribed traumatic or surgical lesion), and (3) the subcortical fiber system (which also affects brain structures and nuclei at considerable distances from the actual site of lesion). Secondary alterations due to sudden lesions include metabolic changes and cellular degeneration; they affect protein synthesis and, in the case of immature brains, the potential for neurogenesis and growth. However, these more far-reaching consequences of sudden tissue destruction are never discussed in the aphasic literature. It is true that we do not know the full range of their effect on behavior, but their very existence should cloud the strict localizationist's crystal ball. There are many insults other than stroke, trauma, and surgical lesions that destroy or alter man's neuroanatomy and neurophysiological processes. Whether these do or do not affect language capacities depends not only on the location of the primary lesion, but also on the mode of onset of the disease, on the co-occurrence of other cerebral lesions (a second lesion may under certain circumstances relieve the symptoms caused by the first), and on various other histo-pathological, metabolic, and biochemical conditions.

Another most important source of data on language function is *abnormal development*, due either to naturally occurring diseases or to man-inflicted deprivations, both environmental and nutritional. The aphasiologists' almost exclusive concentration on a highly selected group of pathologies—pathologies that in one respect are totally different from all others, namely in their mode of onset—has engendered a fairly lopsided view of how the brain controls language. Moreover, lesions and pathological conditions that *fail* to interfere with language should play as important a part in our theory construction as do lesions that do cause interference.

Further, it is difficult to make generalizations about the effect of lesions upon a subject's ability to learn and to form associations. Usually tasks become more difficult for the subject and more training is required to establish learning. But it is at least very rare that simple disconnecting cuts through fiber tracts (excepting the commissures) abolish once and for all the capacity for associative learning. Although an aphasia (say of the second type described) may remain entirely stationary for many years, a patient may nevertheless learn to recognize new faces and to associate names with faces. The age of the patient is of paramount importance here. The young war veteran will have little difficulty in this respect, whereas a patient of sixty or more may be totally unable to learn a single new word or name, even if his general health is fairly good and he continues to live for ten or more years.

Electrophysiological data are beginning to play an increasing role in aphasiology. They fall into two major categories: extra-cranial recordings; and electrical stimulation of live, nervous tissue *in situ* in conscious patients undergoing certain types of neurosurgery. In both categories, one may make observations on the physiology of reception and on the physiology of production of behavior (movements). As far as language is concerned, the extra-cranial recording techniques have not yet added much to our earlier conceptions of brain mechanisms. The perceptual studies, however, have given us further details of the functional asymmetries between the two hemispheres.[10]

As far as speech production is concerned, electroencephalographic data (including averaged potentials) have been disappointing. In 1967, Ertl and Schafer[11] reported studies on cortical electrical activities linked to verbal behavior, but in a subsequent article, they questioned their own earlier interpretations. McAdam and Whitaker[12] reported observing electrical activity over Broca's area that preceded speech acts and that differed from the activity of the homologous area on the right, but their reports have been severely criticized by Morrell and Huntington,[13] whose own experiments along similar lines failed to lend support to the McAdam and Whitaker findings. (See, however, McAdam and Whitaker's reply to Morrell and Huntington.[12])

The electrical stimulation of brain tissues has resulted in some rather startling observations relevant to both the anatomy and the physiology of language mechanisms. At the same time, it is necessary to stress that these data raise new problems and that there is no intuitively *obvious* way to interpret them. In the first place, there is a curious discrepancy between the behavioral consequences of a lesion and the behavioral consequences of electrical stimulation in the same place when the tissue is healthy. The evidence is primarily taken from animal experiments, but there are analogous data for man. One would expect that behavior produced by stimulation of a given spot could be abolished by the destruction of that same place. But this is not so. There is not much symmetry between destruction and stimulation. A given type of behavior may be elicited by stimulation in a wide variety of different loci (and histologically different tissues), but lesions in these areas may affect that behavior only negligibly or not at all. On the other hand, the same behavior may be altered by placing lesions in areas where electrical stimulation does not affect it.

Precisely this kind of condition obtains in man with respect to language. No direct cortical stimulation has ever produced more than vowel-like, drawn-out sounds; and it is rare that patients report hearing articulate utterances when stimulated on the cortical convexity. But cortical destruction can interfere dramatically with language. On the other hand, Schaltenbrand and others[14] have reported observing patients uttering words and whole phrases upon thalamic stimulation, whereas lesions in the same areas do not produce the types of aphasia described earlier. (In about 10 percent of thalamotomized patients certain speech disorders do ensue; these defects, however, are usually of a dysarthric or dysrhythmic nature.) In this connection, it may be well to remember that electrical stimulation is always a rather crude interference with ongoing activity, with many uncontrolled variables. Von Holst and von St. Paul[15] have shown that in the brain of a chicken, at least, the place of electrical stimulation is no more important than the characteristics of the electrical stimulus and the psychophysiological state of the animal at the time of stimulation. They were able to elicit specific sorts of behavior from randomly reached loci by controlling only the nature and moment of the stimulus.

The apparent paradox caused by the incongruity between the consequences of stimulation, on the one hand, and lesioning, on the other, can be resolved if we abandon the simple-minded switchboard model of the brain. The notion of fixed and narrowly located brain centers for specific behavior also has to go. Instead, the circuitry appears to have much more widely distributed networks, with rather richly redundant connectivity; and experiments such as those initiated by von Holst and von St. Paul suggest that the *nature of the activity* that goes on in these networks must also be reckoned with in our attempts at model-building.

It is generally known, and beyond dispute, that focal lesions in young children carry a prognosis different from that of similar lesions in the adult. Pathology confined to the left hemisphere (including dysgenesis or surgical removal) and incurred before the end of the second year of life does not block language development, which may even occur at the normal age. If the insult occurs after the onset of language development, but before the end of the child's first decade, a transient aphasia may ensue, but, if the disease is arrested, language is fully recovered within a year or so, even though the left hemisphere may have a fixed and irreversible lesion.[16] From such evidence we must conclude that the physiological processes of language are not irrevocably destined from the earliest stage of postnatal brain development to be located in the left hemisphere. Instead, lateralization is apparently a gradual process of differentiation or functional specialization concomitant with brain maturation (which in man is much protracted beyond lower primates' maturational histories). At first, both hemispheres can and apparently do partake in the activity patterns that constitute learning and knowing language. As the growing child becomes capable of finer and finer intellectual operations,[17] some specializations, both structural and functional, also occur in the neural substrate, displacing activity patterns instrumental for language to the left, and others, such as those involved in nonverbal processes, to the right.

In support of this view about lateralization, we can also compare the effects of sectioning the corpus callosum in adult life with the clinical picture of adult patients with an embryological agenesis of the corpus callosum. If we allow the brain to come to full maturity with the corpus callosum intact, functional asymmetry can develop. If the corpus callosum is severed after formation of such asymmetry, language is strongly localized to the left, many other functions to the right, and the sectioning produces an isolation of language from other aspects of cognition. However, if there has never been a corpus callosum to begin with, so that the hemispheres with their respective cortices have developed without cross-communication, each hemisphere runs its own differentiation history and never loses its capacity for language activities.[18] Thus, the fiber tracts and especially the commissures play a role in the maturational history and may well have embryological functions that deserve to be studied further. A failure of the language functions to lateralize is not an uncommon event; lifelong seizure-proneness in the left hemisphere, for instance, seems to interfere with lateralization.[19]

In view of these facts, the electrographic evidence of neurophysiological lateralization, cited earlier, should be expanded. Currently, Helen Neville, a graduate student at Cornell University, is attempting to collect similar data in a developmental perspective, in order to obtain a picture of the natural history of the electrical asymmetries. It will be particularly interesting to see whether such a history is changed in children with abnormal language development.

A very important but widely ignored fact of neuropathology is the trade-off between rate of growth and size of a lesion. For instance, a tumor that takes many years to grow may assume rather formidable proportions before any symptoms whatever begin to show. When symptoms do develop, they are frequently of the kind that have little localizing value clinically (seizures, headache, vomiting). Even a faster growing, more malignant tumor that destroys tissues in the classical cortical speech and language areas may manifest itself rather differently from sudden destruction of the same tissue by stroke, trauma, or surgery. The classical types of aphasia are by no means obligatory when the lesion is neoplastic. Even the post-operative prognosis does not depend simply on the location and size of the surgical lesion; it depends also on the pathology and morbid history that have led to surgery. Thus the usual ablation studies on animals differ in a fundamental way from surgical procedures on man. The former are done on healthy brains; the latter are not. Notice, however, that it is possible to simulate a condition in experimental animal surgery that approximates a slowly growing lesion in man, with its subsequent surgical treatment. If ablation on animals is carried out in multiple stages, so that only small parts of tissue are removed at a time, and the total ablation is protracted over a period of months or years, then the animal's behavior is no longer irreversibly interfered with and functions may recover.[20] Once more we see that the activity patterns that correspond to behavioral capacities may be only slightly displaced if the insults expand very gradually. Undoubtedly there are definite limits to this sort of *plasticity*. For example, there are many brain structures whose removal is clearly incompatible with the continuance of given functions, no matter how gradually the destruction takes place. But we are talking primarily of a single and specific type of tissue: the cerebral cortex, where it seems that functional localization enjoys a certain degree of flexibility under the specific circumstances mentioned (insults during immaturity, or very slow impingement). Even here the functions in the area striata are more fixed than those of Heschl's gyrus, and both these cortical fields are more indispensable than the so-called association cortex.

Preliminaries to Theories on Brain Mechanisms of Language

The neurophysiology of behavior comprises three realms of mechanisms: those concerned with input, those with central integration, and those with output. The first realm includes reception, transduction, and tranformation of exogenous stimuli; the third deals with control, regulation, and coordination of muscular activity. The nature of the second realm can be inferred only from the imperfect correlation that exists between input and output. There are many types of input that produce no overt motor output, and many an output (verbal or motor) does not seem to be correlated with any specific environmental input. Registration in our minds of some event need not lead to any immediate or even future predictable motor act. On the other hand, a motor act, or an utterance such as "A black scorpion is not dropping on my plate" (which B. F. Skinner told his students was said to him by A. N. Whitehead during a discussion of verbal behavior) need not be evoked by any closely related physical event in the environment.

Up to the present, experimental neurophysiological research and the interpretation of the respective data have been almost exclusively focused on the first and, to a lesser extent, on the third realms. However, the biology of *knowing language* is essentially a problem of the second realm. Knowing a language means relating, computing, and operating on specific aspects of the environment. Learning language means doing these things in very specific ways. Theorizing about the brain mechanisms of language is made extremely difficult by our nearly complete ignorance of how any of the processes of the second realm function. The difficulty is not merely the absence of specific facts that may shortly become available. The difficulty is the present lack of even a general or abstract *theoretical model* of how this second realm might work—how behavior and cognition might be related to brain function. The theoretical models that enjoy greatest popularity among neurophysiologists today try to explain how physical patterns (such as the configuration of a chair) might be transformed into "the language of the brain," but they do not face the problem of what happens to the transformed data—of what goes on in the second realm.

The map-making aphasiologists endeavor to tell us where the neurally encoded speech signal first arrives in the cortex, where it is shunted next, and where it "exists" to produce speech acts. Quite apart from the innumerable questions that surround such functional maps, they would not actually explain what the physiology of language knowledge is, even were the anatomical locations by now firmly established. A nervous system is not like a trumpet into which the environment can blow and produce a tune. Brains are not passive conveyors of information; they are very active objects, and their activity states are highly unstable, easily perturbed, and subject to modulation from the outside. That is why treating the brain as a communication channel or viewing behavior simply as a function of the input to the system is misleading. It tends to ignore the fact that behavior is in many ways autonomous activity, in the sense that it derives its energy *not* from the stimuli that are behaviorally significant, but from energy stores that are supplied through the body's metabolic activities. Psychologically important stimuli trigger and shape behavior, but the stimuli are not the architects of the principles by which behavior operates; nor is behavior a transform of the brain's input. The relevance of these observations to language is obvious.[21]

The acquisition and maintenance of the language function is a particular example of the general biological problem of how patterns come about and are maintained. It is a special problem within the general problem of biological specificity. We are faced with quite similar problems in the contexts of both evolution and ontogeny. And the problem extends to the field of structure as well as to the field of function and of behavior. Thus, our ability to "explain" language biologically is inextricably tied up with our ability to explain the organism's ontogenesis.

The clinical data, especially the relationship between lesioning and age and the importance of the rate at which cortex is destroyed, emphasize the role of morphogenetic processes during the establishment of language capacities. It is only by bringing the notions of embryological regulation, differentiation, and determination to bear upon the functional organization of the human brain during the critical years of language development that we can hope to understand the occurrence and nonoccurrence of language disturbances. Piaget and his colleagues are the only psychologists who have clearly seen the intimate relationship between embryological processes and the unfolding of cognition.[22] Nothing could illustrate better the direct connections between developmental biology and developmental psychology than the neurology of language. As the behavioral capacities become differentiated during growth,[23] the human brain is undergoing its final structural and functional differentiation as well.[24] It is especially the functional differentiation that should be of interest to the student of behavior and language. Functions do not suddenly start when the "machine has been assembled," as in a computer that is suddenly ready to be used. Cognitive functions and the capacity for language knowledge have an epigenetic history; they are transforms of earlier, less specialized functions and their correlated physiological processes. The family of cerebral activity patterns that constitute the use and knowledge of language have gradually developed characteristics (their modes of functioning, the nature of their perturbability, the types of transitions between their states), and these, in turn, depend in part on the system's anatomical differentiation history and in part on the history of perturbations that the developing system has incurred.

The German neurophysiologists have been more interested in the structure of cerebral activity patterns and the internal interactions among such patterns than their colleagues on this side of the Atlantic. They have pointed out that a "cognitive act" has its own momentary history of formation; that it is the end result of patterned interactions—a topic which has been discussed under various headings, such as *Aktualgenese, Funktionsstruktur*, or *Wirkungsgefuege*. But no one except Piaget has even discussed the epigenetic history of these patterns.

In general, the problem of relating behavior or language to brain mechanisms is to find a model that relates aspects of *dynamic patterns* to the known anatomical and clinical or experimental facts in such a way that the phenomena of so-called plasticity (suggested, for instance, by the age and rate of lesioning data, or by the capacity to learn, forget, or will to do things) become comprehensible without recourse to an implied demon that switches flows of impulses and makes decisions on where and how neuronal action is to take place. We do not yet have such a model. In casting around for possible explanations, we ought to keep two aspects of brain connectivity in mind.

(1) It is possible that in certain limited tissues in the brain, cells are interconnected randomly. If we consider this possibility, together with the fact that the number of synapses between neurons is many times larger than the number of neurons (by an order of magnitude of 10^3 to 10^4), then it becomes plausible to assume that neurons are not functionally autonomous in such areas, but that the areas have their own characteristic cooperative behavior. Such behavior will be a function of each neuron's repertoire of behavior, the nature of the coupling connecting each neuron to others, the number of neurons so connected, and the geometry of the assembly as a whole.

(2) It is possible that the gross connections among nuclei and regions, which are highly regular and predictable, and therefore quite the opposite of random, are essentially channels through which the various structures perturb one another. Assume that every histologically distinct structure in

the brain has its own peculiar activity patterns; add to this the facts that just about every structure of the nervous system has a multiplicity of fiber systems that interconnect it, nonrandomly, to several other structures, and that no nervous tissue is ever "idle"; then one is tempted to think that structures are not independent agencies that send messages to one another, but, rather, that the brain and its activities are in constant functional flux. Even when a steady state is reached, in the sense that different activities in different parts of the brain are relatively constant, the equilibrium of the system as a whole would still be precarious equilibrium. Any alteration of activity in any part of the brain would cause chain reactions of new interactions and cross-perturbations that might take a long time to reach a new steady state. In other words, at any one moment, all the specialized activities in all the different parts of the nervous system can be viewed as a single configuration, and the activity patterns of the brain can be seen as a series of moment to moment transitions from configuration to configuration.

At present, neuroscientists are struggling with the formulation of new models for dealing with activity patterns such as those likely to occur in brains. Of special interest is the activity generated by systems that are composed of very large numbers of autonomously active but coupled elements.[25] The formalisms used in the description of fluid dynamics and their patterns are also under consideration for their possible application to brain function.[26] Concepts such as that of the dissipative structures of nonequilibrium thermodynamics are beginning to interest the neurophysiologists[27] and may open new horizons for studying the brain and its dynamic patterns. The importance of these new endeavors lies in their potential for relating the structuralization of function to the structuralization of form,[28] and for explaining some of the plasticity phenomena I briefly discussed in connection with language development. It is far too early to apply any of these concepts specifically to language mechanisms. But I think it is important to stress, even at this early stage, the existence of a conceptual framework and theoretical constructs that are based on well-defined physical, chemical, and mathematical notions, and that are capable of elevating our picture of brain function from its present plane of switching diagrams to a new conception of four-dimensional dynamic patterns.

REFERENCES

1. K. Conrad, "New Problems of Aphasia," *Brain*, LXXVII (1954), 491-509; C. von Monakow, *Die Lokalisation im Grosshirn* (Wiesbaden: Bergmann, 1914); V. von Weizsäcker, *Der Gestaltkreis* (Stuttgart: Thieme, 1950).

2. N. Geschwind, "Disconnexion Syndromes in Animals and Man," *Brain*, LXXXVIII (1965), 237-294; 585-644.

3. E. Bay, "The Classification of Disorders of Speech," *Cortex*, III (1967), 26-31.

4. A. R. Luria, *Higher Cortical Functions in Man* (New York: Basic Books, 1966).

5. N. Chomsky, *Aspects of the Theory of Syntax* (Cambridge: M.I.T. Press, 1965).

6. J. de Ajuriaguerra and R. Tissot, "Some Aspects of Psychoneurologic Disintegration in Senile Dementia," *Senile Dementia*, eds. C. Müller and L. Ciompi (Berne: Huber, 1968); H. Sinclair, M. Boehme, R. Tissot, and J. de Ajuriaguerra, "Quelques aspects de la désintégration des notions de temps à travers des épreuves morphosyntaxiques de langage et à travers des épreuves opératoires chez des vieillards atteints de démence dégénérative," *Bulletin de Psychologie*, CCXLVII (1966), 8-12.

7. E. Bay, "Aphasielehre und Neuropsychologie der Sprache," *Nervenarzt*, XL (1969), 53-71; Geschwind, "Disconnexion Syndromes in Animals and Man"; K. Goldstein, *Language and Language Disorders* (London: Grune and Stratton, 1948); H. Head, *Aphasia and Kindred Disorders of Speech* (London: Cambridge University Press, 1926); A. R. Luria, "Brain Disorders and Language Analysis," *Language and Speech*, I (1958); *Traumatic Aphasia: Its Syndromes, Psychology, and Treatment* (The Hague: Mouton, 1970); A. Pick and R. Thiele, "Aphasie," *Handbuch der normalen und pathologischen Physiologie*, XV, eds. A. Bethe *et al.* (Berlin: Springer, 1931); A. V. S. de Reuck and M. O'Connor, eds., *Disorders of Language*, CIBA Foundation Symposium (Boston: Little, Brown, 1964).

8. K. Brodmann, *Vergleichende Lokalisationslehre der Grosshirnrinde* (Leipzig: Barth, 1909), quoted in G. von Bonin, *The Cerebral Cortex* (Springfield, Ill.: C. C. Thomas, 1960), p. 215.

9. Luria, *Higher Cortical Functions in Man*, p. 32.

10. M. Buchsbaum and P. Fedio, "Visual Information and Evoked Responses from the Left and Right Hemispheres," *Electroencephalography and Clinical Neurophysiology*, XXVI (1969), 266-278; D. Kimura, "Left-Right Differences in the Perception of Melodies," *Quarterly Journal of Experimental Psychology*, XIV (1964), 355-358; "Functional Asymmetry of the Brain in Dichotic Listening," *Cortex*, III (1967), 163-178; L. K. Morrell and J. Salamy, "Hemispheric Asymmetry of Electrocortical Responses to Speech Stimuli," *Science*, CLXXIV (1971), 164-166; C. Wood, W. Goff and R. Day, "Hemispheric Differences in Auditory Evoked Potentials during Phonemic and Pitch Discrimination," *Science*, CLXXIII (1971), 1248-1251.

11. J. Ertl and E. W. P. Schafer, "Cortical Activity Preceding Speech," *Life Sciences*, VI (1967), 473ff; "Erratum," *Life Sciences*, VIII (1969), 559.

12. D. W. McAdam and H. A. Whitaker, "Language Production: Electroencephalographic Localization in the Normal Human Brain," *Science*, CLXXII (1971), 499-502; Reply to Morrell and Huntington, *Science*, CLXXIV (1971), 1360-1361.

13. L. K. Morrell and D. A. Huntington, "Electrocortical Localization of Language Production," *Science*, CLXXIV (1971), 1359-1360.

14. G. Schaltenbrand, "The Effects of Stereotactic Stimulation in the Depth of the Brain," *Brain*, LXXXVIII (1965), 835-840; G. Schaltenbrand, H. Spuler, W. Wahren, B. Rümmler, "Electroanatomy of the Thalamic Ventro-oral Nucleus Based on Stereotactic Stimulation in Man," *Zeitschrift für Neurologie*, CIC (1971), 269-276.

15. E. von Holst and U. von Saint Paul, "On the Functional Organization of Drives," *The Neurological Basis of Motivation*, eds. S. E. Glickman and P. M. Milner (New York: Van Nostrand, Reinhold, 1963, 1969).

16. E. H. Lenneberg, *Biological Foundations of Language* (New York: Wiley, 1967), Ch. 8; E. C. Wanderley and A. B. Lefèvre, "Afasia adquirida na infancia," *Arquivos de Neuro-Psiquiatria,* XXVII (1969), 89-96.

17. B. Inhelder and J. Piaget, *Genetic Epistemology; The Growth of Logical Thinking from Childhood to Adolescence* (New York: Basic Books, 1964).

18. R. W. Sperry, "Plasticity of Neural Maturation," *The Emergence of Order in De-veloping Systems,* ed. M. Locke, Supplement 2 to *Developmental Biology* (1968); M. Gazzaniga, *The Bisected Brain* (New York: Appleton-Century Crofts, 1970).

19. A. Smith, "Speech and Other Functions after Left (Dominant) Hemispherectomy," *Journal of Neurology, Neurosurgery & Psychiatry,* XXIX (1966), 467-471; K. Ueki, "Hemispherectomy in the Human with Special Reference to the Preservation of Function," *Progress in Brain Research,* CXXI (1966), 285-338. For relevant experimental work on animals demonstrating age-correlated functional differentiation of the cerebral cortex, see D. M. Bowden, P. S. Goldman, H. E. Rosvold, and R. L. Greenstreet, "Free Behavior of Rhesus Monkeys following Lesions of the Dorsolateral and Orbital Prefrontal Cortex in Infancy," *Experimental Brain Re-search,* XII (1971), 265-274; P. S. Goldman, "Functional Development of the Pre-frontal Cortex in Early Life and the Problem of Neuronal Plasticity," *Experimental Neurology,* XXXII (1971), 366-387; P. S. Goldman, H. E. Rosvold, and M. Mish-kin, "Evidence for Behavioral Impairment Following Prefrontal Lobectomy in the Infant Monkey," *Journal of Comparative and Physiological Psychology,* LXX (1970), 454-463; A. Kling and T. J. Tucker, "Sparing of Function Following Localized Brain Lesions in Neonatal Monkeys," *The Neuropsychology of Development,* ed. R. Isaacson (New York: Wiley, 1968). For general comments on critical age in man, see E. H. Lenneberg, "The Effect of Age on the Outcome of Central Nervous System Disease in Children," *The Neuropsychology of Development.*

20. D. G. Stein, J. J. Rosen, J. Graziadei, D. Mishkin, and J. J. Brink, "Central Nervous System: Recovery of Function," *Science,* CLXVI (1969), 528-530; J. D. Rosen, D. Stein, and N. Butter, "Recovery of Function After Serial Ablation of Pre-frontal Cortex in the Rhesus Monkey," *Science,* CVXXIII (1971), 353-356.

21. Lenneberg, *Biological Foundations of Language.*

22. J. Piaget, *Biology and Knowledge: An Essay on the Relations Between Organic Regulations and Cognitive Processes* (Chicago: University of Chicago Press, 1971).

23. R. Brown, *A First Language: The Early Stages* (Cambridge: Harvard University Press, forthcoming); H. Sinclair, *Langage et Opérations. Sous-Systèmes Linguis-tiques et Opérations concrètes* (Paris: Dunod, 1967).

24. Lenneberg, *Biological Foundations of Language;* M. Jacobson, "Brain Development in Relation to Language," *Foundations of Language Development: A Multidisciplinary Approach,* eds. E. and E. Lenneberg (UNESCO, forthcoming).

25. R. Elul, "Brain Waves," *Data Acquisition and Processing in Biology and Medicine,* ed. K. Enslein, V (New York: Pergamon, 1968); W. J. Freeman, "Waves, Pulses and the Theory of Neural Masses," *Progress in Theoretical Biology,* eds. R. Rosen and F. M. Snell, I (1972); O. H. Schmitt, "Biological Information Processing Using the Concept of Interpenetrating Domains," *Information Processing in the Nervous System,* ed. K. N. Leibovic (New York: Springer, 1969).

26. M. Eigen and L. de Maeyer, "Carriers and Specificity in Membranes," *Bulletin of the Neurosciences Research Program*, IX, No. 3 (1971); A. Katchalsky and G. Oster, "Chemico-diffusional Coupling in Biomembranes," *The Molecular Basis of Membrane Function*, ed. D. C. Tosteson (Englewood Cliffs: Prentice-Hall, 1969).

27. R. Blumenthal, J. P. Changeux, and R. Lefever, "Membrane Excitability and Dissipative Instabilities," *Journal of Membrane Biology*, II (1970), 351-374.

28. Eigen and de Maeyer, "Carriers and Specificity in Membranes"; P. Glansdorff and I. Prigogine, *Thermodynamic Theory of Structure, Stability and Fluctuations* (London: Wiley-Interscience, 1971); A. M. Turing, "The Chemical Basis of Morphogenesis," *Royal Society of London Philosophical Transactions*, Series B, CCXXXVII (1952), 37-72.

ROGER BROWN

Development of the First Language in the Human Species

THE FACT THAT one dare set down the above title, with considerable exaggeration but not perhaps with more than is pardonable, reflects the most interesting development in the study of child speech in the past few years. All over the world the first sentences of small children are being as painstakingly taped, transcribed, and analyzed as if they were the last sayings of great sages. Which is a surprising fate for the likes of "That doggie," "No more milk," and "Hit ball." Reports already made, in progress, or projected for the near future sample development in children not only from many parts of the United States, England, Scotland, France, and Germany, but also development in children learning Luo (central East Africa), Samoan, Finnish, Hebrew, Japanese, Korean, Serbo-Croatian, Swedish, Turkish, Cakchiquel (Mayan-Guatemala), Tzeltal (Mayan-Mexico), American Sign Language in the case of a deaf child, and many other languages. The count you make of the number of studies now available for comparative analysis depends on how much you require in terms of standardized procedure, the full report of data, explicit criteria of acquisition, and so on. Brown (1973), whose methods demand a good deal, finds he can use some 33 reports of 12 languages.[1] Slobin (1971), less interested in proving a small number of generalizations than in setting down a large number of interesting hypotheses suggested by what is known, finds he can use many more studies of some 30 languages from 10 different language families.[2] Of course, this is still only about a 1% sample of the world's languages, but in a field like psycholinguistics, in which "universals" sometimes have been postulated on the basis of one or two languages, 30 languages represent a notable empirical advance. The credit for inspiring this extensive field work on language development belongs chiefly to Slobin at Berkeley, whose vision of a universal developmental sequence has inspired research workers everywhere. The quite surprising degree to which results to date support this vision has sustained the researcher when he gets a bit tired of writing down Luo, Samoan, or Finnish equivalents of "That doggie" and "No more milk."

It has, of course, taken some years to accumulate data on a wide variety

121

of languages and even now, as we shall see, the variety is limited largely to just the first period of sentence construction (what is called Stage I). However, the study of first-language development in the preschool years began to be appreciated as a central topic in psycholinguistics in the early 1960s. The initial impetus came fairly directly from Chomsky's (1957) *Syntactic Structures* and, really, from one particular emphasis in that book and in transformational, generative grammar generally.[3] The emphasis is, to put it simply, that in acquiring a first language, one cannot possibly be said simply to acquire a repertoire of sentences, however large that repertoire is imagined to be, but must instead be said to acquire a rule system that makes it possible to generate a literally infinite variety of sentences, most of them never heard from anyone else. It is not a rare thing for a person to compose a new sentence that is understood within his community; rather, it is really a very ordinary linguistic event. Of course, *Syntactic Structures* was not the first book to picture first-language learning as a largely creative process; it may be doubted if any serious linguist has ever thought otherwise. It was the central role Chomsky gave to creativity that made the difference, plus, of course, the fact that he was able to put into explicit, unified notation a certain number of the basic rules of English.

In saying that a child acquires construction rules, one cannot of course mean that he acquires them in any explicit form; the preschool child cannot tell you any linguistic rules at all. And the chances are that his parents cannot tell you very many either, and they obviously do not attempt to teach the mother tongue by the formulation of rules of sentence construction. One must suppose that what happens is that the preschool child is able to extract from the speech he hears a set of construction rules, many of them exceedingly abstract, which neither he nor his parents know in explicit form. This is saying more than that the child generalizes or forms analogies insofar as the generalizations he manifests conform closely to rules that have been made explicit in linguistic science.

That something of the sort described goes on has always been obvious to everyone for languages like Finnish or Russian which have elaborate rules of word formation, or morphology, rules that seem to cause children to make very numerous systematic errors of a kind that parents and casual observers notice. In English, morphology is fairly simple, and errors that parents notice are correspondingly less common. Nevertheless they do exist, and it is precisely in these errors that one glimpses from time to time that largely hidden but presumably general process. Most American children learning English use the form *hisself* rather than *himself* when they are about four years old. How do they come by it? It actually has been in the language since Middle English and is still in use among some adults, though called, for no good reason, a "substandard" form. It can be shown, however, that children use it when they have never heard it from anyone else, and so presumably they make it up or construct it. Why do they invent something that is, from the standard adult point of view, a mistake? To answer that we must recall the set of words most similar to the reflexive pronoun *himself*. They are such other reflexive pronouns as *myself, yourself,* and *herself*. But all of these others, we see, are constructed by combining the possessive pronoun, *my, your,* or *her* with *self*. The masculine possessive pronoun is *his* and, if the English language were consistent at this point, the reflexive would be *hisself*. As it happens, standard English is not consistent at this point but is, rather, irregular, as all languages are at some points, and the preferred form is *himself*. Children, by inventing *hisself* and often insisting on it for quite a period, "iron out" or correct the irregularity of the language. And, incidentally, they reveal to us the fact that what they are learning are general rules of construction—not just the words and phrases they hear.

Close examination of the speech of children learning English shows that it is often replete with errors of syntax or sentence construction as well as morphology (e.g., "Where Daddy went"). But for some reason, errors of word formation are noticed regularly by parents, whereas they are commonly quite unconscious of errors of syntax. And so it happens that even casual observers of languages with a well-developed morphology are aware of the creative construction process, whereas casual observers of English find it possible seriously to believe that language learning is simply a process of memorizing what has been heard.

The extraction of a finite structure with an infinite generative potential which furthermore is accomplished in large part, though not completely, by the beginning of the school years (see Chomsky, 1969, for certain exceptions and no doubt there are others [4]), all without explicit tuition, was not something any learning theory was prepared to explain, though some were prepared to "handle" it, whatever "handle" means. And so it appeared that first-language acquisition was a major challenge to psychology.

While the first studies of language acquisition were inspired by transformational linguistics, nevertheless, they really were not approved of by the transformational linguists. This was because the studies took the child's spontaneous speech performance, taped and transcribed at home on some regular schedule, for their basic data, and undertook to follow the changes in these data with age. At about the same time in the early 1960s, three studies of, roughly, this sort were begun independently: Martin Braine's (1963) in Maryland, Roger Brown's (Brown & Bellugi, 1964) at Harvard with his associates Ursula Bellugi (now Bellugi-Klima) and Colin Fraser (Brown & Fraser, 1963), and Susan Ervin (now Ervin-Tripp) with Wick Miller (Miller & Ervin, 1964) at Berkeley.[5] The attempt to discover constructional knowledge from "mere performance" seemed quite hopeless to the MIT linguists (e.g., Chomsky, 1964; Lees, 1964).[6] It was at the opposite extreme from the linguist's own method, which was to present candidate-sentences to his own intuition for judgment as grammatical or not. In cases of extreme uncertainty, I suppose he may also have stepped next door to ask the opinion of a colleague.

In retrospect, I think they were partly right and partly wrong about our early methods. They were absolutely right in thinking that no sample of spontaneous speech, however large, would alone enable one to write a fully determinate set of construction rules. I learned that fact over a period of years in which I made the attempt 15 times, for three children at five points of development. There were always, and are always, many things the corpus alone cannot settle. The linguists were wrong, I think, in two ways. First, in supposing that because one cannot learn everything about a child's construction knowledge, one cannot learn anything. One can, in fact, learn quite a lot, and one of the discoveries of the past decade is the variety of ways in which spontaneous running discourse can be "milked" for knowledge of linguistic structure; a great deal of the best evidence lies not simply in the child's own sentences but in the exchanges with others on the level of discourse. I do not think that transformational linguists should have "pronounced" on all of this with such discouraging confidence since they had never, in fact, tried. The other way in which I think the linguists were wrong was in their gross exaggeration of the degree to which spontaneous speech is ungrammatical, a kind of hodgepodge of false starts, incomplete sentences, and so on. Except for talk at learned conferences, even adult speech, allowing for some simple rules of editing and ellipses, seems to be mostly quite grammatical (Labov, 1970).[7] For children and for the speech of parents to children this is even more obviously the case.

The first empirical studies of the 1960s gave rise to various descriptive characterizations, of which "telegraphic speech" (Brown & Fraser, 1963) and "Pivot Grammar" (Braine, 1963) are the best known. These did not lead anywhere very interesting, but they were unchallenged long enough to get into most introductory psychology textbooks where they probably will survive for a few years even though their numerous inadequacies are now well established. Bloom (1970), Schlesinger (1971), and Bowerman (1970) made the most telling criticisms both theoretical and empirical, and Brown (1973) has put the whole, now overwhelmingly negative, case together.[8] It seems to be clear enough to workers in this field that telegraphic speech and Pivot Grammar are false leads that we need not even bother to describe.

However, along with their attacks, especially on Pivot Grammar, Bloom (1970) and Schlesinger (1971) made a positive contribution that has turned out to be the second major impetus to the field. For reasons which must seem very strange to the outsider not immersed in the linguistics of the 1960s, the first analyses of child sentences in this period were in terms of pure syntax, in abstraction from semantics, with no real attention paid to what the children might intend to communicate. Lois Bloom added to her transcriptions of child speech a systematic running account of the nonlinguistic context. And in these contexts she found evidence that the child intends to express certain meanings with even his earliest sentences, meanings that go beyond the simple naming in succession of various aspects of a complex situation, and that actually assert the existence of, or request the creation of, particular relations.

The justification for attributing relational semantic intentions to very small children comprises a complex and not fully satisfying argument. At its strongest, it involves the following sort of experimental procedure. With toys that the child can name available to him he is, on one occasion, asked to "Make the truck hit the car," and on another occasion "Make the car hit the truck." Both sentences involve the same objects and action, but the contrast of word order in English indicates which object is to be in the role of agent (hitter) and which in the role of object (the thing hit). If the child acts out the two events in ways appropriate to the contrasting word orders, he may be said to understand the differences in the semantic relations involved. Similar kinds of contrasts can be set up for possessives ("Show me the Mommy's baby" versus "Show me the baby's Mommy") and prepositions ("Put the pencil on the matches" versus "Put the matches on the pencil"). The evidence to date, of which there is a fairly considerable amount collected in America and Britain (Bever, Mehler, & Valian, in press; de Villiers & de Villiers, 1973; Fraser, Bellugi, & Brown, 1963; Lovell & Dixon, 1965), indicates that, by late Stage I, children learning English can do these things correctly (experiments on the prepositions are still in a trial stage).[9] By late Stage I, children learning English also are often producing what the nonlinguistic context suggests are intended as relations of possession, location, and agent-action-object. For noncontrastive word orders in English and for languages that do not utilize contrastive word order in these ways, the evidence for relational intentions is essentially the nonlinguistic context. Which context is also, of course, what parents use as an aid to figuring out what their children mean when they speak.

It is, I think, worth a paragraph of digression to point out that another experimental method, a method of judgment and correction of word sequence and so a method nearer that of the transformational linguist himself, yields a quite different outcome. Peter and Jill de Villiers (1972) asked children to observe a dragon puppet who sometimes spoke correctly with respect to word order (e.g., "Drive your car") and sometimes incorrectly (e.g., "Cup the fill").[10] A second dragon puppet responded to the first when the first spoke correctly by saying "right" and repeating the sentence. When the first puppet spoke incorrectly, the second, tutorial puppet, said "wrong," and corrected the sentence (e.g., "Fill the cup"). After observing a number of such sequences, the child was invited to play the role of the tutorial puppet, and new sentences, correct and incorrect, were supplied. In effect, this is a complicated way of asking the child to make judgments of syntactic well-formedness, supplying corrections as necessary. The instruction is not given easily in words, but by role-playing examples de Villiers and de Villiers found they could get the idea across. While there are many interesting results in their study, the most important is that the children did not make correct word-order judgments 50% of the time until after what we call Stage V, and only the most advanced child successfully corrected wrong orders over half the time. This small but important study suggests that construction rules do not emerge all at once on the levels of spontaneous use, discriminating response, and judgment. The last of these, the linguist's favorite, is, after all, not simply a pipeline to competence but a metalinguistic performance of considerable complexity.

In spite of the fact that the jurisdiction for attributing semantic intentions of a relational nature to the child when he first begins composing sentences is not fully satisfactory, the practice, often called the method of "rich interpretation," by contrast with the "lean" behavioral interpretation that preceded it, is by now well justified simply because it has helped expose remarkable developmental universals that formerly had gone unremarked. There are now I think three reasonably well-established developmental series in which constructions and the meanings they express appear in a nearly invariant order.

The first of these, and still the only one to have been shown to have validity for many different languages, concerns Stage I. Stage I has been defined rather arbitrarily as the period when the average length of the child's utterances in morphemes (mean length of utterance or MLU) first rises above 1.0—in short, the time when combinations of words or morphemes first occur at all—until the MLU is 2.0, at which time utterances occasionally will attain as great a length as 7 morphemes. The most obvious superficial fact about child sentences is that they grow longer as the child grows older. Leaning on this fact, modern investigators have devised a set of standard rules for calculating MLU, rules partially well motivated and partially arbitrary. Whether the rules are exactly the right ones, and it is already clear that they are not, is almost immaterial because their only function is a temporary one: to render children in one study and in different studies initially comparable in terms of some index superior to chronological age, and this MLU does. It has been shown (Brown, 1973) that while individual children vary enormously in rate of linguistic development, and so in what they know at a given chronological age, their constructional and semantic knowledge is fairly uniform at a given MLU. It is common, in the literature, to identify five stages, with those above Stage I defined by increments of .50 to the MLU.

By definition, then, Stage I children in any language are going to be producing sentences of from 1 to 7 morphemes long with the average steadily increasing across Stage I. What is not true by definition, but is true in fact for all of the languages so far studied, is that the constructions in Stage I are limited semantically to a single rather small set of relations and, furthermore, the complications that occur in the course of the Stage are also everywhere the same. Finally, in Stage I, the only syntactic or expressive devices employed are the combinations of the semantically related forms under one sentence contour and, where relevant in the model language, correct word order. It is important to recognize that there are many other things that *could* happen in Stage I, many ways of increasing *MLU* besides those actually used in Stage I. In Stage I, *MLU* goes up because simple two-term relations begin to be combined into three-term and four-term relations of the same type but occurring in one sentence. In later stages, *MLU,* always sensitive to increases of knowledge, rises in value for quite different reasons; for instance, originally missing obligatory function forms like inflections begin to be supplied, later on the embedding of two or more simple sentences begins, and eventually the coordination of simple sentences.

What are the semantic relations that seem universally to be the subject matter of Stage I speech? In brief, it may be said that they are either relations or propositions concerning the sensory-motor world, and seem to represent the linguistic expression of the sensory-motor intelligence which the work of the great developmental psychologist Jean Piaget has described as the principal acquisition of the first 18 months of life. The Stage I relations also correspond very closely with the set of "cases" which Charles Fillmore (1968) has postulated as the universal semantic deep structures of language.[11] This is surprising since Fillmore did not set out to say anything at all about child speech but simply to provide a universal framework for adult grammar.

In actual fact, there is no absolutely fixed list of Stage I relations. A short list of 11 will account for about 75% of Stage I utterances in almost all language samples collected. A longer list of about 18 will come close to accounting for 100%. What are some of the relations? There is, in the first place, a closed semantic set having to do with reference. These include the nominative (e.g., "That ball"), expressions of recurrence (e.g., "More ball"), and expressions of disappearance or nonexistence (e.g., "All gone ball"). Then there is the possessive (e.g., "Daddy chair"), two sorts of locative (e.g., "Book table" and "Go store") and the attributive (e.g., "Big house"). Finally, there are two-term relations comprising portions of a major sort of declarative sentence: agent-action (e.g., "Daddy hit"); action-object (e.g., "Hit ball"); and, surprisingly from the point of view of the adult language, agent-object (e.g., "Daddy ball"). Less frequent relations which do not appear in all samples but which one would want to add to a longer list include: experiencer-state (e.g., "I hear"); datives of indirect object (e.g., "Give Mommy"); comitatives (e.g., "Walk Mommy"); instrumentals (e.g., "Sweep broom"); and just a few others. From all of these constructions, it may be noticed that in English, and in all languages, "obligatory" functional morphemes like inflections, case endings, articles, and prepositions are missing in Stage I. This is, of course, the observation that gave rise to the still roughly accurate descriptive term *telegraphic speech.* The function forms are thought to be absent because of some combination of such variables as their slight phonetic substance and minimal stress, their varying but generally considerable grammatical complexity, and the subtlety of the semantic modulations they express (number, time, aspect, specificity of reference, exact spatial relations, etc.).

Stage I speech seems to be almost perfectly restricted to these two-term relations, expressed, at the least, by subordination to a single sentence contour and often by appropriate word order, until the *MLU* is about 1.50. From here on, complications which lengthen the utterance begin, but they are, remarkably enough, complications of just the same two types in all languages studied so far. The first type involves three-term relations, like agent-action-object; agent-action-locative; and action-object-locative which, in effect, combine sequentially two of the simple relations found before an *MLU* of 1.50 without repeating the term that would appear twice if the two-term relations simply were strung together. In other words, something like agent-action-object (e.g., "Adam hit ball") is made up *as if* the relations agent-action ("Adam hit") and action-object ("Hit ball") had been strung together in sequence with one redundant occurrence of the action ("hit") deleted.

The second type of complication involves the retention of the basic line of the two-term relation with one term, always a noun-phrase, "expanding" as a relation in its own right. Thus, there is development from such forms as "Sit chair" (action-locative) to "Sit Daddy chair," which is an action-locative, such that the locative itself is expanded as a possessive. The forms expanded in this kind of construction are, in all languages so far studied, the same three types: expressions of attribution, possession, and recurrence. Near the very end of Stage I, there are further complications into four-term relations of exactly the same two types described. All of this, of course, gives a very "biological" impression, almost as if semantic cells of a finite set of types were dividing and combining and then redividing and recombining in ways common to the species.

The remaining two best established invariances of order in acquisition have not been studied in a variety of languages but only for American children and, in one case, only for the three unacquainted children in Brown's longitudinal study—the children called, in the literature, Adam, Eve, and Sarah. The full results appear in Stage II of Brown (1973) and in Brown and Hanlon (1970). Stage II in Brown (1973) focuses on 14 functional morphemes including the English noun and verb inflections, the copula *be,* the progressive auxiliary *be,* the prepositions *in* and *on,* and the articles *a* and *the.* For just these forms in English it is possible to define a criterion that is considerably superior to the simple occurrence-or-not used in Stage I and to the semiarbitrary frequency levels used in the remaining sequence to be described. In very many sentence contexts, one or another of the 14 morphemes can be said to be "obligatory" from the point of view of the adult language. Thus in a nomination sentence accompanied by pointing, such as "That book," an article is obligatory; in a sentence like "Here two book," a plural inflection on the noun is obligatory; in "I running", the auxiliary *am* inflected for person, number, and tense is obligatory. It is possible to treat each such sentence frame as a kind of test item in which the obligatory form either appears or is omitted. Brown defined as his criterion of acquisition, presence in 90% of obligatory contexts in six consecutive sampling hours.

There are in the detailed report many surprising and suggestive outcomes. For instance, "acquisition" of these forms turns out never to be a sudden all-or-none affair such as categorical linguistic rules might suggest it should be. It is rather a matter of a slowly increasing probability of presence, varying in rate from morpheme to morpheme, but extending in some cases over several years. The most striking single outcome is that for these three children, with spontaneous speech scored in the fashion described, the order of acquisition of the morphemes approaches invariance, with rank-order correlations between pairs of children all at about .86. This does not say that acquisition of a morpheme is invariant with respect to chronological age: the variation of rate of development even among three children is tremendous. But the order, that is, which construction follows which, is almost constant, and Brown (1973) shows that it is not predicted by morpheme frequency in adult speech, but is well predicted by relative semantic and grammatical complexity. Of course, in languages other than English, the same universal sequence cannot possibly be found because grammatical and semantic differences are too great to yield commensurable data, as they are not with the fundamental relations or cases of Stage I. However, if the 14 particular morphemes are reconceived as particular conjunctions of perceptual salience and degrees of grammatical and semantic complexity, we may find laws of succession which have cross-linguistic validity (see Slobin, 1971).

Until the spring of 1972, Brown was the only researcher who had coded data in terms of presence in, or absence from, obligatory contexts, but then Jill and Peter de Villiers (1973) did the job on a fairly large scale.[13] They made a cross-sectional study from speech samples of 21 English-speaking American children aged between 16 and 40 months. The de Villiers scored the 14 morphemes Brown scored; they used his coding rules to identify obligatory contexts and calculated the children's individual *MLU* values according to his rules.

Two different criteria of morpheme acquisition were used in the analyses of data. Both constitute well-rationalized adaptations to a cross-sectional study of the 90% correct criterion used in Brown's longitudinal study; we will refer to the two orders here simply as 1 and 2. To compare with the de Villiers' two orders there is a single rank order (3) for the three children, Adam, Eve, and Sarah, which was obtained by averaging the orders of the three children.

There are then three rank orders for the same 14 morphemes scored in the same way and using closely similar criteria of acquisition. The degree of invariance is, even to one who expected a substantial similarity, amazing. The rank-order correlations are: between 1 and 2, .84; between 2 and 3,

.78; between 1 and 3, .87. These relations are only very slightly below those among Adam, Eve, and Sarah themselves. Thanks to the de Villiers, it has been made clear that we have a developmental phenomenon of substantial generality.

There are numerous other interesting outcomes in the de Villiers' study. The rank-order correlation between age and Order 2 is .68, while that between *MLU* and the same order is .92, very close to perfect. So *MLU* is a better predictor than age in their study, as in ours of morpheme acquisition. In fact, with age partialed out, using a Kendall partial correlation procedure, the original figure of .92 is only reduced to .85, suggesting that age adds little or nothing to the predictive power of *MLU*.

The third sequence, demonstrated only for English by Brown and Hanlon (1970), takes advantage of the fact that what are called tag questions are in English very complex grammatically, though semantically they are rather simple. In many other languages tags are invariant in form (e.g., *n'est-ce pas*, French; *nicht wahr*, German), and so are grammatically simple; but in English, the form of the tag, and there are hundreds of forms, varies in a completely determinate way with the structure of the declarative sentence to which it is appended and for which it asks confirmation. Thus:

"John will be late, won't he?"
"Mary can't drive, can she?"

And so on. The little question at the end is short enough, as far as superficial length is concerned, to be produced by the end of Stage I. We know, furthermore, that the semantic of the tag, a request for confirmation, lies within the competence of the Stage I child since he occasionally produces such invariant and simple equivalents as "right?" or "huh?" Nevertheless, Brown and Hanlon (1970) have shown that the production of a full range of well-formed tags is not to be found until after Stage V, sometimes several years after. Until that time, there are, typically, no well-formed tags at all. What accounts for the long delay? Brown and Hanlon present evidence that it is the complexity of the grammatical knowledge that tags entail.

Consider such a declarative sentence as "His wife can drive." How might one develop from this the tag "can't she?"? It is, in the first place, necessary to make a pronoun of the subject. The subject is *his wife*, and so the pronoun must be feminine, third person, and since it is a subject, the nominative case—in fact, *she*. Another step is to make the tag negative. In English this is done by adding *not* or the contraction *n't* to the auxiliary verb *can*; hence *can't*. Another step is to make the tag interrogative, since it is a question, and in English that is done by a permutation of order—placing the auxiliary verb ahead of the subject. Still another step is to delete all of the predicate of the base sentence, except the first member of the auxiliary, and that at last yields *can't she?* as a derivative of *His wife can drive*. While this description reads a little bit like a program simulating the process by which tags actually are produced by human beings, it is not intended as anything of the sort. The point is simply that there seems to be no way at all by which a human could produce the right tag for each declarative without *somehow* utilizing all of the grammatical knowledge described, just how no one knows. But memorization is excluded completely by the fact that, while tags themselves are numerous but not infinitely so, the problem is to fit the one right tag to each declarative, and declaratives are infinitely numerous.

In English all of the single constructions, and also all of the pairs, which entail the knowledge involved in tag creation, themselves exist as independent sentences in their own right, for example, interrogatives, negatives, ellipses, negative-ellipses, and so on. One can, therefore, make an ordering of constructions in terms of complexity of grammatical knowledge (in precise fact, only a partial ordering) and ask whether more complex forms are always preceded in child speech by less complex forms. This is what Brown and Hanlon (1970) did for Adam, Eve, and Sarah, and the result was resoundingly affirmative. In this study, then, we have evidence that grammatical complexity as such, when it can be disentangled, as it often cannot, from semantic complexity, is itself a determinant of order of acquisition.

Of course, the question about the mother tongue that we should really like answered is, How is it possible to learn a first language at all? On that question, which ultimately motivates the whole research enterprise, I have nothing to offer that is not negative. But perhaps it is worthwhile making these negatives explicit since they are still widely supposed to be affirmatives, and indeed to provide a large part of the answer to the question. What I have to say is not primarily addressed to the question, How does the child come to talk at all? since there seem to be fairly obvious utilities in saying a few words in order to express more exactly what he wants, does not want, wonders about, or wishes to share with others. The more exact question on which we have a little information that serves only to make the question more puzzling is, How does the child come to *improve* upon his language, moving steadily in the direction of the adult model? It probably seems surprising that there should be any mystery about the forces impelling improvement, since it is just this aspect of the process that most people imagine that they understand. Surely the improvement is a response to selective social pressures of various kinds; ill-formed or incomplete utterances must be less effective than well-formed and complete utterances in accomplishing the child's intent; parents probably approve of well-formed utterances and disapprove or correct the ill-formed. These ideas sound sensible and may be correct, but the still-scant evidence available does not support them.

At the end of Stage I, the child's constructions are characterized by, in addition to the things we have mentioned, a seemingly lawless oscillating omission of every sort of major constituent including sometimes subjects,

objects, verbs, locatives, and so on. The important point about these oscillating omissions is that they seldom seem to impede communication; the other
person, usually the mother, being in the same situation and familiar with
the child's stock of knowledge, usually understands, so far as one can judge,
even the incomplete utterance. Brown (1973) has suggested the Stage I
child's speech is well adapted to his purpose, but that, as a speaker, he is
very *narrowly* adapted. We may suppose that in speaking to strangers or of
new experiences he will have to learn to express obligatory constituents if
he wants to get his message across. And that may be the answer: The social
pressures to communicate may chiefly operate outside the usual sampling
situation, which is that of the child at home with family members.

In Stage II, Brown (1973) found that all of the 14 grammatical morphemes were at first missing, then occasionally present in obligatory contexts, and after varying and often long periods of time, always present in
such contexts. What makes the probability of supplying the requisite morpheme rise with time? It is surprisingly difficult to find cases in which
omission results in incomprehension or misunderstanding. With respect
to the definite and nondefinite articles, it even looks as if listeners almost
never really need them, and yet child speakers learn to operate with the
exceedingly intricate rules governing their usage. Adult Japanese, speaking
English as a second language, do not seem to learn how to operate with
the articles as we might expect they would if listeners needed them. Perhaps it is the case that the child automatically does this kind of learning
but that adults do not. Second-language learning may be responsive to
familiar sorts of learning variables, and first-language learning may not.
The two, often thought to be similar processes, may be profoundly and
ineradicably different.

Consider the Stage I child's invariably uninflected generic verbs. In
Stage II, American parents regularly gloss these verbs in one of four ways:
as imperatives, past tense forms, present progressives, or imminent-inten-
tional futures. It is an interesting fact, of course, that these are just the
four modulations of the verb that the child then goes on, first, to learn to
express. For years we have thought it possible that glosses or expansions
of this type might be a major force impelling the child to improve his
speech. However, all the evidence available, both naturalistic and experimental (it is summarized in Brown, Cazden, & Bellugi, 1969), offers no
support at all for this notion.[14] Cazden (1965), for instance, carried out an
experiment testing for the effect on young children's speech of deliberately
interpolated "expansions" (the supplying of obligatory functional morphemes), introduced for a period on every preschool day for three months.[15]
She obtained no significant effect whatever. It is possible, I think, that
such an experiment done now, with the information Stage II makes available, and expanding only by providing morphemes of a complexity for

which the child was "ready," rather than as in Cazden's original experiment expanding in all possible ways, would show an effect. But no such experiment has been done, and so no impelling effect of expansion has been demonstrated.

Suppose we look at the facts of the parental glossing of Stage I generic verbs not, as we have done above, as a possible tutorial device but rather, as Slobin (1971) has done, as evidence that the children already intended the meanings their parents attributed to them. In short, think of the parental glosses as veridical readings of the child's thought. From this point of view, the child has been understood correctly, even though his utterances are incomplete. In that case there is no selection pressure. Why does he learn to say more if what he already knows how to say works quite well?

To these observations of the seeming efficacy of the child's incomplete utterances, at least at home with the family, we should add the results of a study reported in Brown and Hanlon (1970). Here it was not primarily a question of the omission of obligatory forms but of the contrast between ill-formed primitive constructions and well-formed mature versions. For certain constructions, *yes-no* questions, tag questions, negatives, and *wh-*questions, Brown and Hanlon (1970) identified periods when Adam, Eve, and Sarah were producing both primitive and mature versions, sometimes the one, sometimes the other. The question was, Did the mature version communicate more successfully than the primitive version? They first identified all instances of primitive and mature versions, and then coded the adult responses for comprehending follow-up, calling comprehending responses "sequiturs" and uncomprehending or irrelevant responses "nonsequiturs." They found no evidence whatever of a difference in communicative efficacy, and so once again, no selection pressure. Why, one asks oneself, should the child learn the complex apparatus of tag questions when "right?" or "huh?" seems to do just the same job? Again one notes that adults learning English as a second language often do not learn tag questions, and the possibility again comes to mind that children operate on language in a way that adults do not.

Brown and Hanlon (1970) have done one other study that bears on the search for selection pressures. Once again it was syntactic well-formedness versus ill-formedness that was in question rather than completeness or incompleteness. This time Brown and Hanlon started with two kinds of adult responses to child utterances: "approval," directed at an antecedent child utterance, and "disapproval," directed at such an antecedent. The question then was, Did the two sets of antecedents differ in syntactic correctness? Approving and disapproving responses are, certainly, very reasonable candidates for the respective roles, "positive reinforcer" and "punishment." Of course, they do not necessarily qualify as such because reinforcers and punishments are defined by their effects on performance

(Skinner, 1953); they have no necessary, independent, nonfunctional properties.[16] Still, of course, they often are put forward as plausible determinants of performance and are thought, generally, to function as such. In order differentially to affect the child's syntax, approval and disapproval must, at a minimum, be governed selectively by correct and incorrect syntax. If they should be so governed, further data still would be needed to show that they affect performance. If they are not so governed, they cannot be a selective force working for correct speech. And Brown and Hanlon found that they are not. In general, the parents seemed to pay no attention to bad syntax nor did they even seem to be aware of it. They approved or disapproved an utterance usually on the grounds of the truth value of the proposition which the parents supposed the child intended to assert. This is a surprising outcome to most middle-class parents, since they are generally under the impression that they do correct the child's speech. From inquiry and observation I find that what parents generally correct is pronunciation, "naughty" words, and regularized irregular allomorphs like *digged* or *goed*. These facts of the child's speech seem to penetrate parental awareness. But syntax—the child saying, for instance, "Why the dog won't eat?" instead of "Why won't the dog eat?"—seems to be set right automatically in the parent's mind; with the mistake never registering as such.

In sum, then, we presently do not have evidence that there are selective social pressures of any kind operating on children to impel them to bring their speech into line with adult models. It is, however, entirely possible that such pressures do operate in situations unlike the situations we have sampled, for instance, away from home or with strangers. A radically different possibility is that children work out rules for the speech they hear, passing from levels of lesser to greater complexity, simply because the human species is programmed at a certain period in its life to operate in this fashion on linguistic input. Linguistic input would be defined by the universal properties of language. And the period of progressive rule extraction would correspond to Lenneberg's (1967 and elsewhere) proposed "critical period." [17] It may be chiefly adults who learn a new, a second, language in terms of selective social pressures. Comparison of the kinds of errors made by adult second-language learners of English with the kinds made by child first-language learners of English should be enlightening.

If automatic internal programs of structure extraction provide the generally correct sort of answer to how a first language is learned, then, of course, our inquiries into external communication pressures simply are misguided. They look for the answer in the wrong place. That, of course, does not mean that we are anywhere close to having the right answer. It only remains to specify the kinds of programs that would produce the result regularly obtained.

REFERENCES

1. R. Brown, *A First Language: The Early Stages* (Cambridge: Harvard University Press, 1973).

2. D. I. Slobin, "Developmental Psycholinguistics," *A Survey of Linguistic Science,* ed. W. O. Dingwall (College Park: Linguistics Program, University of Maryland, 1971).

3. N. Chomsky, *Syntactic Structures* (The Hague: Mouton, 1957).

4. C. Chomsky, *The Acquisition of Syntax in Children from 5 to 10* (Cambridge: M.I.T. Press, 1969).

5. M. D. S. Braine, "The Ontogeny of English Phrase Structure: The First Phase," *Language,* XXXIX (1963), 1-14; R. Brown and U. Bellugi, "Three Processes in the Acquisition of Syntax," *Harvard Educational Review,* XXXIV (1964), 133-151; R. Brown and C. Fraser, "The Acquisition of Syntax," *Verbal Behavior and Learning: Problems and Processes,* eds. C. N. Cofer and B. S. Musgrave (New York: McGraw-Hill, 1963); W. Miller and S. Ervin, "The Development of Grammar in Child Language," *Monographs of the Society for Research in Child Development,* XXIX, No. 1 (1964), 9-34, from U. Bellugi and R. Brown, eds., *The Acquisition of Language.*

6. N. Chomsky, "Formal Discussion of Wick Miller and Susan Ervin. The Development of Grammar in Child Language," *Monographs of the Society for Research in Child Development,* XXIX, No. 1 (1964), 35-40, from U. Bellugi and R. Brown, eds., *The Acquisition of Language;* R. Lees, "Formal Discussion of Roger Brown and Colin Fraser. The Acquisition of Syntax. And of Roger Brown, Colin Fraser, and Ursula Bellugi. Explorations in Grammar Evaluation," *Monographs of the Society for Research in Child Development,* XXIX, No.1(1964), 92-98, from U. Bellugi and R. Brown, eds., *The Acquisition of Language.*

7. W. Labov, "The Study of Language in Its Social Context," *Studium Generale,* XXIII (1970), 30-87.

8. L. Bloom, *Language Development: Form and Function in Emerging Grammars* (Cambridge: M.I.T. Press, 1970); I. M. Schlesinger, "Production of Utterances and Language Acquisition," *The Ontogenesis of Grammar,* ed. D. I. Slobin (New York: Academic Press, 1971); M. Bowerman, "Learning to Talk: A Cross-Linguistic Study of Early Syntactic Development with Special Reference to Finnish" (Ph.D. diss., Harvard University, 1970).

9. T. G. Bever, J. R. Mehler, and V. V. Valian, "Linguistic Capacity of Very Young Children," *The Acquisition of Structure,* eds. T. G. Bever and W. Weksel (New York: Holt, Rinehart and Winston, forthcoming); J. G. de Villiers and P. A. de Villiers, "Development of the Use of Order in Comprehension," *Journal of Psycholinguistic Research,* II (1973), 331-341; C. Fraser, U. Bellugi, and R. Brown, "Control of Grammar in Imitation, Comprehension, and Production," *Journal of Verbal Learning and Verbal Behavior,* II (1963), 121-135; K. Lovell and E. M. Dixon, "The Growth of Grammar in Imitation, Comprehension, and Production," *Journal of Child Psychology and Psychiatry,* V (1965), 1-9.

10. P. A. de Villiers and J. G. de Villiers, "Early Judgments of Semantic and Syntactic Acceptability by Children," *Journal of Psycholinguistic Research*, I (1972), 299-310.

11. C. J. Fillmore, "The Case for Case," *Universals in Linguistic Theory*, eds. E. Bach and R. T. Harms (New York: Holt, Rinehart and Winston, 1968).

12. R. Brown and C. Hanlon, "Derivational Complexity and Order of Acquisition in Child Speech," *Cognition and the Development of Language*, ed. J. R. Hayes (New York: Wiley, 1970).

13. J. G. de Villiers and P. A. de Villiers, "A Cross-sectional Study of the Development of Grammatical Morphemes in Child Speech," *Journal of Psycholinguistic Research*, II (1973), 267-278.

14. R. Brown, C. Cazden, and U. Bellugi, "The Child's Grammar from 1 to 3," *Minnesota Symposium on Child Psychology*, vol. 2, ed. J. P. Hill (Minneapolis: University of Minnesota Press, 1969).

15. C. B. Cazden, "Environmental Assistance to the Child's Acquisition of Grammar" (Ph.D. diss., Harvard University, 1965).

16. B. F. Skinner, *Science and Human Behavior* (New York: Macmillan, 1953).

17. E. H. Lenneberg, *Biological Foundations of Language* (New York: Wiley, 1967).

COURTNEY B. CAZDEN

Problems for Education: Language as Curriculum Content and Learning Environment

Language as Curriculum Content

LANGUAGE POSES multiple problems for education because it is both curriculum content and learning environment, both the object of knowledge, and a medium through which other knowledge is acquired.[1]

Usually, education in the institutions we call schools imparts knowledge about something without considering the context in which that knowledge is to be used. Language poses a particular challenge to curriculum designers because it is not certain that teaching knowledge about language helps us in any way. The unclear role of knowledge entails two further curriculum problems: inciting motivation and providing opportunities for practice. I will discuss these related questions with reference, in turn, to first languages, second languages, and dialects.

I

Communicative competence[2] implies a knowledge of both linguistic and sociolinguistic rules: a knowledge, in other words, both of language (in the narrow sense of phonology, syntax and semantics), and of the social world in which it must be used.

To date, we know far more about the child's acquisition of linguistic rules than about his acquisition of sociolinguistic rules, and the two processes may be quite different. About the acquisition of linguistic rules, we know that, during the most dramatic language learning period from two to five years old, children are not taught syntax directly. Parents correct erroneous labels and factual inaccuracies, and they try to teach what they think of as speech etiquette (a matter of sociolinguistic rules) by censuring taboo words and admonishing the child to say "please" or to be quiet; but they do not correct immature grammatical forms. One may, after the fact, conjecture about what information on language structure is conveyed by parental utterances.[3] But parents themselves talk without any

137

intent to teach language structure, and the child's immature grammatical forms assume a transparency through which parents and children engage in reciprocal communication from the very beginning.

Somehow, by means of the speech they engage in or overhear, children do internalize abstract rules. One example of these rules can stand for many: the contrasting meanings of English indefinite and definite articles, "a" and "the," investigated experimentally by Maratsos.[4] A child was seated at a table with a group of identical toy cars in front of him. The experimenter sat facing the child across the table. At the experimenter's request, the child handed him one of the cars. The adult then asked one of the two questions:

"Do you have a car?"
"Do you have the car?"

The questions were asked in random order, with normal intonation. To the first question, most children as young as three years old answered "yes" or nodded their heads; to the second question they said "no" or shook their heads. Somehow, many children, at least by the time they are three, have learned the contrast in meaning between what we label "definite" and "indefinite," a very abstract distinction which no one tries to teach a child directly.

Furthermore, all the evidence[5] shows that teaching grammatical rules in school has no effect on students' actual performance in speech or writing. In other words, grammatical performance seems to be based on implicit grammatical knowledge, which is unaffected by explicit teaching. One reason, therefore, why language is such a difficult subject for curriculum planners is that we do not understand the relationship between what is in some way *learned* and what can be *taught*.

Polanyi's distinction between two kinds of awareness may be helpful. When hammering in a nail, we see the nail as the *focal* point and the hammer as a mere *subsidiary* instrument.

Subsidiary awareness and focal awareness are mutually exclusive. If a pianist shifts his attention from the piece he is playing to the observation of what he is doing with his fingers while playing it, he gets confused and may have to stop. This happens generally if we switch our focal attention to particulars of which we had previously been aware only in their subsidiary role. . . . All particulars become meaningless if we lose sight of the pattern which they jointly constitute.

When we use words in speech or writing we are aware of them only in a subsidiary manner. This fact is usually described as the *transparency* of language.[6]

In Polanyi's scheme, *maxims*—rules about aspects of a skill—can play a role:

Maxims are the rules, the correct application of which is part of the art which they govern. The true maxims of golfing or of poetry increase our insight into golfing or poetry and may even give valuable guidance to golfers or poets;

but these maxims would instantly condemn themselves to absurdity if they tried to replace the golfer's skill or the poet's art. Maxims cannot be understood, still less applied by anyone not already possessing a good practical knowledge of the art.[7]

If we accept Polanyi's view, it does not follow that maxims of effective communication cannot be taught, but only that the maxims selected should be at the level of functional effectiveness and style, not at the level of grammar. It may be argued, of course, that English teachers have always given style some consideration. But it is all too easy to ignore Polanyi's insistence on intentionality. Neither practice for practice's sake, nor maxims for maxims' sake will suffice. Both must serve a personal purpose, an intentionality that alone binds the parts into a whole.

Thus, to realize the goals of language as curriculum content, it is necessary to design a particular kind of environment for language use, one in which the contrast between language as curriculum content and as learning environment is reduced. We must create environments in which (1) each individual is motivated by a powerful communicative intent (2) to use language in ways which extend his repertoire beyond what he uses out-of-school, and in which he can receive (3) feedback on the effectiveness of his efforts in speech or writing, and even (4) generalizations (Polanyi's maxims) that go beyond the individual case.

Critical problems in designing such environments vary according to the age of the learner. For young children, consistency of adult-child relationships, distribution of adult talking time, and the character of the adult-child interaction seem to be important;[8] for older children and adults, the problem of motivation probably overwhelms all others.[9]

II

Traditionally, we have believed that a second language was learned by a different process from a first language; recently that belief is being questioned. Dulay and Burt review the evidence[10] that, at least for young children, first and second language learning processes are very similar.

Consider just one interesting comparison. Brown[11] has described some nine basic kinds of two-word utterances used by monolingual children at about two years of age around the world. One kind, for example, indicates *possession* ("Mommy sweater" or "My ball"), another *location* ("Sweater chair" or "Pencil cup"). But time relations, which could also be expressed in two-word utterances like "Fall yesterday," do not appear.

By contrast, Dodson, Price and Williams report[12] on five-year-old children, initially monolingual in English, who attended the reception class of a Welsh Infant School where they spent two hours in a Welsh-speaking environment each afternoon. These children also went through a period of using two-word utterances, in this case in Welsh. One of the relationships expressed by these five-year-olds is time:

> Shirley wedyn   "Shirley afterwards"

This is as it should be if, as Brown argues, conceptual complexity as opposed to grammatical complexity determines order of acquisition at this early stage. Children learning a first language are at this stage at about age two. The Welsh children were five and their age shows. Five-year-olds should be thinking in terms of time as well as space.

Dodson, Price, and Williams also separated these children's utterances into those in which correct Welsh is structurally different from English and those which are a direct translation and found that: "This association with or discrimination from the mother tongue had little effect on the children's response, and they seemed to use the apparently more difficult patterns as readily as the easier ones."[13] Examples of the children's Welsh utterances expressing possession are:

> esgidiau Dadi   "Daddy's shoes"
> blodyn gwyn Karen   "Karen's white flower"
> cadair y babi   "the baby's chair"

It is visually clear that in Welsh the possessor is named last, rather than first as in English. The children were evidently able to learn the reversed order without confusion.

On the basis of scanty evidence to date, it seems likely that the nature of second language learning changes with age, and that younger learners resemble first language learners more than older ones do. But the age of that turning point, or even whether there is only one, is a matter of controversy. At Geneva, H. Sinclair and her student, Margarite Levalée, suggest that a change takes place between five and seven years.[14] Lenneberg's work[15] would suggest that it takes place at the onset of adolescence. It is undoubtedly no coincidence that the two ages suggested coincide with the change in Piaget's developmental progression to concrete and formal operations respectively. But exactly how language learning, in this case second language learning, interlaces with other aspects of cognitive development is not yet clear.

What is clear is the supremely important role of attitude in second language learning. How can we create educational environments which activate the natural language learning abilities which all children have? Here, probably, is the source of the problems some foreign language speaking minorities have in learning English.

At least that seems to be the implication of one success story of second language learning in school. Lambert, Just and Segalowitz[16] describe two classes of monolingual English children in Montreal who received their first years of schooling entirely in French. The kindergarten program, which the authors think may be crucial, "conducted almost entirely in French by two very skilled and experienced teachers from Europe, stressed vocabulary development and listening comprehension through art, music and play, and encouraged spontaneous verbal expression in French."[17] French was the only language used from first grade on, and the children achieved dramatically both in languages and in mathematics. Furthermore, the children transferred what they had learned about reading from French to English with little trouble.

Ervin-Tripp asks the obvious question: Why does being taught in a foreign language work for these Montreal children and fail for Chicano, Puerto Rican, and Navajo children in the United States? In her words, "the differences are social."[18] In commenting on the same contrast, Haugen agrees:

We need to think in terms of dominant and nondominant, but these are terms we don't like to talk about because they are ultimately political. . . . Children are sensitive to the pressure of society through their parents and their peers. I think the opposition of dominant and nondominant is so important that I wonder if Lambert's good results may not be accounted for by the fact that he is teaching the members of a dominant group a nondominant language which has potentialities of dominance, while in Texas or New Mexico we are teaching a dominant language to a nondominant group. This alters the educational picture totally.[19]

The same conclusions about the importance of attitudes was reached by Tax and his colleagues in the Carnegie Corporation Cross Cultural Education Project of the University of Chicago[20] which was concerned with raising the literacy level of Cherokees in eastern Oklahoma. Cherokee history is particularly interesting because in the nineteenth century 90 percent of the Cherokees were literate in their native language—using a writing system developed in 1819 by Sequoyah, a Cherokee with no formal education—and they were more literate in English than the whites in neighboring communities in Texas and Arkansas. Walker suggests what it would take for them to regain this status:

It seems clear that the startling decline during the past sixty years of both English and Cherokee literacy in the Cherokee tribe is chiefly a result of the recent scarcity of reading materials in Cherokee and of the fact that learning to read has become associated with coercive instruction, particularly in the context of an alien and threatening school. . . . For the Cherokee community to become literate once again, Cherokees must be convinced that literacy does not imply the death of their society, that education is not a clever device to wean children away from the tribe. This is not a uniquely Cherokee situation. Identical attitudes toward education and the school no doubt can be found in Appalachia, in urban slums, in Afro-Asia, and indeed, in all societies where the recruitment of individuals into the dominant society threatens the extinction of a functioning social group.[21]

III

Children learn to speak like the people important to them in their home community. On some nonconscious level, children pick their parents and later their peers as language models despite the fact that they listen, during long periods of watching television, to standard American patterns of pronunciation and grammar. Around the world, people retain their speech patterns as expressions of self-identity and community solidarity, despite the potentially homogenizing effect of the mass media.

This selection of speech patterns, and the linguistic pluralism that results, is a source of both potentialities and problems: potentialities because rich alternative forms of expression are available to their users; problems because if speech patterns are a form of self-identification, they can be used for discriminatory purposes in a discriminatory society. Unlike the grammatical immaturities of young children, dialect features are not transparent. Quite the opposite. They are often so opaque that true reciprocal communication is impossible as judgments are formed about the educability of a child or the employability of an adult.

In the long run, these problems produce the "Pygmalion effect" and the pressure to include instruction in Standard English in the curriculum. There is no empirical evidence (only heated arguments) that dialect differences *per se* have any direct adverse affect on a child's educability.

But there is empirical evidence of an indirect adverse effect—the effect of a child's speech on his teacher's attitudes toward him, and thereby on the learning environment that she creates. Seligman, Tucker and Lambert,[22] for example, report that a recorded speech pattern had more influence on third grade teachers' ratings than the quality of a child's composition or drawing.[23] Here a curriculum on language is sorely needed—but for teachers, not children.

Whether schools should attempt to teach standard English is a matter of values—whether parents wish to maintain their distinctive culture, encourage their children to learn the standard speech patterns of the larger society, or both. Despite our current American failure to teach Standard English effectively in school, Fishman and Lueders-Salmon[24] offer a convincing description of how such language pluralism is achieved in another country—the area around Stuttgart, Germany. There, where standard German is taught successfully, teachers and students are often members of the same speech community, the teachers respect the children's home dialect, accept its spontaneous use in classroom discussions, and emphasize both in their own speech behavior and in their language instruction the functional value of being able to shift among varied verbal repertoires.

Language as Learning Environment

Since language is the medium of instruction for most curriculum content, including itself, it is a large part of any learning environment.

School language may differ in function from that used outside; for example, language in school is used more often to refer to nonperceptible people, events and relationships. School language may differ from other language even when used for functions which are also common outside school, such as influencing the behavior of others.[25]

Two criteria for analyzing the role of language in learning environments will be applied here: situational appropriateness and functional effectiveness. (One could well add another: aesthetic taste, a criterion raised too rarely by curriculum planners. Despite its importance, however, the matter of aesthetics will be omitted here because I feel unqualified to give more than opinions.)

IV

We know that all speakers of a language can speak in more than one way and unconsciously shift their style of speaking to adapt to different situations. They switch pronunciation, syntax and word selection. Even in a seemingly homogeneous speech community, such code selection occurs. For example, Fisher[26] discovered switching between "-ing" and "-in'" in a semirural New England village. Children from three to ten years old varied their pronunciation, depending on the formality of the setting, the change in their mood as they became more relaxed within a single interview, and even (for one boy) the connotations of specific verbs: "reading" and "criticizing" versus "swimmin'" and "punchin'." Children can also shift their styles of interacting from peer groups, where no one controls who talks when, to mixed groups where children are expected to respond only to adults or to be seen but not heard.[27]

Yet there is evidence that such shifts do not always occur where they would be appropriate and beneficial to the speaker. Three problems stand out: cultural conflict between the norms of interaction at home and those at school, failure to transfer apparent classroom learning to performance on tests, and probable differences between the learning of linguistic and sociolinguistic rules.

Consider first possible conflicts between home and school. "Those brought together in classrooms, even though having the language of the classroom in common, may not be wholly members of the same speech community. They may share a speech situation, but bring to it different modes of using its language and of interpreting the speech that goes on there."[28] The styles of language use children learn at home may inhibit their participation in the learning environment of the school or, to describe it in the reverse way, the learning environment of the school may repress rather than maximize the participatory skills of children or may favor some (even a majority) at the cost of others.

The work of two anthropologists is illustrative. Laura Lein, an anthropology student of Claudia and Keith Kernan's at Harvard, has been living in upstate New York with black families from Florida who migrate north every summer as farm laborers. In studying selected aspects of the language used by these migrant children, in the migrant camp and at school, she became interested in how the children respond to commands. Responses to parents are of two kinds. "Reasonable" commands, such as "You can't go outside now, it's dark," are immediately obeyed. But commands without obvious justification, like "Wipe that smile off your face," or "Come stand over here by me," are treated differently. The children understand the latter quite correctly as invitations to engage in a routinized verbal game in which the children resist, the adults repeat, with escalating insistence until the adults appeal to higher status members of the family or community to enforce the command. The game often lasts fifteen to twenty minutes, and everyone understands it as such. One can easily imagine what Lein found in school. The children thought that the situation for this game was defined by the content of the commands and did not understand that it was defined also by the setting (home but not school). Thus, they resisted playfully when their teachers gave the meaningless commands which teachers are apt to give, were labeled "defiant" by the teachers, and never understood the source of the problem.[29]

Philips[30] studied the speech patterns of children on the Warm Springs Indian Reservation in Oregon, both in and out of the classroom. Philips refers to structural arrangements of interaction as "participant structures." In the public school classrooms on the War Springs Reservation, teachers use four participant structures:

In the first type of participant structure the teacher interacts with all of the students. . . . And it is always the teacher who determines whether she talks to one or to all, receives responses individually or in chorus, and voluntarily or without choice. In a second type of participant structure, the teacher interacts with only some of the students in the class at once, as in reading groups. In such contexts, participation is usually mandatory rather than voluntary, individual rather than chorus, and each student is expected to participate or perform verbally.
A third participant structure consists of all students working independently at their desks, but with the teacher explicitly available for student initiated [and private] verbal interaction.
A fourth participant structure, and one which occurs infrequently in the upper primary grades, and rarely, if ever, in the lower grades, consists of the students being divided into small groups which they run themselves.[31]

Outside the home, in the Warm Springs communities, social (speech) events are open to all: each individual decides the degree, form, and time of participation for himself, and there is no leader who has the right to enforce the participation of one person in the presence of others. It is not surprising that, under these contrasting conditions, teachers label Indian children as "shy."

The relationship between eliciting context, sociolinguistic rules, and valid inferences is critical in all education—in everyday classroom events in which children's words are taken as indicators of what they have learned, and even more in the special situations we call "tests," whether administered by experimenters or teachers. After viewing videotapes of psychological experiments, Emanuel Schegloff suggested that such situations are "interactionally impoverished."[32]

Children are differently prepared—by age or experience in home and school—to cope with the special interaction requirements of tests. Shapiro, concerned that first grade children who were clearly learning in the classroom were not responding well on tests, puts the problem this way:

Since situations are sociologically and psychologically apprehended, their sociological and psychological parameters must be described and specified. . . . Specifically, for studies like the present one, the relevance and appropriateness of the classroom and the test situation as locations for studying the impact of schooling on children requires re-evaluation. Each can supply useful information, but in both instances the evidence is situation-bound.

Determining the appropriate timing for the evaluation of impact demands that we know when [at what age] it is plausible and valid to expect children to be able to function readily and competently in a variety of situations, to switch from one form of communication to another, to be able to produce on demand. At what point and as a consequence of what kinds of experience does the restrictive influence of situational factors become less crucial?[33]

An important contrast implicit in this paper must be made explicit, even if it cannot be explained: that between linguistic and sociolinguistic interference in learning. According to Labov:

The development of formal rules of discourse is a necessary ingredient in the analysis of subcultural differences. . . . Where subcultures differ in such rules, the consequences for personal interaction can be strong. Though native speakers of a given dialect show an extraordinary ability to interpret the grammatical rules of another dialect, they do not necessarily show the same ability in dealing with the broader aspects of communicative competence. The rules of discourse tend to differ not in obligatory sequencing rules, but in the interpretation of the social significance of actions—differences in the forms of politeness, ways of mitigating or expressing anger, or of displaying sincerity and trust. This is an area where ethnographic and linguistic description has an important role to play.[34]

This is also an area where we need to know more about the learning processes involved. The way we learn about appropriate and effective language use may be quite different from the way we learn language structure. Perhaps here an explicit sociolinguistic curriculum could be valuable.

Lest we despair of the possibilities, it may be a healthy antidote to academic obsessions to be reminded how quickly changes in people's lives can produce changes in their behavior, sociolinguistic behavior included. Fanon, a black French psychiatrist assigned to an Algerian hospital, analyzes the "new attitudes adopted by the Algerian people in the course of the fight for liberation with respect to a precise technical instrument: the radio."[35] According to Fanon, before 1945, when the only station available was Radio-Alger, the voice of France in Algeria, 95 percent of all receivers were in the hands of European settlers, and hundreds of Algerian families who could easily afford radios did not have them. Fanon describes one reason that was given for this passive resistance to radios, one which has an authentic sociolinguistic ring:

Pressed with questions as to the reasons for this reluctance, Algerians rather frequently give the following answer: "Traditions of respectability are so important for us and are so hierarchical, that it is practically impossible for us to listen to radio programmes in the family. The sex allusions, or even the clownish situations meant to make people laugh, which are broadcast over the radio cause an unendurable strain in a family listening to these programmes.
The ever possible eventuality of laughing in the presence of the head of the family or the elder brother, of listening in common to amorous words or terms of levity, obviously acts as a deterrent to the distribution of radios in Algerian native society. . . .
Here, then, at a certain explicit level is the apprehension of a fact: receiving sets are not readily adopted by Algerian society. By and large, it refuses this technique which threatens its stability and the traditional types of sociability.[36]

Fanon then goes on to show "how artificial such a sociological approach is, what a mass of error it contains." At the end of 1956, a new station went on the air: Voice of Free Algeria. In less than twenty days the entire stock of radio sets in Algeria was bought up and battery-operated receivers were in great demand in the rural regions of the country.

Traditional resistances broke down and one could see in a *dewar* groups of families in which fathers, mothers, daughters, elbow to elbow, would scrutinize the radio dial waiting for the Voice of Algeria. Suddenly indifferent to the sterile, archaic modesty and antique social arrangements devoid of brotherhood, the Algerian family discovered itself to be immune to the off-colour jokes and the obscene references that the announcer occasionally let drop.
Almost magically—but we have seen the rapid and dialectical progression of the new national requirements—the technical instrument of the radio receiver lost its identity as an enemy object [and] Algerian society made an autonomous decision to embrace the new technique and thus tune itself in on the new signalling systems brought into being by the Revolution.[37]

It is probably harder to change the way people act than the way they respond, the way they speak than the way they listen. Even when feelings of self-identity change, well-practiced habits may make new forms of behavior difficult to maintain. But the two factors implicit in Fanon's report of a change in listening habits—a dramatic shift in the symbolic value of a stimulus that comes from a change in the underlying social reality, and strong support for change from within the speaker's reference community—probably apply to changes in ways of speaking too.

V

We cannot, of course, evaluate learning environments solely on the basis of whether the home and the school have the same expectations for children.

Take Ward's ethnographic study of language learning in Rosepoint, Louisiana as a case in point. She compares the language learning of young children—such as Mark—with the children studied by Roger Brown. A few quotes convey the quality of the language environment in Rosepoint:

Speaking is often equated with the quality "bad." A twelve-month baby sat absolutely still on the couch for an hour. His mother commented that her baby was "good": he could not yet talk. When babies learn to talk they are "bad children."

Mark [28 months old] has never been rewarded for verbal advances; no one expects him to say more than the bare minimum. . . . In fact, as the conversations indicate, the children hold their parent's attention longer *if they say nothing.* [emphasis in the original]

A child's requests for information are not treated as a demand for knowledge (which adults are expected to supply) or as an attempt to open the lines of communication. . . . A child actively seeking information will be treated as a noisy child, not as an inquiring, curious one.[38]

We have all seen or read of classrooms where the same kind of sociolinguistic rules obtain, in which quiet passivity is valued over active inquiry.

In considering these learning environments, we need to know not only whether the home and school function consistently—as they may for Ward's children but do not for Lein's playful migrant children or for Philips' shy Indian children—but also whether that functioning is conducive to learning. Speaking for myself—and in this value-laden area I can do no more—I would want to remove home-school discontinuities for Philips' children by making the interactional setting of the school more like that of the home, whereas I would be reluctant to accept the same solution for Ward's children. Admittedly such decisions imply definite notions about what experiences promote maximum mental functioning.

In making decisions about whether or how to "intervene," an outsider must remember that any system functions as a whole, in terms both of the relationship among its parts and of its relationship to some larger social unit. Robert L. Munroe of the Child Development Research Unit in Nairobi, Kenya, reported an open discussion following the presentation of research data on traditional child rearing practices. When Munroe suggested that some of these practices might have the effect of depressing the development of what we call "intelligence" in children, a Ghanian colleague replied that even if that were true, he would be unwilling to attempt to change to more "western" styles at the price of a decrease in courtesy and obedience—qualities more important in tribal life than the "intelligence" which westerners value so highly.[39] The Ghanian did not want to disrupt the internal cohesiveness of his culture.

Emanuel Jackson, Director of the Martin Luther King Family Center in Chicago's West Side, focused on the relationship of black family life to the larger world:

My concern would be, if a kid's not talking, to understand why and why not before one goes in and undermines defenses that are very necessary. Some little kids are hostile, they're suspicious, they're alert, and it's diagnosed as pathology. In our community, if you're not suspicious and alert, you're not going to live. . . .
We're trying to understand what it is about language and Black people that may make Black people seem more non-verbal. Maybe Black people need to be more non-verbal. When my Mother tells me "Now don't you tell the teacher this" and "Don't you tell the teacher that," we get a message about talking. I'm saying that the world makes my Mother have to tell me to shut up or she'll be done in.[40]

Advisors and supervisors working with teachers are also aware of how the teacher's behavior—e.g., how much child activity and talk she allows in her classroom—is affected by the system of which she is a part. Perhaps all that we as outsiders can do is what Munroe did—point out the possible implications as we understand them, suggest alternatives, and do all we can to help work out the ensuing problems for those who do wish to change.

REFERENCES

1. I am grateful to Betty H. Bryant for critically reviewing this paper from a black perspective. Not all her criticisms have been met, but the paper is better for her sharp comments.

2. D. Hymes, "Competence and Performance in Linguistic Theory," *Language Acquisition: Models and Methods,* eds. R. Huxley and E. Ingram (New York: Academic Press, 1971), pp. 3-28.

3. Cf. C. E. Snow's study of the speech of college-educated mothers, "Language Acquisition and Mothers' Speech to Children," *Child Development,* XLIII (1972), 549-565; and C. Ward's study of the speech of mothers in the ex-plantation community of Rosepoint, Louisiana, *Them Children: A Study in Language Learning* (New York: Holt, Rinehart and Winston, 1971).

4. M. P. Maratsos, "The Development of Definite and Indefinite Reference." Unpublished doctoral dissertation, Harvard University, 1972.

5. J. Moffett, *Teaching the Universe of Discourse* (Boston: Houghton Mifflin, 1968).

6. M. Polanyi, *Personal Knowledge: Towards a Post-Critical Philosophy* (New York: Harper Torchbooks, 1964), pp. 56-57.

7. *Ibid.*, p. 31.

8. C. B. Cazden, "Two Paradoxes in the Acquisition of Language Structure and Functions," *The Development of Competence in Early Childhood,* eds. J. S. Bruner and K. J. Connolly (New York: Academic Press, forthcoming).

9. C. B. Cazden, *Child Language and Education* (New York: Holt, Rhinehart and Winston, 1972), Ch. 10.

10. H. Dulay and M. K. Burt, "You Can't Learn without Goofing (an Analysis of Children's Second Language Errors)," *Error Analysis—Perspectives in Second Language Acquisition,* ed. J. Richards (London: Longmans, forthcoming).

11. R. Brown, *A First Language, the Early Stages* (Cambridge: Harvard University Press, forthcoming).

12. C. J. Dodson, E. Price, and T. I. Williams, *Towards Bilingualism: Studies in Language Teaching Methods* (Cardiff: University of Wales Press, 1968).

13. *Ibid.*, p. 42.

14. H. Sinclair and Margarite Levalée, personal communication, 1971.

15. E. H. Lenneberg, *Biological Foundations of Language* (New York: John Wiley, 1967).

16. W. E. Lambert, M. Just, and N. Segalowitz, "Some Cognitive Consequences of Following the Curricula of the Early School Grades in a Foreign Language," *Twenty-first Annual Round Table: Bilingualism and Language Contact,* ed. J. E. Alatis, Monograph Series on Languages and Linguistics, No. 23 (Washington, D.C.: Georgetown University Press, 1970), pp. 229-262.

17. *Ibid.*, p. 233.

18. S. Ervin-Tripp, "Structure and Process in Language Acquisition," *Twenty-first Annual Round Table: Bilingualism and Language Contact,* p. 314.

19. E. Haugen, *Twenty-first Annual Round Table: Bilingualism and Language Contact,* p. 310.

20. S. Tax and R. K. Thomas, "Education for American Indians: Threat or Promise," *The Florida FL Reporter,* VII, No. 1 (1969), 15-19ff; W. Walker, "Notes on Native Writing Systems and the Design of Native Literacy Programs," *Anthropological Linguistics* (1969), 148–165.

21. W. Walker, "An Experiment in Programmed Cross-cultural Education: The Import of the Cherokee Primer for the Cherokee Community and for the Behavioral Sciences," Mimeo (Middletown, Conn.: Wesleyan University, March 1965), p. 10.

22. C. R. Seligman, G. R. Tucker, and W. E. Lambert, "The Effects of Speech Style and Other Attributes on Teachers' Attitudes toward Pupils," *Language in Society,* I (1972), 131-142.

23. F. Williams, J. L. Whitehead, and L. Miller, "Relations between Language Attitude and Teacher Expectancy," *American Educational Research Journal,* IX

(1972), 263-277; F. Williams, N. Hewlett, L. M. Miller, R. C. Naremore, and J. L. Whitehead, *Explorations of the Linguistic Attitudes of Teachers* (Austin: University of Texas, 1972).

24. J. A. Fishman and Erika Lueders-Salmon, "What Has the Sociology of Language to Say to the Teacher? On Teaching the Standard Variety to Speakers of Dialectal or Sociolectal Varieties," *Functions of Language in the Classroom*, eds. C. B. Cazden, V. P. John and D. Hymes (New York: Teacher's College Press, 1972), pp. 67-83.

25. *Functions of Language in the Classroom;* H. Mehan, "Language Using Abilities," *Language Sciences* (Bloomingdale: Indiana University Research Center for the Language Sciences, 1972).

26. J. L. Fisher, "Social Influence in the Choice of a Linguistic Variant," *Word*, XIV (1958), 47-56. Reprinted in *Language in Culture and Society*, ed. D. Hymes (New York: Harper & Row, 1964), pp. 483-488.

27. Ward, *Them Children.*

28. D. Hymes, "Introduction," *Functions of Language in the Classroom*, p. xxxvii.

29. Lein, Language seminar, Harvard Graduate School of Education, 1971.

30. S. U. Philips, "Acquisition of Rules for Appropriate Speech Usage," *Functions of Language in the Classroom*, pp. 370-394.

31. *Ibid.*

32. Emanuel Schegloff, personal communication.

33. E. Shapiro, "A Pilot Study of a Bank Street Follow Through Program for First Grade Children in Three Geographic Regions," Final Report to Project Follow Through, U.S. Office of Education, VI (New York: Bank Street College of Education, December 1971), pp. 8-10.

34. W. Labov, "The Place of Linguistic Research in American Society," *Linguistics in the 1970's* (Washington, D. C.: Center for Applied Linguistics, 1970), pp. 64-65.

35. F. Fanon, *A Dying Colonialism* (Middlesex, England: Penguin Books, 1970), p. 53.

36. *Ibid.*, p. 54.

37. *Ibid.*, p. 67.

38. Ward, *Them Children*, pp. 29, 46-47, 52.

39. Munroe, personal communication, 1971.

40. Emanuel Jackson, Colloquium at the Harvard Graduate School of Education, 1971.

PETER STREVENS

Second Language Learning

PERHAPS 250 MILLION people alive today have received instruction in at least one foreign language. Yet, unlike the scientific disciplines of linguistics and psychology with which it has been linked in the past two decades, language teaching has remained an art and a craft whose theoretical and philosophical foundations are only now being elaborated. The average rate of success in learning a foreign language achieved by learners today is probably much higher than that of their parents; nevertheless, language teachers continue to seek means to improve the ease and effectiveness of language learning, through modifications in their ways of teaching.

The seminal work of Henry Sweet,[1] Otto Jespersen,[2] and Harold Palmer[3] notwithstanding, there is no well-articulated theory taking account of all the complex elements entailed in the teaching and learning of languages; the history of language teaching during the past fifty years describes, chiefly, a search for the single most effective "method" of optimizing learning while standardizing and, hopefully, minimizing teaching, together with a quantity of experimentation whose results have often been ambiguous or too specific to lend themselves to generalization.

In the 1920's, the *direct method* sought to replace the classical, literature-based *grammar-translation method;* it advocated learning by hearing the language spoken, forbidding all use of the learner's native language in class; in the 1930's, strict control of the vocabulary and grammatical structures presented sought to systematize the work of the teacher and to provide principles for feeding the learner with an input designed to match his presumed learning tactics; in the 1940's, the U.S. Army Specialized Teaching Program (ASTP) and its counterpart in Britain incorporated some of the ideas of Bloomfieldian and European descriptive linguistics respectively, into intensive specialized courses for teaching languages to service personnel by *audio-lingual methods;* in the 1950's, in the United States, the audio-lingual method was consciously developed on the theoretical bases of the findings of Bloomfieldian structuralist linguistics and of behaviorist psychology, while in France a composite *audio-visual method* was elaborated, using integrated texts, recordings and illustrations, and based on the teaching

151

concepts of *psycho-pédagogie* rather than on linguistics, and in Britain (where teachers are perhaps less eager than their American counterparts to justify their teaching procedures by reference to a theory) improvements in methodology largely consisted of techniques for teaching younger children in the school systems of developing countries; in the 1960's, American audio-lingual methods were expanded for use with younger learners, especially with those learning English as a foreign language overseas, and language teachers everywhere, affected at one remove by dramatic developments in theoretical linguistics and especially in psycholinguistics, began to question their principles and procedures, to express dissatisfaction with the short-comings of language teaching methods, and to seek new ways of improving their effectiveness.

During the twenty-year period since 1950, during which language teach-ing has been dominated by linguistics, the belief in a unique, best method has perhaps been fed by the heated partisanship of the various schools of linguistics. All the more frustrating then is the inevitable discovery that a particular teaching method, though demonstrably used with spectacular suc-cess in one place, gives poor results in another.

Experimentation has also brought its disappointments. It may not seem difficult to design a range of critical experiments to compare the effective-ness of method X and method Y; equally, it may seem plausible that by such experiments the general or inherent superiority of X or Y could be established. Alas, twenty-five years of such experiments reveal only the multiplicity of confounding variables and the astonishing particularity of such separate school, class, teacher, and learner. From the Keating Report of 1960,[4] whose inflated and tendentious claims were based on poor experi-mental procedures, to the *before-and-after* experiments of 1964 on teaching English in the Philippines;[5] from the *with-or-without-language-lab* experi-ments of Scherer and Wertheimer in 1966,[6] to the massive and meticulous statistical surveys of the Pennsylvania Project in 1970,[7] or to the elegant, simple, small-scale, single-school experiments at York reported by Eric Hawkins and others in 1973,[8] the lessons are clear and repeated: first, it is extremely difficult to design experiments in comparative methodology that are not falsified by unforeseen or fortuitous circumstances, and second, the great variability of learning-teaching situations renders the results of any single valid experiment only partially applicable to the precise conditions in which any particular learners are working.

It is doubtful, in fact, whether even perfect experimentation or complete success in seeking the best teaching method could produce the desired re-sult, since both types of methodological inquiry rest upon a pair of unstated assumptions: first, that language learning is sufficiently homogeneous for a single method to fit all circumstances; and second, that the achievement of relative success or failure in language learning is to be ascribed, above all, to method, and not significantly to other factors.

Both these assumptions are probably false. In the first place, the complex circumstances of teaching and learning languages—with different kinds of pupils, teachers, aims and objectives, approaches, methods and materials, classroom techniques, and standards of achievement—make it inconceivable that any single method could achieve optimum success in all circumstances. Indeed, there are so many factors in the achievement of success—and method is only one of them[9]—that there is no reason to suppose that any single factor is solely or even largely responsible for success, still less that method is such a factor. As Stern points out:

we cannot say that we have found as yet a completely satisfactory solution to the basic difficulties of second language learning. The primary weakness . . . lies in the *search for single or restricted solutions of major problems*. . . . Language teaching . . . suffers from oversimplification and primitivism.[10]

The most recent method to gain a following is that of *cognitive-code* learning and teaching.

According to this theory, learning a language is a process of acquiring conscious control of the phonological, grammatical and lexical patterns of a second language, largely through study and analysis of these patterns as a body of knowledge. . . . Provided the student has a proper degree of cognitive control over the structures of the language, facility will develop automatically with the use of the language in meaningful situations.[11]

There is no doubt that this approach, concentrating as it does on the cognitive processes of the learner rather than on mechanistic procedures imposed upon him by the teacher, is in keeping with the anti-authoritarian, learner-centered educational outlook which is sweeping through much of the world. At the level of psychological learning theory, the *cognitive-code* method signals a rejection of stimulus-response models; at the level of linguistic theory, it signals rejection of the view that language is external to the mind of the individual; and at the level of teaching techniques, it signals the encouragement of deliberate grammar teaching as an aid to learning.

Herein lies a paradigm for the fallacy of trying to find a unique methodological approach. In the audio-lingual method, teachers are warned *not* to tell the learner *about* the language—roughly speaking, not to teach them grammar. This is a general interdiction intended to apply to all learners since it is based on principle and theory. In the cognitive-code method, teachers are *required* to tell the learner *about* the language, and this too is a general theory-based proposition. The fallacy is in the presupposition that one prescription must be right for the generality of learners, and the other false. In fact, it is the common experience of teachers that some kinds of learners are indeed helped by overt knowledge about the language they are learning (especially sophisticated adults with much previous foreign language learning experience) but that others are impeded by such techniques (especially young children).

Language teachers have overlooked the existence of crucial factors in learning and teaching which lie outside both linguistics and psychology, but which fall squarely within the study of the processes of instruction. Yet there are encouraging signs of new developments here that will give greater depth and perspective to language learning.

Depth can be expected to come from a new surge of theoretical studies on teaching. Among these are the application to language teaching of Bloom's taxonomy of educational objectives;[12] the interdisciplinary approach of *applied linguistics* (using the term as it is used in Europe and in the work of the Center for Applied Linguistics in Washington, D.C.) whereby linguistics, psychology, educational research, educational technology and other potential sources of illumination are brought together;[13] the work of Stern, still in preparation, toward "a general model for second language teaching"; and new work on the analysis of teacher-student interaction.[14] Perhaps the most significant evidence of this surge of interest is the imminent appearance of a new journal, *Instructional Science*, devoted to theoretical studies of practical teaching and learning. We understand all too little how teaching promotes or inhibits learning, and what range of delicate interactions and subtle choices between encouragement and neutrality, nudging and bludgeoning, characterizes good teaching at any given moment. There is some hope, however, that the new wave of practical-theoretical studies of teaching will deepen our understanding of these matters.

If depth is promised by theoretical studies, another desirable quality, perspective, is likely to be achieved through new and illuminating analyses of different learning-teaching situations and of conditions which foster or impede maximum success in learning and teaching. These analyses highlight the inherent improbability of finding any single teaching method approprate in all circumstances, for any search for the fundamental variables or dimensions of foreign language learning indicates that different teaching situations are characterized by different dimensions and relate to crucially different kinds of learning, or teaching, or both.

II

The dimensions of language learning seem to embrace the following variables: the age of the learner; his educational aims; whether he is learning of his own free will; the level of proficiency he has attained; the language in which instruction is given; and the general perspective within which he is learning.

Pupil Age. As learners, human beings display different qualities at different ages. Young children have a spontaneous enthusiasm for learning, but they are easily bored, and their attention span is short, so the teacher needs to create variety to maintain their learning stance. The adult has learned how to learn; unlike the child, he often knows exactly *why* he is learning a language; he may have previous experience learning foreign languages and a highly visual, writing-centered bias to the way he learns; he can concentrate for long periods and persevere by balancing short-term discomforts of boredom and fatigue against long-term rewards of achieving certain goals; he can intellectualize his learning and apply shortcuts or make use of abstract rules.

The adolescent retains the younger child's ability, at least when he is sufficiently motivated and interested, to learn with enthusiasm, and he has begun to acquire the adult's ability to balance present effort against future achievement. But he is subject to sudden changes of attitude toward learning (and especially toward his teacher); his attention is readily distracted by the sight of a member of the opposite sex, or by casual mention of current emotional trigger words, like "pollution," "revolution," "Vietnam," or "efficiency"; and he is prone to exaggerated reactions toward evidence of his own success or failure.

We do not know to what extent the mental processes of the young child are the same as those of the adolescent or the adult; there are, however, regular, observable differences among learners of different ages in how they approach the task of learning. Three major learning stages need to be recognized, corresponding roughly to *the young child, the adolescent,* and *the adult.*

Educational Aims. A second crucial set of variables relates language learning to wider questions concerning the education of the individual. At one extreme, foreign language is learned as part of a humane school or college education, as a means of opening the door to another culture and especially to its literature. The great majority of foreign language instruction is organized with this cultural-literary orientation. Yet at the other extreme, many students of language derive their satisfaction not from studying literature but rather from gaining a practical command and mastery of the language, or from using it as a tool for communication. Others again want to learn a defined subset of the language for use in their occupations. Obviously, from the point of view of both teacher and learner, a literary course, a practical course for communication, and a restricted special purpose course, are different kinds of language learning situations.

Free Will. Entwined with the educational aims of the language learning situation is the question of whether the learner is there of his own free will as a·volunteer, or whether he is learning a language because he cannot escape doing so. There is a subtle difference between the two situations with regard to the student-teacher relationship. The personal commitment to success of the volunteer is rarely matched by that of the drafted learner. Only two main subdivisions on the free will scale need to be distinguished: *volunteer* and *nonvolunteer*.

Present Proficiency. Organized instruction seeks to lead the learner along the path of progress from zero command of the language toward native-like proficiency; the kinds of approaches and materials that can best profit a learner change according to the place he has reached along the path. The near beginner, for example, is in a stage of learning where the range of meanings he can convey is very small and his rate of errors rather high. Learners at this stage can express themselves only when they are led by the teacher or the course book; later they begin to construct sentences for themselves, to understand material that they hear or read beyond that which they have actually met in class, and perhaps to replace the mere game sentences of early training with sentences that have some tiny spark of originality or creativity, reflecting their own needs and ideas.

Once the learner has reached this stage he has ceased to be a beginner, and becomes an intermediate learner who needs materials of a different type from those which satisfied him as a beginner. Then he needed spoon feeding; now he needs an increasing opportunity to follow his own interests through the medium of the foreign language, still with guidance and help available when he overreaches his linguistic capability.

The advanced learner is different yet again. For him, voracious reading and listening are essential, with guidance of some kind about unexpected difficulties or discriminations. Variety, quantity, and subtlety of teaching are important in helping the advanced learner to learn quickly and effectively.

As the learner progresses, his needs as a learner change, and in consequence the most successful teaching techniques change also. One can distinguish at least three subdivisions of proficiency: the *beginning, intermediate,* and *advanced* stages of learning.

Language of Instruction. It makes an important difference whether the language used as the medium of instruction is the learner's own first language. Three possibilities exist: the target language can be taught by the use of that same foreign language (the typical case in second language situations, among others); the target language can be taught through a different language also foreign to the learner (an Algerian, for example, whose first language is Arabic but who was educated in French, could learn English through the medium of French); or the target language can be taught through the learner's mother tongue. Which of these three situations obtains crucially affects learning and teaching.

Perspective. There is a fairly large set of constraints upon the teaching-learning process deriving from its organizational framework. These constraints latch into the complex questions of the administration of education, the training of teachers, the provision of school buildings, and so on, right to the core of social and educational policy. The learner can be seen in three perspectives, as an *individual,* as a member of a *class,* and as a unit in the educational system of a whole *nation.*

Dimensions of Language Learning and Teaching

Dimensions	Main Subdivisions
PUPIL AGE	—child —adolescent —adult
EDUCATIONAL AIMS	—general educational, cultural, literary —for practical communication —for special purposes
FREE WILL	—volunteer —nonvolunteer
PRESENT PROFICIENCY	—beginner —intermediate —advanced
LANGUAGE OF INSTRUCTION	—target language —second language —mother tongue
PERSPECTIVE	—individual —class —nation

The foregoing breakdown of dimensions shows that the extreme complexity and diversity of a task engaged in by millions of people can nevertheless be reduced to managable proportions; they support the argument that any approach to teaching and learning languages which does not take account of at least these dimensions is to that extent deficient.

III

But even if a particular learning-teaching situation has been described in terms of these variables, a prescription for successful teaching and learning is not automatically produced. Before success or failure can be assessed, the aims of the teaching and the learning have to be adequately stated: they must be *relevant* to the learner, and *realistic.* There are many parts of the world where inadequate results can be traced, in part, to unrealistic or incoherent aims. Even in the relatively sophisticated school systems of North America and Europe, *de facto* changes in the aims of language learning brought about by the evolution of social needs or of public opinion have not always been recognized.

Furthermore, the choice of which variety of a foreign language it is proper to teach is no longer always self-evident, being much influenced by the growth of national, ethnic and regional feelings of identity. The British have long accepted that in teaching English overseas there are some areas where it is appropriate to set the goal of speaking English like an Englishman (or an American), but that elsewhere such a goal is unacceptable and must be modified in the direction of, for example, speaking educated West African English. The French-Canadian learning English expects to speak Canadian English; but does the English-speaking Canadian learning French expect to speak Canadian French? What of relations between Black English and Standard American English? Is it reasonable for the black American to be expected to learn Standard English as a second dialect, or should white Americans accept the co-existence of a different dialect in their society? The days are long past when learning a particular language obviously and unequivocally meant learning a single, universally acknowledged standard form. Nowadays the precise aims and goals of language learning need to be in line with public needs, and revised as these needs change.

Even given an adequate formulation of aims, there remain to be considered a number of negative factors or constraints which interact to determine the degree of success likely to be achieved in any given case. What are these additional restraints on optimum learning and teaching of a second language? These conditions for success or failure seem to fall into the following categories: quantity and intensity of instruction; absence of impediments to learning; make-up of the learner; make-up of the teacher; and methods and materials.[15]

Quantity and Intensity of Instruction. For any given set of objectives, there is a minimum number of hours of instruction below which the target cannot be reached by the average learner; there is probably an upper limit also, beyond which additional hours of instruction only lead to thin lessons and consequent tedium. Within broad limits, however, the more intensive the teaching, the more effective the learning. Below four or five hours per week, special precautions have to be taken against boredom; above fifteen hours per week, precautions are needed against fatigue, although rates of intensity of twenty to thirty hours per week are becoming common with adult learners, and are generally associated with good success, while forty hours or more per week is not unknown.

Absence of Impediments. Large numbers of learners face conditions where learning is seriously impeded. Overcrowding, for instance, almost guarantees that teaching and learning will be largely ineffective. Conversely, other factors being equal, a class size of one, two, or three establishes a high probability of satisfactory learning progress by all pupils. Physical distractions from excessive noise, or heat, or cold, or fatigue, all impede learning; among psychological impediments one must cite *exam neurosis* which can be generated by the learner, the teacher, or the learner's family.

Make-up of the Learner. It now seems likely that individuals differ much less than was previously thought in their possession of inherent factors, such as intelligence, verbal ability, and a good ear, at least for purposes of acquiring a practical command of spoken language. On the other hand, the roles of the learner's willingness to learn, of his expectations of success or failure, and of his conscious attention and effort to the task of learning the language are greater than was earlier believed.

Make-up of the Teacher. To succeed in imparting foreign language competence to a learner, a teacher must possess three basic qualities: a nondiscouraging personality; an adequate command of the language being taught; and the skills and wisdom to teach effectively.

Constraints upon Optimum Learning and Teaching of a Second Language

QUANTITY AND INTENSITY OF INSTRUCTION	—sufficient total number of hours, but not too many —as intensive as possible up to an optimum of fifteen hours per week; if below four hours per week, special precautions are needed against boredom; if above sixteen, against fatigue
ABSENCE OF IMPEDIMENTS	—free from impediments to learning (overcrowding, distraction, exam neurosis, and so on)
MAKE-UP OF THE LEARNER	—inherent factors: intelligence and ability —volitional factors: willingness to give attention and effort to learning
MAKE-UP OF THE TEACHER	—encouraging personality —adequate command of the language being taught —skill in teaching techniques
METHODS AND MATERIALS	—relevant —interesting

Methods and Materials. The analysis of teaching methods and materials is a vast subject. For purposes of successful learning and teaching, we must insist on two fundamental features: *relevance* and *interest.* The methods and materials should be appropriate to the learner as an individual, suitable for attaining his aims, and related to his circumstances as a learner; they should also contain enough variety and interest to help the learner maintain his willingness to devote time and attention to learning.

IV

What, then, are the salient features of second language learning as we approach the last quarter of the century? First, it is moving away from teacher-centered, mechanistic, automated approaches to learning, toward learner-centered, creativity-engendering, custom-designed approaches. Second, teachers are abandoning overly simplistic ideas about teaching and learning, including the fallacy of the unique preferred methodology, in favor of a more difficult and complex but more realistic outlook based on analyzing the dimensions of the learning situation for each set of learners. Third, it is becoming possible to identify the factors that maximize success and minimize failure so that those responsible for the organization of teaching can, by conscious acts, improve its effectiveness. Fourth, after a period of close dependence on linguistics and psycholinguistics, when it seemed to many that these disciplines could, between them, generate all the effective learning of languages that men might desire, and only that, the profession is engaged afresh, with improved intellectual tools, in increasing its scientific understanding of the nature of teaching.[16] Having avoided domination by the useful but essentially trivial assistance provided by technology in such forms as recording devices, language labs, and teaching machines, second language learning now emerges as a process and a task which for its further improvement requires an ever-deepening knowledge of its three equipollent elements: the mind of the learner, the nature of language, and the skill of the teacher.[17]

REFERENCES

1. Henry Sweet, *The Practical Study of Languages: A Guide for Teachers and Learners* (London: 1899; reprinted London and New York: Oxford University Press, 1964).

2. Otto Jespersen, *How to Teach a Foreign Language* (London: Allen & Unwin, 1904).

3. H. E. Palmer, *The Principles of Language-Study* (London: 1922; reprinted London and New York: Oxford University Press, 1964); *The Scientific Study and Teaching of Languages* (London: 1917; reprinted London and New York: Oxford University Press, 1968).

4. R. F. Keating, *A Study of the Effectiveness of Language Laboratories* (New York: Teachers' College, Columbia University, 1963).

5. Donald A. Bowen, "English in the World Today," *Department of English Working Papers* (Los Angeles: U.C.L.A., 1971).

6. George A. C. Scherer and Michael Wertheimer, *A Psycholinguistic Experiment in Foreign-Language Teaching* (New York: McGraw-Hill, 1964).

7. P. D. Smith, *A Comparison of the Cognitive and Audio-Lingual Approaches to Foreign Language Instruction* (Philadelphia: Center for Curriculum Development, 1970).

8. Peter Green, ed., *The School Language Laboratory: Performance and Prediction* (Edinburgh: Oliver and Boyd, forthcoming).

9. William F. Mackey, *Language Teaching Analysis* (London: Longmans, 1965).

10. H. H. Stern, "Perspectives on Second Language Teaching," *Modern Language Centre Publications*, No. 1 (Toronto: Ontario Institute for Studies in Education, 1970).

11. John B. Carroll, "The Contributions of Psychological Theory and Educational Research to the Teaching of Foreign Languages," *Trends in Language Teaching*, ed. A. Valdman (New York: McGraw-Hill, 1966).

12. Rebecca Valette and R. Disick, *Performance Objectives in Language Teaching and Individualization* (New York: Harcourt Brace, 1972). Eric Bauer has told me that he is also preparing work on this problem.

13. G. E. Perren and J. L. M. Trim, eds., *Applications of Linguistics: Selected Papers of the Second International Congress of Applied Linguistics, 1969* (Cambridge: Cambridge University Press, 1971); Paul Pimsleur and Terence Quinn, eds., *The Psychology of Second Language Learning: Papers from the Second International Congress of Applied Linguistics, 1969* (Cambridge: Cambridge University Press, 1971).

14. Guy C. Capelle, Robert J. Jarvella, and Eleanor Revelle, *Development of Computer-assisted Observational Systems for Teacher Training* (University of Michigan: Center for Research on Language and Language Behavior, 1972); C. De Landscheere, "La prédiction et l'évaluation de l'efficacité des professeurs," *Revue Belge de Psychologie et de Pédagogie*, XXV (1963); N. A. Flanders, *Interaction Analysis in the Classroom: A Manual for Observers* (Ann Arbor: University of Michigan School of Education, 1966).

15. Einar Haugen, "From Army Camp to Classroom: The Story of an Elementary Language Text," *Scandinavian Studies*, XXIII, No. 3 (August 1951). It is interesting to note that Haugen, describing the ASTP and commenting on the success of the operation, says: [There existed] "unusually favourable conditions for our teaching, realizing almost the language teacher's dream, by giving us 15-17 hours a week of class time, mature students, whose attention was not distracted by outside activities, and clearly stated objectives."

16. See particularly the following books: Denis Girard, *Linguistics and Foreign Language Teaching* (London: Longmans, 1972); Leon A. Jakobovits, *Foreign Language Learning: a Psycholinguistic Analysis of the Issues* (Rowley, Mass.: Newbury House, 1970); Leon A. Jakobovits, *The New Psycholinguistics and Foreign Lan-*

guage Teaching (Rowley, Mass: Newbury House, 1972); D. A. Wilkins, *Linguistics in Language Teaching* (London: Arnold, 1972); F. Smith and G. A. Miller, *The Genesis of Language: A Psycholinguistic Approach* (Cambridge, Mass.: M.I.T. Press, 1966); ed. Albert Valdman, *Trends in Language Teaching* (New York: McGraw-Hill, 1966).

17. Further discussion of these issues will be found in several papers in *The Psychology of Second Language Learning*, eds. P. Pimsleur and T. Quinn (Cambridge: Cambridge University Press, 1971), notably in the papers by Dean H. Obrecht, "Fundamentals of Language and Fundamentals of Teaching: The Necessity of Cross-breeding"; John W. Oller, "Language Communication and Second Language Learning"; D. A. Reibel, "Language Learning Strategies for the Adult." See also H. H. Stern, "Foreign Language Learning and the New View of First-Language Acquisition," *Child Study*, XXX, No. 4 (Winter 1968/9), 119.

THE FUNCTIONS OF LANGUAGE

ERIC WANNER

Do We Understand Sentences from the Outside-In or from the Inside-Out?

THE HISTORICAL ironies which await the founding father are legendary. As every undergraduate knows, it was Wilhelm Wundt, the nineteenth century physiologist and philosopher, who introduced experimental work into psychology. He was also the first to undertake a psychology of language. Nevertheless, Wundt staunchly believed that our understanding of the mental processes underlying the use of language could not be advanced through experiment. Today, the experimental study of linguistic behavior is flourishing in both Europe and America; it has a name, *experimental psycholinguistics*, and the amount of work in the area is expanding rapidly. Indeed, although we are still far from answering many of the questions Wundt posed, it might not be too much to hope that even the master would be impressed.

In retrospect, Wundt's pessimism is not hard to understand. The nature of psychological experimentation has changed a good deal since the days when he founded his laboratory in Leipzig. So too has the conception of the mind. In Wundt's view, knowledge of the mind derived from immediate, conscious experience. Hence for Wundt, psychology's chief method of experimentation was introspection: stimulus conditions were arranged; a trained subject reacted and then reported the conscious accompaniments of his reaction. As Wundt realized, this method is practically useless when applied to language. The conscious accompaniments of speaking or understanding a sentence are ordinarily nil. So Wundt was forced to conclude that the mental processes underlying our ability to speak and understand cannot be studied experimentally.

Modern psychology has largely detached itself from Wundt's commitment to introspection. We tend now to think of the mind not as something we can look into with an inner eye, but rather as something we infer in order to account for observable behavior. Reports about consciousness are only one of a large variety of observable behaviors which can be studied in this way. Indeed, many of the mental processes which appear to underlie overt behavior are quite unconscious. Some are surprising. In this article we will discuss one example of the way in which behavioral experiments can be used to reach conclusions about the unconscious processes underlying the listener's ability to understand the sentences of his language. The example is interesting because it upsets some of our common sense notions about the way language is used, as well as some of our beliefs about the human nature of the language user.

To introduce our illustration, suppose that you and I have just attended a lecture on a difficult subject. Suppose further that it has been delivered in barely audible tones and that the acoustics of the hall are poor. If, as we leave, I ask you whether you understood the lecture, it is plausible that you might respond, not without exasperation:

(1) Understand it? I couldn't even hear it.

But suppose I had asked you instead whether you had been able to hear the lecture. It seems rather unlikely that you would answer:

(2) Hear it? I couldn't even understand it.

Why is (1) plausible where (2) is not? Presumably because we believe that understanding a sentence or a discourse is contingent upon hearing it; that is, upon recognizing the component speech sounds.[1] Hence a failure to hear entails a failure to understand, as in (1). But we apparently do not believe that our ability to recognize speech sounds depends upon our ability to understand meanings, so (2) sounds quite bizarre.

Like most of our common sense, this little bit of everyday psychology is partly correct. As far as we know, it is quite impossible to grasp the meaning of a spoken word without hearing it first. So to this extent it is easy to answer the question we have used as a title: comprehension is surely an outside-in process. But it is not exclusively outside-in. In the past twenty years of psycholinguistic investigation into what the listener does when he understands a sentence, we have come to understand that there is no simple correlation between the properties of the acoustic stimulus and the listener's interpretation of the sentence. The listener makes an active contribution to what he hears and understands, and it is this contribution which makes the problem of comprehension both difficult and interesting.

Although we are by no means certain of everything that a listener must do when he understands a sentence, we can start with a rough list of what seem to be obvious tasks. For example, the listener must recognize the appropriate set of words in the flow of speech directed at him. This will require him to find a match between some internal representation of the way each word sounds and properties of the incoming information about the speech waveform. Once a word is recognized, its meanings must be retrieved. If there are several such meanings, the one appropriate to the current context must be selected and combined with the meanings of other words in order to form an interpretation of the entire sentence. Wherever the appropriate manner of combination depends upon syntactic properties of the sentence, such as word order or the grouping of words into phrases, these syntactic properties must be determined and put to use.

For almost every task on this list, there is evidence that the listener's solution involves an important inside-out component. Here we consider two such tasks: namely, the recognition of words and the determination of certain semantically relevant aspects of syntax. To begin, consider the deceptively simple matter of how words are recognized. If word recognition is exclusively outside-in, then we can formulate the following expectations:

(3) In the speech which conveys a sentence there should be a region of sound corresponding to each word which contains all the physical cues that are necessary and sufficient for the recognition of the word in question.

(4) Such regions should be *local* to the words they represent in the sense that they should conform, in nature and extent, to the patterns of sound which convey the same word in isolation.

In fact neither of these expectations has proved to be completely correct. In a simple experiment which has become a classic, Miller, Heise, and Lichten compared the intelligibility of single words in two conditions: one in which the words are embedded in sentences and another in which the same words are spoken in isolation.[2] The strength of the signal relative to background noise was varied over a wide range in both conditions.[3] Basically, Miller and his colleagues found that sentential context makes words easier to identify. Adding context, it appears, improves intelligibility by about the same amount as turning down the volume of the background noise enough to raise the signal-to-noise ratio by six decibels. The moral of this result is straightforward: information which is outside the region of sound that is local to a given word may nevertheless play a role in its identification. Miller, Heise, and Lichten thought that context plays its part by limiting the number of words which the listener might expect at any given point in the sentence. With a smaller set of possibilities to decide among, the listener may need less information about the physical characteristics of the sound in order to reach his decision.

This is still our best guess about how context improves intelligibility. In a related experiment, Miller, Heise, and Lichten showed that the listener's ability to recognize a word presented in isolation could be improved by giving him foreknowledge of the set from which the test word would be drawn. The smaller the set of alternatives, the better the listener's performance. Sentential context may narrow the listener's expectations in a comparable way, but we still do not know how this narrowing takes place. The reason we don't is simple enough: a proper account of the operation of context will probably require a complete theory of comprehension; for it is by understanding the meaning of what has already been said that the listener forms opinions about what is going to be said.

Despite our inability to produce a complete account of these results, Miller's experiments provide a nice demonstration of the co-existence of outside-in and inside-out processes in word recognition. Evidently we can improve performance either by making the signal clearer or by increasing the subject's knowledge of what to expect. In the first case, we make the task easier to solve from the outside-in; in the second case, we make it easier to solve from the inside-out. But how, one might ask, are these two processes balanced in listening to ordinary conversation? An experiment by Pollack and Pickett demonstrates the surprising importance of inside-out processes.[4]

Pollack and Pickett lured subjects into an anechoic chamber, ostensibly to record stimulus materials for a subsequent experiment. At some point during the recording session, each subject was told that the tape recorder had broken down. During a delay of fifteen minutes or so, one of the experimenters engaged the subject in conversation while the subject was still seated directly in front of the microphone. These conversations were surreptitiously recorded. The point was to obtain recordings of conversational speech in acoustically optimal circumstances, and from speakers who were unaware that they were being recorded. Pollack and Pickett selected about a hundred samples from each of four speakers who were recorded in this way. Every sample contained eight words and was about two seconds long. Electronic gating techniques were then used to produce eight recordings of each sample such that the first recording included only the first word, the second included only the first two words, and so on up to the eighth recording which contained all eight words.

The eight recordings of each sample were then played in order of increasing size to a crew of listeners. Each recording was scored in terms of the percentage of words correctly identified. The surprising result is that these intelligibility scores are simply much lower than one would expect if word recognition were a strictly outside-in process. In order to achieve 90 percent intelligibility, listeners had to hear recordings containing an average of 7.5 words and lasting over 1.5 seconds. Only 60 percent intelligibility was obtained with recordings which were about two words and half a second long. When single words were played to listeners, average intelligibility dropped as low as 30 percent for some speakers. It is worth noting that these poor scores were obtained despite the high quality of the recordings,[5] despite the fact that the listeners were told how many words to expect on each trial, and despite a method of presentation which provided repeated exposures to some portion of most of the speech tested.

Why was performance so poor under these conditions? The obvious answer is that conversational speech is simply not clear enough to permit the listener to recognize one word at a time, using only the sounds local to each word. Expectations (3) and (4) above are incorrect for conversational speech. To be convinced, it is only necessary to listen to a tape recording of an ordinary conversation. Stripped of its social context, the fits, starts, slurs, and omissions become glaringly obvious. Evidently the speaker knows that the listener is capable of employing contextual information to compensate for deficiencies in the quality of his own speech. Indeed there is even evidence that the quality of the speaker's pronunciation deteriorates as contexts become increasingly informative.[6]

One final point. Notice that it would be possible to maintain an outside-in view of word recognition in the face of Pollack and Pickett's results by abandoning our expectation (4). Recognition is outside-in, one could hold, but speech is recognized in terms of units which are much longer than the single word. Hence the poor performance on Pollack and Pickett's shorter segments. This is not a silly argument. As we will see, there is reason to believe that speech recognition does not take place in terms of minimal units. However, if we advance the argument that the average length of the recognition unit must be about 7.5 words (to choose a segment length at which Pollack and Pickett's subjects performed acceptably), then we run into the problem that there are simply too many such units to learn in the average lifetime. Rough calculation suggests that there are about 10^{14} different seven-word sequences possible in English. To appreciate the size of this number, we need only observe that the number of seconds per century is only about 3.15×10^9. In short there appears to be no alternative to the conclusion that our recognition processes are fundamentally influenced by knowledge derived from context. It is in this sense that word recognition is partially an inside-out process.

Much the same point can be made about the processes which determine the semantically relevant syntactic properties of a sentence. Consider first the matter of word segmentation. In the large majority of sentences, the listener probably solves the problem of determining the boundaries between words simply as a by-product of his solution to the word recognition problem. In some cases, however, a given stretch of sound can be analyzed as several different strings of words. Here the placement of word boundaries can have important semantic effects. For example, speech which can be analyzed syllabically as

(5) light-house-keep-er

could result from either of two wordings:

(6) light hóusekeeper

(7) lighthouse keeper

How does the listener distinguish between these two possibilities? Following the outside-in notions of common sense again, we should expect to find local physical cues which signal the segmentation that the speaker has in mind. Indeed, such cues do exist. But they are not the ones we might anticipate; nor are they as important as outside-in notions would lead us to believe.

When asked how (6) and (7) sound different, English speakers will often state that the contrast depends upon emphasis or stress. Stress, in turn, is supposed to be a matter of loudness. According to this view, the speaker produces "house" most forcefully when he intends the segmentation of (6) (which we will subsequently designate as *l-hk*); and he comes down heavily on "light" when he has (7) (hereafter *lh-k*) in mind. Intuitively sensible as this hypothesis is, it does not turn out to fit the facts. When we look at measures of loudness and forcefulness, such as the total energy in the speech spectrum or the speaker's subglottal air pressure, we find no tendency for such measures to correlate with perceived stress. Typically both measures peak at the vowels in the syllables "light" and "house." Sometimes one peak is higher than the other; but within individual speakers there is no tendency for the highest peak to shift from "light" in *lh-k* to "house" in *l-hk*.[7]

Bolinger and Gerstman were the first to observe that the relevant cue was not the height of the vowel peaks but the temporal intervals between them.[8] They backed up this observation by showing that they could artificially change a tape recording of *lh-k* into *l-hk* simply by splicing in short sections of empty tape between "light" and "house." Lieberman has successfully repeated this demonstration.[9] Moreover he has estimated that the elapsed time between "light" and "house" is roughly five times as great for *l-hk* as for *lh-k* when these phrases are read as part of ordinary sentences. Lieberman calls this temporal cue *disjuncture,* but it is important to recognize that a *disjuncture* is not simply a silent pause. As anyone who has looked at a spectrogram of ordinary speech knows,[10] there are no uniform intervals of dead time between spoken words corresponding to the blank spaces between written words. The interval between the vowels of "light" and "house" is filled, among other things, with the sound deriving from the fricative /h/.

How important is *disjuncture* in ordinary speech? Two lines of evidence suggest that its importance is limited. First, Lieberman reports that when speakers are asked to read phrases such as "light heavyweight," where the

of a single linguist were compared with measurements of the fundamental frequency of the speech sound, it turned out that a given pitch level did not correspond consistently to a discrete frequency range. Even within the transcriptions of a single linguist for a single utterance, the fundamental frequency corresponding to the "lowest" pitch level transcribed was sometimes equal to or greater than the fundamental frequency transcribed as "intermediate."

Lieberman also asked his two linguists to transcribe the intonation contours of a continuous vowel sound which had been synthesized in such a way that it reproduced the fundamental frequency and amplitude contours of the originally tested speech. Given these sounds, the linguists changed about half of their previous decisions. Interestingly, the changed transcriptions proved to be a more accurate reflection of fundamental frequency than the transcriptions of the original speech. This is strong evidence against the simple notion that phrase structure is determined from perceived intonation which is in turn determined from changes in the speaker's fundamental frequency. In unambiguous sentences at least, perceived intonation has no simple relation to fundamental frequency. Lieberman's trained observers seem to have been paying attention to something else besides the speaker's fundamental frequency when assigning intonation contours. Lieberman has even suggested that this something else might be the phrase structure of the sentence, as determined not by acoustic cue, but from the parsing which the listener imposes on the sentence given his knowledge of English syntax. Before we accept this avowedly inside-out argument, we will need to check the possibility that other acoustic cues, besides the speaker's fundamental frequency, are operative. To this end we turn to an entirely independent line of research, and something of an excursion into modern cognitive psychology.

The story begins with the work of Ladefoged and Broadbent who, for reasons we can ignore, were interested in whether the perceived order of a sequence of sounds always reflects its actual physical order.[19] To put this question to the test, Ladefoged and Broadbent made tape recordings of sentences and of sequences of digits. At some point in each recording a brief electronic click sound was superimposed on the speech. These stimuli were played to listeners who were simply asked to indicate the point in the speech sequence at which the click sound occurred. Most people find it difficult to believe that they can make errors on such a simple test; but the task is by no means as easy as it seems. On the average, Ladefoged and Broadbent's subjects mistakenly located those clicks which occurred during sentences about two positions prior to their true location (here each word and each interword boundary was counted as a position). For the digit sequences, performance was somewhat better, but hardly perfect: on the average, clicks were perceived .7 position prior to their actual location.

As Ladefoged and Broadbent point out, the very existence of these errors indicates that "items do not pass along sensory paths in rigid succession."[20] In other words, if we imagine the flow of auditory information through the nervous system as a sort of parade passing from the ear to the mechanism in the brain which recognizes speech sounds, then our inability to perceive the true location of a superimposed click suggests that the marchers in this parade may not maintain a rigid order. One way to conceive of how auditory items might get out of order can be built upon Broadbent's suggestion, illustrated here in *Figure 1*, that incoming auditory information may be stored briefly in a buffer memory before it is subject to recognition.[21] If incoming information is stored in a buffer before recognition takes place, then the order in which items are recognized need not reflect the order in which they enter the buffer. For example, a word which arrives before a click might be stored in the buffer and recognized at some point after the detection of the click. Before developing this possibility in detail, however, we need to review a few of the reasons for postulating buffer memory in the first place.

Figure 1

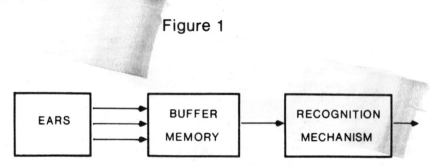

The Buffer Memory Model. The multiple arrows leading from "Ears" to "Buffer Memory" represent the hypothesis that signals may enter the buffer in parallel. Thus several simultaneous sounds may be stored at one time. The single arrow leaving the "Recognition Mechanism" indicates that the output of this hypothetical device is serial; only one sound can be identified at a time. Finally, note that although we have drawn only a single arrow from the "Buffer Memory" to the "Recognition Mechanism," we do not wish to be committed to the notion that only one signal can be input to the recognition mechanism at a time. Indeed, current work suggests that the recognition mechanism may receive multiple inputs. However, there is a long history of controversy on this point which goes by the name of research on *selective attention*.[21]

Perhaps the most important of these reasons runs as follows. Everything we know about auditory recognition indicates that its output is serial: basically, we can only recognize one sound at a time. Yet it is easy to demonstrate that if an experimental subject is exposed to two simultaneous messages, say one in each ear, then he can report both messages accurately as long as they are both short. We can account for this ability and maintain our serial view of recognition if we hypothesize a buffer memory system which is capable of storing one message while the other is being recognized. Conceivably the fact that one's ability to handle simultaneous messages is limited to inputs of brief duration reflects the limited capacity of the buffer, or the speed with which information in the buffer decays, or both.

A second argument for adopting the buffer memory hypothesis arises from the obvious fact that auditory information is, by its very nature, spread over time. We ordinarily assume that recognition (at least outside-in recognition) depends upon making a successful match between some internally stored (or generated) representation of an auditory item and incoming auditory information. Hence complete identification of any auditory item must be delayed until all the incoming information necessary to make the match has arrived. One way to accomplish such a delay is by means of a buffer memory in which the information relevant to each item accumulates before recognition takes place. So, for example, if we recognize speech, say, one phoneme at a time, then we might imagine a buffer which preserves stretches of information about the incoming sound that are long enough to permit the identification of each phoneme. Of course, if speech is recognized in terms of larger units such as the syllable, word, or phrase, then longer delays will be involved and a larger buffer will be required to store the longer stretches of auditory information which pertain to such units.

Returning now to the click phenomenon, we can advance a very tentative account of Ladefoged and Broadbent's observation that clicks are generally perceived as occurring prior to their true location. Suppose a click actually occurs in the middle of some perceptual unit, ignoring for the moment what the nature of that unit may be. Suppose further, as we have suggested, that the recognition of any unit is delayed until all information pertinent to its identification has accumulated in the buffer memory. Then a click which occurs in the middle of a unit will arrive at a point when the last output of the recognition mechanism was the immediately preceding unit, but when the output for the current unit has yet to be produced. Thus, if the click is perceived as soon as it actually occurs, it will appear to have arrived *between* the immediately preceding and the current unit, not *during* the current unit. We will call this account of click migration Hypothesis I. *Figure 2* provides an illustration of how Hypothesis I works out in detail.

Applying Hypothesis I to Ladefoged and Broadbent's results, we can make the case that the size of the click displacements which they observed indicates that speech is not perceived in terms of minimal, phoneme-sized chunks. For if speech were perceived in terms of phonemes, then we should expect that the largest displacement of a click co-occurring with a given phoneme should be to the point between that phoneme and its

Figure 2

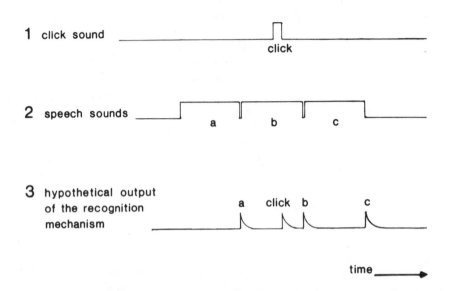

An Illustration of Hypothesis I. Line 1 indicates the arrival time of a click relative to a sequence of three speech sounds (*a, b, c*) of unspecified type represented on line 2. Line 3 indicates the times at which the sounds would be perceived, assuming (1) that the recognition of any speech sound is delayed until
all information pertinent to it is received and (2) that the click is perceived
immediately upon its arrival. Note that on the basis of these assumptions the
click would be perceived as occurring *before* speech sound *b* even though it actually occurs *during* speech sound *b*.

predecessor. We would clearly not expect a click occurring in the middle of
a word to migrate as far as the preceding word boundary. But the average
distance for click displacement in digit strings (.7 position) indicates that
a click occurring during a spoken digit was frequently perceived at the
interdigit boundary preceding its true location. Moreover, clicks in sentences typically migrate further than clicks in digit strings—often as far
as several words away from their true locations. The fact that click displacements are larger in sentences than in digit strings suggests that sentences may be perceived in terms of larger perceptual units. Ladefoged
and Broadbent eschewed any attempt to say what the perceptual unit for
sentences might be. However, one difference between sentences and digit
strings is that sentences are structured into phrases. So it is a short step
to the hypothesis that the greater click mislocations in sentences are due to
the listener's tendency to recognize sentences a phrase at a time.

Fodor and Bever were the first to entertain this notion.[22] Reanalyzing Ladefoged and Broadbent's results, Fodor and Bever found that the strength of the tendency for clicks to migrate to a nearby word boundary was positively correlated with the number of phrases which bordered on that boundary. Moreover, this tendency appeared to hold in both directions. For example, in a sentence such as

(17) $((\text{Because }(\text{Bill }_1 \text{ quit}))_2 ((\text{the }_3 \text{ team}) \text{ lost}))$

a click objectively located in the middle of the word "the" should be perceived more frequently in the word boundary we have labeled 2 than in word boundary 3 because more phrases (indicated above by parentheses) abut on boundary 2 than on boundary 3. However, a click objectively located in the word "quit" should be perceived more frequently in boundary 2 than in boundary 1, again because boundary 2 is "deeper" in the sense that a greater number of phrases border upon it. According to Fodor and Bever then, the tendency to prepose clicks which Ladefoged and Broadbent observed arises at least in part from the accidental fact that in Ladefoged and Broadbent's sentences, deep boundaries tend to precede the true location of the click.

To verify their observation that clicks tend to move towards deep boundaries, Fodor and Bever conducted the following experiment. They devised a number of sentences, each of which contained one particularly deep boundary. Multiple recordings of each sentence were made; and a single click was located in each recording so that over the full set of recordings of each sentence, the objective click locations surrounded the deep boundary. Sentence (18) illustrates such a set of recordings.

(18) $((\text{That }(\text{he }(\text{was happy})))$ * $(\text{was }(\text{evident }(\text{from }((\text{the way})$
$(\text{he smiled}))))))).$

Here arrows mark click locations; the asterisk indicates the deep boundary; and as before, parentheses designate phrases. In statistical terms, Fodor and Bever's experiment confirmed that clicks tend to migrate to deep boundaries. 80 percent of all attempts to locate the click were erroneous. Of these errors, 65 percent were in the direction of the deep boundary, and 35 percent were in the deep boundary proper. Moreover, the tendency for clicks to migrate toward the deep boundary was quite consistent over both sentences and subjects. These results seem to demonstrate that click migration is sensitive to phrase structure. However, the sensitivity is not quite of the sort specified by Hypothesis I. Recall that Hypothesis I predicts that a click will always be perceived as occurring at a point prior to the perceptual unit with which it co-occurs. Hence if phrases are perceptual units, clicks should always be preposed to the beginning of the concurrent phrase. But in Fodor and Bever's data, clicks appear to converge on deep boundaries from both directions. In view of this result, Fodor and Bever chose to replace Hypothesis I with the following account of click migration, which we will call Hypothesis II. Hypothesis II contains two assumptions and a single inference:

(19) There is a general psychological tendency for "a perceptual unit to preserve its integrity by resisting interruptions."[23]

(20) The phrase is a perceptual unit in the comprehension of sentences.

(21) Therefore clicks migrate in either direction to deep boundaries because deep boundaries are the points in any sentence which interrupt the fewest phrases.

Fodor and Bever were content to leave their statement of Hypothesis II in these general terms, but it is not difficult to see how Hypothesis II might be translated into the more detailed specifications of the perceptual system outlined above in connection with Hypothesis I. For example, note that however recognition proceeds, the matching operations involved must take time. Since a phrase is a reasonably long and complicated unit, we might guess that the amount of time involved is not negligible. Indeed it may well be the case that in order to complete the identification of a phrase within a brief period after all the information relevant to the phrase has arrived, recognition operations must be initiated at a point well before the end of the phrase has been reached. If we assume in addition that these operations require the entire capacity of the recognition mechanism, then the perception of a click which arrives during the recognition of a phrase must be deferred. Such a postponement can be accomplished by storing the click in the buffer memory until after the input phrase has been recognized. On the basis of these assumptions, a click which arrives after the initiation of recognition operations for a given phrase will be perceived following that phrase. A click arriving before the initiation of recognition operations for a given phrase will be perceived prior to the phrase just as in Hypothesis I. In this way clicks may move either direction to the borders of a phrase. *Figure 3* provides a detailed illustration of the way in which this movement might occur.

The results of Fodor and Bever's experiment are consistent with Hypothesis II, in either its general or its more specific form; but there are reasons to remain suspicious. One problem is that we have no baseline against which to compare Fodor and Bever's results. Clicks *might* migrate in the way Fodor and Bever observed even if sentences were not

Figure 3

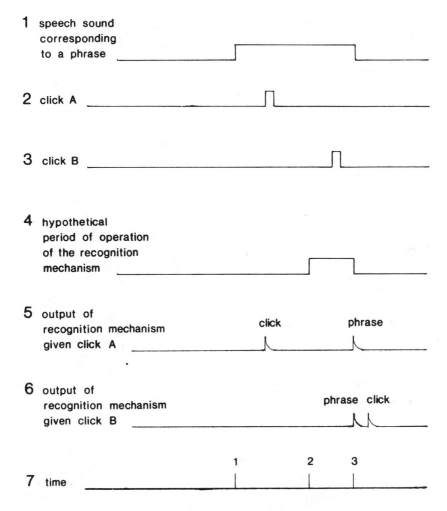

1 speech sound
corresponding
to a phrase

2 click A

3 click B

4 hypothetical
period of operation
of the recognition
mechanism

5 output of
recognition mechanism
given click A

click   phrase

6 output of
recognition mechanism
given click B

phrase click

7 time

1   2   3

An Illustration of Hypothesis II. Assume the input speech is a phrase lasting from time 1 to time 3, as indicated on line 1. Assume further that recognition operations for the phrase are initiated at time 2 and completed by time 3, as indicated on line 4. Now if a click (such as click A on line 2) arrives between times 1 and 2, it should be perceived immediately since the recognition mechanism is not yet occupied with the phrase. In this case, the click will be perceived *before* the phrase as indicated on line 5. However, if a click (such as click B on line 3) arrives between times 2 and 3 when the recognition mechanism is engaged in processing the phrase, it will be perceived *after* the phrase has been recognized, as indicated on line 6, as long as we assume that once it is applied to the phrase, the recognition mechanism must defer all other input.

perceived in terms of phrases. For instance, we know now that although Hypothesis II may be correct, there are many additional factors which influence the perceptual localization of clicks. In particular, clicks tend to be preposed if they are played through earphones to the subject's right ear, but postposed if played to the left ear. Clicks tend to be preposed in the early trials of an experiment, but postposed as the experiment continues. Moreover, click location appears to be subject to what psychologists call a "response bias": quite independent of any effect due to syntactic structure, clicks which co-occur with a word or item early in a sentence or stimulus series tend to be postposed, while clicks which occur late tend to be preposed. Reber and Anderson have argued that this tendency for clicks to move toward the middle of a sentence might account for Fodor and Bever's observations, since most of their deep boundaries were located towards the center of their test sentences.[24] However, Fodor's group has obtained results which appear to parry this attack on the generalization that clicks move to phrase boundaries. Interestingly enough, these results stem from an attempt to determine whether click migration is due to inside-out or outside-in processes.

Suppose, for the moment, that we accept Fodor and Bever's results as evidence that clicks migrate to phrase boundaries. If we admit the phenomenon, then we can inquire into its cause. Once again we face inside-out and outside-in alternatives. Are the phrases which appear to displace clicks determined by the listener on the basis of syntactic knowledge? Or are there physical cues which determine the phrasing and hence attract the click to deep boundaries? In earlier work, Garrett had shown that clicks have a tendency to migrate to a point in a sequence of spoken digits which is marked by a relatively long pause.[25] Coupling this result with Bolinger and Gerstman's demonstration that temporal junctures can signal word boundaries,[26] Fodor and Bever entertained the possibility that acoustic pauses at the deep boundaries were the cause of the observed migration of clicks. As a check, they measured the degree of energy drop at the deep boundary in each sentence and compared it with the observed strength of the click migration. If pauses attract clicks, then there should have been more errors in the direction of the deep boundary for the boundaries at which energy dropped most. But Fodor and Bever found no such correlation. Even in four sentences in which the deep boundary exhibited no measurable pause, 80 percent of all errors were in the predicted direction.

If click migration is a function of phrase structure, then this result rules out one more possibility in the search for a physical cue to phrase grouping. Of course, the determined outside-in theorist could protest that still another cue might be operating. However, Garrett, Bever, and Fodor have put an ingenious end to this line of complaint, for they have been able to demonstrate that click migrations will change direction when the deep boundary is shifted, even though the shift changes none of the physical cues which are local to the deep boundary.[27] The details of their demonstration are as follows. Pairs of sentences were devised which share one segment in common but which are parsed differently because of the nature of the unshared segment. The following pair provides an example:

(22) (In *her* hope of marrying) (Anna   was surely impractical.)
                                 ↑   ↑

(23) (*Your* hope of marrying   Anna) (was surely impractical.)
                                 ↑   ↑

These sentences differ only in their (italized) initial word or two, but the difference is enough to shift the major phrase break from one side of "Anna" to the other. This shift is indicated above by parentheses. Garrett, Bever, and Fodor made a single recording of the common portion of pairs such as this and then used splicing techniques to attach it to the different initial segments. The result was a pair of sentences which had different deep boundaries but which were acoustically identical in the region of those boundaries. Thus if clicks migrate in response to some physical cue, the distribution of subjective locations ought to be the same in both sentences. But if clicks move to the deep boundary, there should be more in the juncture between "marrying" and "Anna" in (22) than in (23), and more in the juncture between "Anna" and "was" in (23) than in (22).

Garrett, Bever, and Fodor tested these predictions with clicks placed as the arrows in (22) and (23) indicate. The results strongly support the inside-out hypothesis. Clicks did distribute themselves differently within the two sentences of each pair: in every case, clicks were perceived more frequently in a given word boundary when it was the deep boundary than when it was not. Notice that these results cannot be attributed to any response bias of the sort argued by Reber and Anderson. Such a bias must operate uniformly over the two versions of each sentence. Yet clicks are perceived differently in each version; and the difference is predictable on the basis of phrase structure. Hence although we cannot give a complete account of the psychological factors underlying click migration, we have reasonable evidence that syntactic factors are involved.

With this result, we would appear to have witnessed the final demise of the outside-in hypothesis as it applies to the determination of phrase structure. As is so often the case in research, however, there are new results which threaten to unravel the story we have told. But none of these appears to jeopardize our conclusions about inside-out processes. On the contrary they tend to reinforce such conclusions.

For example, as is detailed elsewhere in this volume, Chomsky has created something of a revolution in the study of syntax by showing that a simple bracketing of a sentence into its component phrases does not sufficiently represent all the syntactic information which is semantically relevant.[28] Chomsky's solution to this insufficiency has been to add a level of representation which he calls *deep structure* and which displays the basic grammatical relations of any sentence (e.g. subject of the sentence, object of the main verb, etc.) in a uniform way. Deep structure accomplishes this by representing any sentence, however complex, as an arrangement of structures, each of which looks a little like a simple active sentence. This resemblance is useful because just as we know how to find the subject, say, of a simple active sentence because it always precedes the verb, so we can determine the grammatical role of any phrase by observing its position in deep structure. Now it seems fairly certain that the listener must determine grammatical relations such as subject and object if he is to understand such matters as who, according to some sentence, is the actor, who the one acted upon, and so forth. So Chomsky's demonstration that deep structure provides a definition of such relations has led rather directly to the hypothesis that the listener determines deep structure in the course of comprehension.

Some of the work on this hypothesis has involved the click phenomenon. For example, Bever and his associates noticed that many of the boundaries which attracted clicks were not only the major breaks in phrase structure but also the junctures between deep structure sentences.[29] Typically this happens where the deep boundary falls at a juncture between clauses, as in (22). Bever's group has conducted a series of experiments to pick apart the possible effects of superficial phrases and deep structure sentences. Firm pronouncements about these results would be premature, but there is now some evidence that deep sentence boundaries provide a better way of predicting click migration than simple phrase structure. This suggests that the listener processes all the information relevant to a given deep structure sentence before switching attention to any extraneous stimulus, such as the click. If something like this turns out to be true, then we can be fairly certain that the processes which cause clicks to migrate are of the inside-out variety. For it appears that the details of deep structure cannot be communicated through the speaker's pronunciation. Thus, as we have noted, when all else is equal, the speaker *can*, by means of his pronunciation, make the listener select a particular phrase grouping where several are possible; but efforts to pronounce a sentence in such a way as to make a listener select one of many deep structures have been shown to fail.[30]

Suppose then that we accept the claim that comprehension is, in many important respects, an inside-out process. What are the consequences?

Some are technical. For example, in inside-out processing the listener brings his knowledge of the regularities of language and the tendencies of speakers to bear on the problems of identifying words and segmenting them properly. Moreover, the speaker behaves as if he expected the listener to make use of such knowledge, for he delivers clear local cues only where he suspects that prior context is insufficient. It follows that certain devices —such as typewriters which will type what we tell them, or computers which we can talk to—may be very difficult to build. For unless we embark on a program of speech reform, such devices must incorporate some approximation of the knowledge which the listener deploys during comprehension.

Some consequences are practical. Given a noisy environment which can obscure the details of speech at random, and given speakers who are subject to error, it is simply very useful for the listener to have the ability to select an interpretation on the basis of contextual cues. It is useful as well for the communications engineer who can sometimes get by with providing a listener with communications systems which are less than optimal.

Finally, there are consequences which are theoretical. Inside-out processing poses a thorny problem for the psycholinguist. It is his task to explain how the listener uses what he knows about linguistic regularities in order to respond to speech in a way which is sensitive to prior context. So far the most important effect of the kinds of experimental results we have discussed has been negative. They have served to rule out any model of comprehension based exclusively on outside-in mechanisms. So, for example, we know that we cannot build a satisfactory model of comprehension out of simple stimulus-response connections in which a given stimulus uniformly triggers an invariant response. The responses of the model must be contingent and the contingencies are complicated. To date, several ways of handling such contingencies have been proposed, but none is ascendant. For the moment then, we must be satisfied with knowing a little bit about what the listener does when he understands a sentence, without quite knowing how he does it.

REFERENCES

1. The verb *to hear* has several senses which appear to vary with the object construction which co-occurs with it in a given sentence. Consider the following examples:

   (a) Did John hear the noise?
   (b) Did John hear what Bill said?
   (c) Did John hear them announce the plane's departure?

To answer (a) affirmatively, it need only be true that John perceived or sensed the noise referred to. A "yes" to (b), however, requires John to have successfully recognized the speech sounds Bill uttered. But he need not have understood them. Note that it is perfectly possible to anwer (b) by saying,

   (d) Yes, but he couldn't make any sense of it.

Finally, notice that an affirmative answer to (c) does require that John have understood the content of the flight announcement.

In our examples (1) and (2), it may be somewhat ambiguous whether *hear* is intended in the sense of (a) or (b). Note that whichever sense is chosen (2) is a strange answer, where (1) is not. Here, however, we are only interested in the case in which *to hear* means *to recognize*. For while there is evidence that recognition depends partially upon comprehension, there is obviously no comparable evidence that auditory sensation depends upon comprehension. Hence the bizarre quality of (2) reveals an incorrect assumption in our common sense psychology, but only when *to hear* is taken in the sense of *to recognize*.

2. G. Miller, A. Heise, and W. Lichten, "The Intelligibility of Speech as a Function of the Context and the Test Materials," *Journal of Experimental Psychology*, XL (1951), 329-335.

3. Specifically, the signal-to-noise ratio was varied between −12 and +18 decibels at intervals of 6 decibels.

4. I. Pollack and J. Pickett, "The Intelligibility of Excerpts from Conversation," *Language and Speech*, VI (1964), 165-171.

5. Pollack and Pickett report that the signal-to-noise ratio of the electronic gating system was about 30 decibels. Thus it is likely that their recordings made in quiet circumstances provided a signal which was a good deal clearer than any of those which Miller and his colleagues used in their experiments.

6. P. Lieberman, "Some Effects of Semantic and Grammatical Context on the Production and Perception of Speech," *Language and Speech*, VI (1963), 172.

7. P. Lieberman, *Intonation Perception and Language* (Cambridge, Mass.: M.I.T. Press, 1967).

8. D. L. Bolinger and L. J. Gerstman, "Disjuncture as a Cue to Constructs," *Journal of the Acoustic Society of America*, XXIX (1957), 778.

9. P. Lieberman, *Intonation Perception and Language*.

10. A spectrogram, sometimes called a voiceprint, displays continuous changes over time in the way the energy in a sound is distributed over the frequency spectrum.

11. P. Lieberman, *Intonation Perception and Language*.

12. *Ibid.*

13. Note that these readers produced the disjuncture contrast in these sentences even though the context selects the proper segmentation. The reason may be that they had read both sentences several times in the recording session. Hence they were undoubtedly aware of the contrast between the two versions of the critical phrase.

14. Each pair of parentheses encloses a phrase. The labels on the parentheses should be interpreted as follows:

    VP = verb phrase
    NP = noun phrase
    PP = prepositional phrase

15. G. L. Trager and H. L. Smith, "Outline of English Structure," *Studies in Linguistics*, No. 3 (Norman, Oklahoma: Battenburg, 1951).

16. In this crude representation of pitch contour, the elevation of the curve above the line of type is used to represent the relative height of the pitch for each point in the sentence.

17. P. Lieberman, "On the Acoustic Basis of the Perception of Intonation by Linguists," *Word*, XXI (1965), 40-54.

18. G. L. Trager and H. L. Smith, *Outline of English Structure.*

19. P. Ladefoged and D. Broadbent, "Perception of Sequence in Auditory Events," *Quarterly Journal of Experimental Psychology*, XII (1960), 162-170.

20. P. Ladefoged and D. Broadbent, "Perception of Sequence in Auditory Events," p. 168.

21. For a more complete description of Broadbent's buffer memory hypothesis and the results which support it, see D. E. Broadbent, *Decision and Stress* (London: Academic Press, 1971).

22. J. Fodor and T. Bever, "The Psychological Reality of Linguistic Segments," *Journal of Verbal Learning and Verbal Behavior*, IV (1965), 414-421.

23. J. Fodor and T. Bever, "The Psychological Reality of Linguistic Segments," p. 415.

24. A. Reber and J. Anderson, "The Perception of Clicks in Linguistic and Non-linguistic Messages," *Perception and Psychophysics*, VIII (1970), 81-89.

25. M. Garrett, *Structure and Sequence in Judgments of Auditory Events* (Urbana: Institute of Communications Research, University of Illinois, 1964).

26. D. L. Bolinger and L. J. Gerstman, "Disjuncture as a Cue to Constructs."

27. M. Garrett, T. Bever and J. Fodor, "The Active Use of Grammar in Speech Perception," *Perception and Psychophysics*, I (1966), 30-32.

28. N. A. Chomsky, *Aspects of a Theory of Syntax* (Cambridge, Mass.: M.I.T. Press, 1965), and *Syntactic Structures* (The Hague: Mouton, 1957).

29. T. Bever, J. Lackner and W. Stoltz, "Transitional Probability Is Not a General Mechanism for the Segmentation of Speech," *Journal of Experimental Psychology*, LXXIX (1969); T. Bever, J. Lackner and R. Kirk, "The Underlying Structure Sentence Is the Primary Unit of Speech Perception," *Perception and Psychophysics*, V (1969), 225-234.

30. Anne R. Dow, *The Relation of Prosodic Features to Syntax* (Harvard University, unpublished master's thesis, 1966).

EDWARD L. KEENAN

Logic and Language

THE DEVELOPMENT of formal logic in the twentieth century illustrates one of the most elegant and successful pieces of linguistic analysis of modern times. In this essay, we shall extract from this development a model of semantic analysis for natural language. We shall use this model to analyze the meanings of some English sentences and then to compare differences in the expressive power of different languages.

Logic as a Paradigm of Linguistic Analysis[1]

Standard predicate logic is what linguists would call a *universal grammar*—universal not with respect to natural languages such as English, but rather with respect to the languages of the mathematical sciences, such as elementary arithmetic, Euclidean geometry, and set theory.

The purpose of the mathematical sciences is to discover and state truths about particular mathematical objects, such as natural numbers, points and lines, or sets. Each of these sciences needs and has a language in which to express these truths. A grammar of the language lists the basic symbols of the language, places them in grammatical categories, and states rules for combining them into sentences (or formulae). Now standard logic provides a *universal syntax* for these languages in that it defines the set of possible grammatical categories and possible syntactic rules from which each language draws its stock. The syntactic rules are of two types: those that generate simple sentences by combining naming expressions with predicate symbols, and those that generate complex sentences from simpler ones. An example of a simple sentence in arithmetic might be $(0 < 1)$, read in English as "Zero is less than one." Examples of more complex sentences would be: $(\exists x)(x < 1)$ "There is a number x which is less than one"; and $(0 < 1)$ v $(1 < 0)$ "Either zero is less than one or one is less than zero."

The point to notice about the syntactic rules of standard logic is this: although the number of distinct sentences of, for example, arithmetic is unbounded, that is, infinite, the number of different ways of deriving

187

complex sentences from simpler ones is very limited. Thus the rules of standard logic enable us to represent an infinite set in a finite way.

But standard logic is more than a universal syntax, it is also a *universal semantics*. As we have seen, the principal use of a mathematical language is to state truths about mathematical objects. To do this, certain sentences, called axioms, are taken as basic truths; then other sentences are shown to be truths by demonstrating that they are entailed by the axioms.

Of course, whether a given sentence entails another depends on the meanings of the sentences. To take an example from English, consider that the sentence, "Every student in Cambridge studies hard," is entailed by "Every student in Cambridge has rich parents and studies hard," but is not entailed by "Every student in Cambridge either has rich parents or studies hard." And this fact is quite sufficient to establish that these latter two sentences differ in meaning. Entailment then is clearly a semantic relation, and standard logic provides a universal semantics for mathematical languages by defining this relation.

Indeed the formal definition of entailment is one of the major achievements of modern logic. The definition captures the following informally stated intuition: one sentence is entailed by another if (and only if) it is true in every state of affairs in which the other is true. Consequence then is defined in terms of the notion: *true in a state of affairs*. In effect, standard logic defines the truth conditions for each sentence in each of the mathematical languages.

This impressive achievement may appear somewhat less mysterious once we examine the principle behind the definition. The truth conditions for simple sentences, such as $(1 < 0)$, are given somewhat arbitrarily. They merely say that the sentence is true in exactly the cases in which the world is the way the sentence says it is. Then the truth conditions for complex sentences are given in terms of those for the simpler sentences they are formed from. That is, for each of the limited number of syntactic rules which are used to derive a complex sentence from simpler ones, we explicitly state how the truth conditions of the derived sentence are determined by those of the simpler ones. Clearly, for example, the truth of a sentence of the form "either A or B" is determined according to the same states of affairs in which the truth of A and the truth of B are determined. Thus, by defining the truth of a sentence in terms of its syntactic structure we can represent the entailments of an infinite number of sentences in a finite way.

In fact the reason why the syntactic rules of standard logic are designed the way they are is precisely so that the correct definition of truth can be given. The definition is judged correct because the sentences which it determines to be entailed by others are judged to be correctly entailed by people whose understanding of the meaning of mathematical sentences is good. If the definition had determined, for example, that some sentence of arithmetic, A, entailed some other one, B, but mathematicians judged that B could be false in certain cases where A was true, then the definition of truth would not be correct.

Thus, the model of semantic analysis that logic provides is this: *To represent the meanings of a large number of sentences, one should formally define the major ways in which the sentences are semantically related to each other.* Logic then is primarily concerned with semantic relations, not with the "absolute" meaning of single sentences.

Some Major Semantic Relations in Natural Language

To use the logical model to analyze the meanings of natural language sentences we must first identify the semantic relations obtaining among natural language sentences. Entailment of course will be one such relation, since stating truths and making inferences is a part of ordinary speaking. This relation illustrates nicely the soundness of adopting the logical model of semantic analysis. For it often happens that the "absolute" meaning of certain natural language sentences is not completely clear. Even as innocuous a sentence as "John loves Mary" is subject to much uncertainty with regard to its meaning. Certainly, in a particular case, individuals might well disagree as to whether John does, or does not, really love Mary. But these same individuals will readily agree that if the sentence "John loves Mary," is true, then the sentence, "Someone loves Mary," is also true. In other words, they would agree that the two sentences are in the entailment relation even though they disagreed about the absolute meanings of the sentences.

It may come as a surprise therefore to learn that the entailment relation cannot be defined directly for natural language sentences. The reason is that such sentences are often ambiguous; that is, they often have more than one meaning, and can be true in a given situation considered in terms of one meaning, but false in that same situation considered in terms of the other meaning. For example, take the sentence, "Some boy danced with every girl." We can easily imagine a situation in which that sentence is false if understood to mean "There was one particular boy who danced with each of the girls," but true if understood to mean "For each girl there was a boy who danced with her." Similarly the sentences, "The chickens are ready to eat," "John thinks he's Napoleon and so does Fred," and "Flying planes can be dangerous," are also logically ambiguous. Logically ambiguous sentences then will have two (or more) sets of entailments depending on how we understand them. A sentence in one of the entailment sets but not in the other could plausibly be argued both to be and not to be entailed by the ambiguous original sentence. And this is precisely to say that the entailment relation is not well defined in this case. It is partly for this reason that arithmetic is not formally conducted in English. A sentence like "Every number is less than some number" would have different entailments depending on whether we understood it to mean "There is some particular number which every number is less than," or "For every number there is another number which it is less than." Thus to represent unambiguously the meanings of sentences we must have recourse to symbols such as variable signs and parentheses which are not part of the syntax of everyday speech.

Granted that entailment is an important semantic relation of natural language; it must be acknowledged, however, that we must do more than define entailment if we are to represent the meanings of natural language sentences, even of those which are not ambiguous. Many sentences, such as questions and commands, are not used to make statements or inferences, and are not naturally considered to be either true or false. Hence they do not even have entailments in the standard sense. Yet clearly a natural semantic relation exists between a question and its possible answers, and so an adequate semantic analysis of natural language must define this relation.

Unfortunately much less is known, formally speaking, about the question-answer relation than about entailment. The need to define this relation can be explained on two grounds. First, there are declarative sentences which have the same entailments but which are natural answers to different questions; hence they differ in meaning. This difference, however, cannot be stated in terms of differences of entailments. As an example, consider sentences formed from converse verbs like "buy-sell" and "rent-rent." Clearly, "Mary bought a coat from John," is true in exactly the same situations in which "John sold a coat to Mary" is true. So the two sentences have the same entailments. Yet they differ in meaning, for one talks about something John did and the other about something Mary did. And indeed only the first is a natural answer to "What did Mary do yesterday?" while only the second is a natural answer to "What did John do yesterday?" and these questions clearly request different information.

Secondly, there are sentences which have different entailments when they are considered as answers to different questions. Thus the entailment relation is not completely independent of the question-answer relation. As an example,[2] consider that these questions are clearly different in meaning:

(1) Which girls will study abroad next year?

(2) Which history students will study abroad next year?

Now suppose that the following is uttered as an answer to (1):

(3) The girls with scholarships will study abroad next year.

Clearly in such a case (3) entails that all the girls with scholarships will study abroad next year. But if (3) is uttered as an answer to (2) it does not have that entailment. Rather it only entails that girls with scholarships who are history students will study abroad next year.

A third semantic relation which cuts across both declaratives and questions is *logical presupposition*. It is this relation that we shall use to argue that languages differ in logical expressive power.

A claim made in everyday speech, in distinction to a statement of standard logic, is not usually intended to hold in an arbitrary state of affairs. Rather, in making a claim we usually take it for granted (presuppose) that the world is a certain way, and what we say is only meant to apply in that case. If the world is different from the way we have presupposed it to be, then what we have said is simply irrelevant and is considered logically *vacuous*. Take, for example,

(4) It is surprising that Fred attended the meeting.

(4) tells us both that Fred attended the meeting and that that fact is surprising. But these two pieces of information are presented on different, unequal levels. Notice that the natural denials of (4), "No it isn't," or "No, it is not surprising that Fred attended the meeting," do not deny that Fred attended the meeting, but only that that fact is surprising. Now (4) is naturally considered false if its natural denial is true. But notice that if Fred did not attend the meeting then (4) is again not true. And neither is its natural denial above. In fact, if Fred did not attend the meeting it simply does not make any sense to argue about whether the "fact" that he did is surprising or not. We distinguish then two ways a declarative sentence can fail to be true: one, a sentence will be called *false* if its natural denial is true; and two, it will be called *vacuous* if neither it nor its natural denial is true. The presuppositions of a declarative sentence S, then, can be defined as those sentences which must be true for S to be *nonvacuous*. Thus (4) above presupposes that "Fred attended the meeting." It merely *asserts* that that fact is surprising. And in general the *assertions* of a sentence S will be defined to be those entailments of S which are not presuppositions—that is, those sentences which must hold if S is true but need not hold if S is false.

This definition of assertion and presupposition is further established by considering *questions*. In the same way that only the assertions of a sentence can be naturally denied so it is only the assertions of a sentence which are naturally questioned. Thus,

(5) Is it surprising that Fred attended the meeting?

does not question whether Fred attended the meeting, but only whether that fact is surprising or not. In general we may define the presuppositions of a question to be those sentences which must hold for the question to have a true answer. For yes/no questions, such as (5) above, it is easily seen that either *yes* or *no* is a true answer depending on whether the corresponding declarative is true or false. Thus the presuppositions of a yes/no question are the same as the presuppositions of the corresponding declarative, and so it is only the assertions of a sentence which can be naturally questioned.

Notice that the class of English predicates which, like "surprising," make presuppositions is rather large and includes "strange," "ironic," "regrettable," and "annoying." Such predicates contrast with ones like "possible," "probable," and "necessary." "It is probable that Fred left" does not presuppose that "Fred left." This distinction in predicate type also extends to verbs like "regret," "resent," "realize" as compared with ones like "think," "believe," "hope," and "doubt." Thus "Mary regretted that Fred attended the meeting" presupposes that Fred did attend the meeting, and so does its natural denial, "No she didn't." However, if "regretted" is replaced by "thought" in the above examples, the corresponding sentences do not presuppose that Fred attended the meeting. So "regret" is presuppositional whereas "thought" is not.

Presuppositional predicates then determine one class of presupposition structure in natural language; a second such class is determined by definite, restrictive relative clauses like this one:

(6) *The only doctor who is taking the course* needs money.

Clearly (6) presupposes that some doctor, in fact just one, is taking the course. The natural denial of (6), "No he doesn't," does not deny the existence of such a doctor but only denies that he needs money. If no such doctor exists, then neither (6) nor its natural denial is true, so (6) is untrue in the vacuous way. Furthermore, the natural way to question (6), "Does he really?" does not question the existence of the doctor, but only whether he needs money. In general then, it is easy to see that the information in a declarative sentence is presented on two unequal levels: what is presupposed and what is explicitly asserted. And it is also easy to see how sentences which are true in the same conditions and therefore have the same entailments can differ in meaning: they merely partition the entailments differently between those which are presupposed and those which are merely asserted. One sentence may explicitly assert, for example, much of what the other presupposes. Compare in this regard (6) "The only doctor who is taking the course needs money," with (7):

(7) Exactly one doctor is taking the course and any doctor who is taking the course needs money.

A little reflection shows that (6) and (7) are true in the same conditions. But (7) explicitly asserts that exactly one doctor is taking the course whereas (6) presupposes it. And in general when we "paraphrase" a complex sentence by a conjunction of sentences, each of which captures one of the ideas of the original, we elevate some presupposed material to the level of assertion. And since assertions are more explicit than presuppositions this explains our informal feeling that (7) is more explicit than (6).

The distinction between assertion and presupposition is not only logical but psychological as well. For example, it is more of an affront to challenge what someone has presupposed than what he has merely asserted. In the latter case we are merely saying that the speaker is mistaken on a point of fact. But in the former case we are saying that what the speaker has said does not make logical sense. Thus one might naturally deny the assertion of the sentence, "The girl John went out with last night is engaged to be married," merely by saying, "No she isn't. You're mistaken." But in denying the presuppositions of that sentence, an emotional response like "What are you talking about!? John was right here with me last night!" would be more natural.

The fact that presuppositions are difficult to challenge is often cleverly used. Consider the sign in a restaurant which says, "The management regrets that no dogs are allowed on the premises." This communicates by presupposition the idea that you can't bring your dog to the table. But it asserts only that the management regrets that fact. It would be pointless to disagree with the assertion of the sign, for the management is surely the proprietor of its own emotions. The prohibiting information is put in the presupposed position, as though its truth were independent of the policies of the management.

A Model for Translation

We have argued that the meaning of a sentence is, at least in part, the different ways the sentence is semantically related to other sentences. So to say that two sentences have the same meaning is to say, for example, that they answer the same questions and make the same assertions and presuppositions. Our model of semantic analysis then provides a natural model for translation from one language to another: *for two sentences of different languages to be exact translations of each other they must be semantically related to other sentences of their respective languages in exactly the same ways.* For example, if, in some language, a sentence S presupposes a sentence T then any exact translation of S into another language must presuppose the exact translation of T.

To take a concrete example, we have already seen that (7) "Exactly one doctor is taking the course and any doctor who is taking the course needs money" does not mean exactly the same thing as (6) "The only doctor who is taking the course needs money," because the two sentences do not have exactly the same presuppositions and assertions. For the same reason (7) is not an exact translation of (8) below although (6) presumably is.

(8) Le seul médecin qui suit le cours a besoin d'argent.

Using this translation paradigm it is natural to consider that two languages are the same in logical expressive power if each sentence of one has an exact translation in the other. We can now sensibly ask whether all natural languages are equal in expressive power, or are there ideas expressible in one language that cannot be *exactly* expressed in some other?

We shall argue that in fact languages are not all equivalent in expressive power. This is because they differ systematically with respect to presupposition structures. Specifically we will show that languages differ in the syntactic means they use to form restrictive relative clauses which as we have seen in (6) are presuppositional structures. Some languages allow us to form relative clauses in contexts where English, for example, does not. Sentences containing these relative clauses are not naturally translatable into English in a way that preserves the presuppositions of the original.

Thus consider the English relative clause in (9) and its natural translation in Hebrew, (10).

(9)   the woman that *John gave the book to*

(10) ha- isha   she- *Yon natan la*   *et ha- sefer*
    the woman that John gave to her   the book

The Hebrew differs from the English in that the subordinate clause (italicized) contains a personal pronoun, *la,* in the indirect object position after the verb *natan* "gave." In fact in Hebrew the subordinate clause is a full sentence which identifies the woman referred to in (10). It is the sentence which would normally be used to say, "John gave the book to her," in a situation in which a woman was known to the speaker and hearer. In the English relative clause (9), on the other hand, the subordinate clause is not a sentence because the verb *gave* lacks an indirect object. The Hebrew relative clause is logically more transparent than the English one then, since it presents explicitly an entire sentence identifying the person referred to by the relative clause.

Not surprisingly, then, Hebrew allows relative clauses to be formed in syntactic contexts not possible in English. For example, in English we cannot relativize into the position of one member of a coordinate noun phrase. (11b) is not an acceptable way to refer to the man mentioned in (11a):

(11) a. The man and his son went to New York

    b. * I see the man $\begin{Bmatrix} who \\ that \end{Bmatrix}$ and his son went to New York

Yet the corresponding relative clause is well formed in Hebrew:

(12) *Ani roa et ha- ish she- hu   uvno   halxo le New York*
    I   see   the man that he and his son went to New York

Similarly, in English it is not possible to relativize into a position already contained in a relative clause. (13b) cannot be used to refer to the woman of (13a):

(13) a. I know the man who gave the woman a book
    b. * This is the woman that I know the man that gave a book

But again the corresponding relative clause in Hebrew is possible:

(14) *Zot   ha- isha   she- ami makir et ha- ish   she- natan*
    That is the woman that I   know   the man that gave
    la   et ha- sefer
    to her   the book

In a detailed study[3] I have compared relative clause formation in languages like English which do not retain pronouns in the subordinate clause with languages[4] like Hebrew which do. The results of this investigation overwhelmingly support the claim that pronoun retention extends the class of well-formed relative clauses. We conclude, then, that languages differ systematically with respect to the possibility of relative clause formation.

Translating sentences like (14) containing "impossible" relative clauses into English is a definite problem. The relative clause part cannot, as we have seen, be naturally translated as a relative clause in English. The only alternative we know of would factor the information in (14) in two parts, each simpler than (14) itself. We might try, for example, "I know a man that gave some woman a book and this is that woman." But this sentence fails to be an exact translation of (14). For one thing, it asserts "I know some man" whereas this information is presupposed in (14). And, as any translation that factors (14) into distinct conjuncts will similarly assert some of what is presupposed in (14), we can tentatively conclude that there is no translation of (14) into English which has exactly the same pattern of assertions and presuppositions. Consequently languages are not exactly identical in expressive power.

This conclusion must not of course be read as implying that Hebrew is in any general way logically more expressive than English. We have merely shown that there are certain types of relative clauses that can be formed in Hebrew but not in English. Conversely there are also relative clauses that can be formed in English but not in Hebrew. For example, it is possible in English to "stack" relative clauses as in (15).

(15) The students who left early who were drunk began to fight.

But "stacking" relative clauses is not, in general, possible in Hebrew. The general way to translate sentences like (15) is as in (16) where the two subordinate clauses are conjuncted.[5]

(16) The students who left early and who were drunk began to fight

Our main conclusion is not that some languages are logically more expressive than others, but merely that languages are not exactly equivalent in logical expressive power.

REFERENCES

1. My presentation of standard logic owes much to the lectures on logic given by Dr. John Corcoran at the University of Pennsylvania in 1966-1967.

2. This type of example was first pointed out to me by Robert D. Hull.

3. The initial results are presented in Edward L. Keenan, "On Semantically Based Grammar," *Linguistic Inquiry,* III, No. 4 (1972), 413-461.

4. The languages investigated were Hebrew, Arabic, Welsh, Persian, Batak (spoken in Sumatra), Urhobo (spoken in Nigeria), Aoba (spoken in the New Hebrides), and Gilbertese (the language of the Gilbert Islands in the Pacific).

5. I am indebted to Asa Kasher for pointing out to me the logical difference between conjoining and stacking subordinate clauses.

D. TERENCE LANGENDOEN

The Problem of Linguistic Theory in Relation to Language Behavior: A Tribute and Reply to Paul Goodman

LINGUISTIC SCIENCE coexists uneasily with the facts of human verbal behavior. Most theoretical linguists have a tendency to abstract away from the way people talk to an idealized conception of what it is to talk. Thus they fail to take into account a great deal of what people in fact say and how they say it, and at the same time insist on considering many things that no one has ever said or is ever likely to say. Every once in a while someone comes along to castigate those linguists on this curious relation of their work to actual speech behavior. One of the most recent spokesmen for the individual language user is the late Paul Goodman. With characteristic bluntness, he wrote, in *Speaking and Language: Defence of Poetry:*[1]

Again and again I find myself dissenting from the main line of the scientific linguists of the past fifty years—the anthropologists, the positivists, and the structuralists. (The authors I mean are [Edward] Sapir, [Benjamin Lee] Whorf, [Ferdinand de] Saussure, Leonard Bloomfield, Louis Hjelmslev, Zellig Harris, [Roman] Jakobson, [Noam] Chomsky, [Lev] Vygotsky.) It seems to me that in abstracting language from speaking and hearing in actual situations, they make three fundamental, and connected mistakes: (1) They exaggerate constancy and supra-individuality as against the variability and interpersonality of natural language; the "language" that they discuss, with its constant forms and self-contained rules, is sometimes an artifact of their method of investigation. (2) They say that the forms of language can rarely, if ever, be explained by meanings in experience and practical use, and the forms themselves do not have meaning. (3) They have a disposition to treat language and communication as a calculus of forms and a processing of information that could dispense with human speakers and hearers altogether.

Goodman was careful to point out that he did not think that the results of such theorizing have been totally worthless: on Hjelmslev's dictum that "[t]he linguistic theoretician . . . sets up a general calculus in which all conceivable cases are foreseen," he commented: "Incidentally, I have a lot of respect for this kind of musico-mathematical enterprise. It is often beautiful in itself, and it sometimes does cast light on real things."[2] Rather, Goodman argued, it would be better to do linguistic analysis like art or literary

197

criticism, in a "reasoned but *a posteriori*" manner, not like mathematics. In this way, linguistics would not operate merely on the made-up samples of human speech that it characteristically analyzes; instead it would have to come to grips with "the most intimate speech, the most convivial speech, the most expressive speech, the most poetic speech,"[3] most of which linguistic science currently labels deviant.

Goodman pointed out that much of what he had to say about the nature of language and its use was said forty years ago or more by such anthropologists as Edward Burnett Tyler, Franz Boas, and most pointedly, Bronislaw Malinowski.[4] It is interesting to speculate why Malinowski's view that the proper study of language is the study of speech events in their original "contexts of situation"[5] never caught on at all in anthropology and only marginally in linguistics. Its failure to be adopted cannot have been due to its having been out of step with the prevailing theoretical goals of the social sciences of the times, since his approach was rigidly behavioristic and behaviorism was then in the ascendant. The reason, I believe, is that Malinowski's techniques could not be applied in any thoroughgoing way by other anthropologists and linguists, because training in those techniques was simply not available to graduate students. Although, in linguistics, Malinowski's banner was indeed taken up by the British linguist John Rupert Firth, he never did more than argue abstractly for the concept of studying language use in context; he never took it upon himself to show anyone how to do so effectively.[6]

In the past few years, however, the situation has changed. First of all, structural linguistics is a very different discipline now from what it was ten years ago, not to mention forty years ago. The dominant figure in linguistics today, as everyone acknowledges, is Noam Chomsky, and while Chomsky's name is properly listed by Goodman as one who may be accused of "abstracting language from speaking and hearing in actual situations," he must also be credited with having greatly enriched our collective conception of what it is to be human beings, for only human beings possess the wonderfully intricate system of rules that underlies language. Second, there has now grown up around pure linguistic science a host of cross-disciplinary approaches to language that study it in relation to human development, to human anatomy and physiology (notably that of the ears, nose, throat, mouth, and brain); and to social structures, conventions, and institutions. Recently, that is, just those sorts of things Goodman was interested in seeing studied are, in fact, being studied, but in conjunction with and in relation to the abstract study of language, not in place of it.

One way of looking at these contemporary developments is to examine how scholars today analyze an individual's *verbal ability*. They distinguish three separate components; first, the ability to understand speech and to listen, the faculty for speech *perception;* second, the ability to talk, the faculty for speech *production;* and third, the ability to judge what count as samples of a given language in a laboratory setting, the faculty for speech *prediction*. The first two components of verbal ability, perception and production, relate primarily to language in actual use. The third component, which is partially independent of the other two, accounts for each individual's ability to deal with his native language (or languages) as an autonomous system (or systems); it is this component, in other words, which corresponds to Chomsky's notion of an internalized grammar. This grammar must be assumed to exist in order to account for a person's ability to predict whether something not previously encountered belongs to his language. It is now generally recognized, however, that the processes of ordinary speaking and listening go on essentially independently of this internalized grammar. Speaking does not require a mental construction of what one says by means of one's grammar, nor does listening require a mental reconstruction of what one hears. In the latter case, we can now point to the existence of gestalt-like rules by which a person maps what he hears directly onto an image indicating what he thinks that acoustical event means.[7]

With this division of verbal ability in mind, it should come as no surprise to find that some things which people spontaneously say and understand will, when taken out of context, be judged by the same people as not part of their language. Similarly, it should not be surprising to learn that they will judge as part of their language some things which are never spontaneously said and which would be difficult or impossible to understand. In other words, the tension that we noted at the beginning of this essay between linguistic science and the facts of language use exists within each individual.

Before illustrating these points with examples, let me introduce a further terminological distinction. We say that an expression is *acceptable* if it may be used spontaneously in a given context, and that it is *grammatical* if it may be judged, independent of context, to be part of the language. It is easy to construct examples of sentences that are grammatical but unacceptable in any context. Consider, for example, one way in which we modify a noun in English, namely by adding a clause after the noun in which the noun is understood as the direct object. Thus, if we have a sentence which is both acceptable in some contexts and grammatical, such as "The tiger died," we can form a new sentence, also acceptable and grammatical, "The tiger the elephant gored died." The clause "the elephant gored" modifies the noun "tiger"; "tiger," moreover, is understood as the direct object of the verb "gored." Grammatically, the noun "elephant" in the latter sentence can in turn be modified in exactly the same way, but if it is, the resulting sentence is likely to be unacceptable in all contexts: "The tiger the elephant the fly bit gored died." Such a sentence may *seem* ungrammatical, but in fact it is not, as anyone can readily convince himself, once he understands the underlying mechanism for constructing such sentences. Conversely, many ungrammatical sentences are acceptable in certain contexts, and their deviance from full grammaticality may go completely unnoticed. Literature abounds with examples. Rebecca West has been cited for the following striking example: "A copy of the universe is not what is required of art; one of the damned thing is ample."[8] The first paragraph of Charles Dickens's *Bleak House*, which consists entirely of sentence fragments, is an even more spectacular case of this sort.

Confusion about acceptability and grammatically has led some people, Goodman included, to wonder whether grammaticality judgments are reliable, or even possible. Goodman's statement of his skepticism is quite typical: "If I am asked if a sentence is grammatical or idiomatic, I often find it quite impossible to answer without considerable speculation about its meaning in possible contexts. My immediate spontaneous judgment of an isolated sentence is not reliable."[9] It is quite right to say that grammaticality judgments, except in the very simplest cases, cannot be rendered spontaneously, but speculating about the appropriateness of expressions to possible contexts is not the way to obtain correct judgments of grammaticality. At most such speculations can lead only to judgments of potential acceptability. Judgments of grammaticality can be rendered, in complex cases, only under controlled conditions, in which comparisons with other examples and perhaps conscious reflection on grammatical processes are undertaken.

Goodman was confused about meaning as well as grammaticality. In this case, too, the contemporary view concerning the partitioning of verbal ability is helpful. When considered in isolation, linguistic expressions can be seen to have meaning solely by virtue of their form: the words that appear in them and their internal syntactic organization. This we may call the *conventional meaning* of those expressions. There is also, however, meaning by virtue of context, specifically the context of interpersonal communication that interested Goodman so much. Paul Grice, who has done significant study on this aspect of meaning, labels it *conversational meaning* (following an older tradition, this would be one aspect of pragmatics). To illustrate the distinction between conventional and conversational meaning, we may consider the question, "Will you be busy tonight?" and its answer, "No." Conventionally, the question asks for information, whether the hearer will be occupied later that day. The answer indicates, conventionally, that the hearer will not be occupied. Conversationally, however, the questioner may be indicating that he is about to extend an invitation to the hearer, and the hearer may be indicating that he would be receptive to that as yet unspoken invitation.

The systematic study of conventional meaning has of course been pursued for a long time within both linguistics and philosophy; the systematic study of conversational meaning is of more recent vintage. Broadly speaking, two major lines of investigation have been developed to deal with conversational meaning. The followers of what might be called the *func-*

tional approach (associated with the philosophers John Austin, John Searle and Paul Grice) have examined speech in given situations and tried to identify its specific functions and to create axioms which define the nature of the acts it performs. The followers of the *structural* approach (associated with the sociologists Harvey Sacks, Emanuel Schegloff and others) attempt, on the other hand, to relate the structural relations within and among utterances to specific aspects of the situations in which the conversations take place. Functionalists hold that the conversational meaning of an expression may be deduced from an examination of its conventional meaning plus the application of axioms based on *a priori* functional considerations. Thus a conversational axiom might be: "If, conventionally, a person appears to be contributing nothing new to the conversation (by uttering a logical truth), then, conversationally, he must be saying something different." Structuralists relate what is said more directly to the situation at hand; they analyze conversational meaning by referring to the structure of the interpersonal situation as well as to the structure of the verbal material itself. It is important to note that the two groups unite in their belief that something systematic can be said about conversational meaning, whereas earlier, such philosophers as Charles Morris and Rudolf Carnap thought that whatever was pragmatic was necessarily idiosyncratic. They do, however, tend to focus on different aspects of conversational meaning: the functionalists on substantive aspects such as what was actually said; the structuralists on formal aspects such as how closure and turn-taking are determined.

The basic problem with the functionalist approach is that one cannot create a reasonably delimited list of workable axioms without first sharply limiting the kinds of interactions to be accounted for. Thus, functionalists have not been able to deal with conversational meaning that is at any great remove from conventional meaning. To deal with more complex conversational meanings, something along the lines of Goodman's "reasoned but *a posteriori*" approach is still necessary.

The structuralists, however, by paying close attention to interactional and verbal detail, and then manipulating their observations in the manner of a grammarian manipulating syntax, may be able to discover when certain fairly subtle conversational rules of interpretation operate. Consider, for example, the verbal exchange we used earlier:

A. Will you be busy tonight?

B. No.

Remember that we contend that if A and B are friends, then A's question may be interpreted conversationally as an expression of desire to extend an invitation to B and B's response can be seen as an indication of his receptiveness.

Let us make some further observations. First, note that the conversation is naturally continued by A's actually extending the invitation and by B's accepting or modifying it to suit his desires:

A. Then how about I pick you up at 8:00 to go bowling?

B. O.K. But let's make it for 8:30 instead.

It would be unnatural for B to turn A down flatly at this point. If he really wasn't going to be busy but wanted to be left alone, he would probably have said so or made up a story about being busy in reply to A's first question. Second, note that B can anticipate A's invitation by asking, in reply to A's first question, what A has in mind, or by stating that he is open to suggestions. These kinds of replies would only be intelligible if, in fact, B thought that A had an invitation up his sleeve. Third, A's initial question can be varied syntactically, without making any significant change in its conversational meaning as long as its conventional meaning inquires about what B will or will not be doing that evening. For example, A could ask, among other things, "Are you busy tonight?" "Are you doing anything tonight?" "What are you going to be doing tonight?" or "Will you be free this evening?" Fourth, the conversational meaning we have been describing vanishes as soon as we alter the social roles of A and B in certain ways. For example, if A is the person who precedes B on a work shift, and he asks B "Will you be busy tonight?" as he is going off duty, then that question will be interpreted as a literal inquiry as to whether much will be going on that evening. A may be intending to ask B to do him a favor, but B, unless he is wary, or A is a known asker of favors, would have no reason to anticipate such a request.

All of this suggests the existence of a conversational rule. Put in the form of a conversational axiom, the rule is that if a person asks a friend about what that friend is doing during a stretch of time in the near future, then he is asking the friend to make that time available for friendly joint pursuits.[10]

In the foregoing account of the conversational meaning of a particular kind of verbal exchange, I used the structuralist's method, but ended with a functionalist's statement. This is because I believe that this particular blend of the two approaches to conversational meaning yields the most significant and interesting results.[11] The functionalists provide the better overall theoretical framework, and the structuralists the better working method. But, however conversational meaning is gotten at, it is clear that it exists side by side with conventional meaning, just as we saw earlier that acceptability coexists with grammaticality. One pair (acceptability and conversational meaning) is needed for dealing with how language is used; the other (grammaticality and conventional meaning) for dealing with how it is structured.

REFERENCES

1. Paul Goodman, *Speaking and Language: Defence of Poetry* (New York: Vintage Books, 1972), pp. 86-87.

2. *Ibid.*, p. 99.

3. *Ibid.*, p. 137.

4. *Ibid.*, pp. 52-53.

5. This is the phrase Malinowski used in *Coral Gardens and Their Magic*, II, the work that provides the most complete account of his mature thinking about language (New York: American Book Company, 1935).

6. For detailed discussion of Malinowski's theory of language, and Firth's development of it, see D. Terence Langendoen, *The London School of Linguistics* (Cambridge: M.I.T. Press, 1968).

7. For examples, see Thomas G. Bever, "The Cognitive Basis of Linguistic Structures," *Cognition and the Development of Language*, ed. John Hayes (New York: Wiley, 1970).

8. Noam Chomsky, *Problems of Knowledge and Freedom* (New York: Pantheon Books, 1971), pp. 32-33.

9. Goodman, *Speaking and Language*, p. 90.

10. In case the friends are particularly close, so that A may in fact presume upon B's time for a favor (such as baby-sitting), the purpose for which A is asking B to make time available may be different. To handle this, we may generalize the conversational rule by deleting the phrase "for friendly joint pursuits"; what use A wishes to make of B's time will then be based on the strength of their friendship.

11. For an outstanding structuralist-functionalist account of "sounding" among New York City black adolescents, see William Labov, "Rules for Ritual Insult," *Studies in Social Interaction*, ed. David Sudnow (New York: Free Press, 1972).

· app·

DAVID G. HAYS

Language and Interpersonal Relationships

How DOES LANGUAGE engender love?

This problem has been examined by poets and mystics, by psychoanalysts and social psychologists, by linguists and laymen for a long time. My purpose is to show some of the elements of a possible scientific treatment. Science is always a matter of detail, of explaining the gross in terms of the minute, of passing from macroscopic description to microscopic analysis. When science is successful, the statements that it makes about minute details are powerful generalizations, as when the physicist discovers that a few forces, or a handful of particles, are all he needs to explain phenomena of enormous macroscopic variety. A scientific discussion of how language provides a vehicle for social relationships must therefore consist, as I see it, of an analysis of the mechanism of human affection, an analysis of the mechanism of speech, and a comparison of the two. Unfortunately, any discussion of this fundamental problem must be highly speculative. Nevertheless, I feel that the present discussion is justified by the value of summarizing the speculations of a number of predecessors and contemporaries, by the existence of a few rather recent observations and experiments that may be the precursors of a new wave, and by the resulting possibility of speculating today on a slightly deeper level than heretofore.

My first concern is to set forth the general understanding of social interaction that I have gained from my early training in social psychology; next I offer some speculations about our capacity to form images of one another as the core of our system of social interaction. Next I discuss the notion that both our social nature and our linguistic skill are part of us in a way that more superficial learnings are not. I ask what kind of mechanism might account both for this difference, and for the use of social skills and linguistic skills together in conversation. Then I apply the mechanism I suggest to the question of how both language and social relationships grow and change. Finally, I describe a hypothetical system consisting of three coordinated models which I think might explain human behavior if it could be constructed.

Social Interaction

Contrary to a vein of popular anti-intellectual sentiment, most professional opinion holds that language is the vehicle of socialization, of group solidarity, of tension release, of psychotherapy, and of love. Language could not exist without culture, according to A. L. Kroeber, the great anthropologist, nor culture without language:

> Speculatively, different conclusions might be reached. It is difficult to imagine any generalized thinking taking place without words or symbols derived from words. Religious beliefs and certain phases of social organization also seem dependent on speech: caste ranking, marriage regulations, kinship recognition, law, and the like.[1]

According to Martin Buber, the conversation of friends and of lovers serves, at its best, to confirm them as particular human beings. The psychoanalyst Leslie H. Farber puts it this way: "Real talk between a man and a woman offers the supreme privilege of keeping the other sane and being kept sane by the other."[2] To which I would add that good talk also makes each aware of his own sanity.

The question is how. For nothing else on the face of the earth has the same effect as conversation between human beings. The nature of this situation is illuminated somewhat by a small experiment that I conducted in 1956. (The experiment grew naturally out of my Ph.D. thesis. John Kennedy, then my department head at RAND and later professor and chairman of psychology at Princeton, was my senior collaborator. Since we never completed a version of the experiment that we deemed publishable, the results must be taken with a grain of salt.)

The experiment strips conversation down to its barest essentials by depriving the subject of all language except for two pushbuttons and two lights, and by suggesting to him that he is attempting to reach an accord with a mere machine. We brought two students into our building through different doors and led them separately to adjoining rooms. We told each that he was working with a machine, and showed him lights and pushbuttons. Over and over again, at a signal, he would press one or the other of two buttons, and then one of two lights would come on. If the light that appeared corresponded to the button he pressed, he was right; otherwise, wrong. The students faced identical displays, but their feedback was reversed: if student A pressed the *red* button, then a moment later student B would see the *red* light go on, and if student B pressed the *red* button, then student A would see the *red* light. On any trial, therefore, if the two students pressed matching buttons they would both be correct, and if they chose opposite buttons they would both be wrong.

We used a few pairs of RAND mathematicians; but they would quickly settle on one color, say *red*, and choose it every time. Always correct, they soon grew bored. The students began with difficulty, but after enough experience they would generally hit on something. Some, like the mathematicians, chose one color and stuck with it. Some chose simple alternations (*red-green-red-green*). Some chose double alternations (*red-red-green-green*). Some adopted more complex patterns (four *red*, four *green*, four *red*, four *green*, sixteen mixed and mostly incorrect, then repeat). The students, although they were sometimes wrong, were rarely bored. They were busy figuring out the complex patterns of the machine.

But where did the patterns come from? Although neither student knew it, they arose out of the interaction of two students. I think that certain fairly simple patterns are common knowledge, and that by searching their histories for hypotheses the students provided patterns which, when their partners recognized them, formed the basis for agreement and success. I take this as a greatly oversimplified metaphor for social interaction. What patterns, then, do people bring from their common experience into a new situation that enable them to coordinate their behavior in the way the students did?

The terms generally used are *role* and *status*. In Ralph Linton's formulation, "A status . . . is simply a collection of rights and duties." Each student comes to the experiment with no fixed plan, only a generalized sense of *duty* to get as many right as he can or, perhaps, to figure out the machine. He thinks that he has, in turn, a *right* to expect reasonable behavior from the machine. After a time, each student concocts much more detailed specifications about his rights and duties. He feels a duty to punch *red* on certain trials and *green* on others; and a right, in turn, to expect corresponding behavior from the machine. "A role represents the dynamic aspect of a status. . . . When he puts the rights and duties which constitute the status quo into effect, he is performing a role."[3]

In daily life, however, the roles we play have *conditional elements*; if a condition is met, then we emit a gesture, a word, or a behavior that rewards or punishes the partner who met the condition. The condition not being met, we act differently. Since each person acts according to such conditions, social relationships have a special complexity. Talcott Parsons distinguishes simple contingency from *double contingency*: The animal in a learning experiment has something to learn "which is stable independently of what the animal does. . . . But in social interaction alter's possible 'reactions' may cover a considerable range, selection within which is contingent on ego's actions."[4]

Let us look at the way people operate in conversations by imagining them to be playing a game. The game-playing situation excludes many variables, but permits us to see more complexity than was apparent in my pushbutton experiment. The gameplayer sets up *conditions* or expectations which are less than *rights* definitely due him and somewhat dependent on the nature of the game. Each player responds according to how his

partner meets these conditions. Since each player knows that the other
is looking at him and making just the same kind of judgments as he is, he
is operating in a *double contingency* situation; the effect of a move is
determined in part by the rules of the game and the roll of the dice, and in
part by what the other player thinks the effect is *intended* to be. In
Strategic Interaction, Erving Goffman considers the problems of Harry,
a hard-pressed player in a hypothetical game. He suggests that Harry must
look at the other player and think about

(a) What the other side could possibly do.
(b) What the other side wants, and what style of play it has adopted.
(c) What resolve the other side exhibits.
(d) What information the other side has.
(e) What resources the other side has.
(f) How gameworthy the other side is.

In addition, Goffman describes the characteristics which tend to make
a person a successful game player:

the intellectual proclivity to assess all possible courses of action and their consequences ... ; the practice of setting aside all personal feelings and all impulsive
inclinations in assembling the situation and in following a course of action; the
ability to think and act under pressure without becoming either flustered or transparent; the capacity to refrain from indulging in current displays of wit and character at the expense of long-term interests; and, of course, the ability and willingness to dissemble about anything.[5]

We come now to the most complex situation of all, that of ordinary
conversation. The philosophers of language present us with another slant
on double contingency. Grice analyzed the notion of saying something
and meaning it, and John Searle expanded his analysis.[6] To begin with,
saying something consists of a speaker's uttering a sentence. *Meaning it*
has to do with the speaker's *purpose.* He intends his utterance to produce
in the hearer the knowledge that the state of affairs specified by the
sentence do obtain. The knowledge produced in a listener is what Searle
calls the *illocutionary* effect of an utterance. The speaker intends his
utterance to produce its illocutionary effect by means of the hearer's
recognition of his first intention. Clearly, saying something and meaning it
are different from being understood. However, the speaker expects that his
first intention will be recognized by virtue of the hearer's knowledge. At
least when dealing with a person of the same language and background,
he assumes that his hearer knows the rules of communication and expects
him to apply them. Hence a conversation is a serial interchange of remarks within a social setting that gives each participant some *role,* narrowly or broadly defined, to act out, and a *status* with which to analyze
what others do.

On closer inspection, however, conversation proves even more complex. Harold Garfinkel is a student of conversation. He sets his undergraduate students preposterous assignments, and some critics consider the conclusions he draws equally preposterous. My own opinion is rather more favorable than that. For example, Garfinkel asked some students to write down what the participants in a conversation actually said, then in parallel what they understood the participants to be talking about. He drew the following conclusions.

(a) Much was left unsaid.

Each participant in a conversation has a great store of factual knowledge, both general and particular—I like to call it his *encyclopedia*—and each knows more or less what is in the others' encyclopedias. If a speaker assumes too much knowledge, his hearer does not understand. If the speaker assumes too little, the hearer is irritated by his obtuseness. For example, Schegloff has observed transactions involving place names. Many correct ways of referring to a given place are always available, but the social relationships of the conversants make some ways right, others wrong. If, for example, I am asking my wife to meet me at our common home for dinner between the day's work and the evening's excursion, and name it by street address, city, and state, she will question my sanity.[7]

(b) To understand what was said required knowledge of what was left unspoken. The speaker, in other words, depends on the hearer to fill in missing links from his store of knowledge.

(c) "Many matters were understood through a process of attending to the temporal series of utterances as documentary evidences of a developing conversation rather than as a string of terms."

What I think this means is that the participant understands the conversation as a whole, using various portions of it to control the interpretation of other parts.

(d) Understanding required that both participants see the conversation as pointing to "an underlying pattern of matters" they already shared.

(e) The participants used the "biography and prospects of the present interaction" as an aid to understanding.

(f) "Each waited for something more to be said in order to hear what had previously been talked about, and each seemed willing to wait."[8]

Garfinkel's findings, insofar as they can be trusted, warn us against a simple-minded model of conversation. We might imagine that the hearer absorbs and understands each remark from the speaker, perhaps issuing from time to time a warning that he has not understood or a request for clarification. Garfinkel claims, on the contrary, that understanding develops gradually throughout the interchange, the earlier remarks being, as it were, half understood and held over for later re-examination.

Finding something suitable to say at a given moment in a conversation is often a delicate matter. What one says can alter one's relationship with another person. Little seems to be known about this problem, but Michael Moerman hypothesizes a process he calls *finding a breach*.[9] In his illustration, one participant has complained repeatedly about a child's tardiness. Noticing that an account of the absent one's tardiness is needed (finding a breach), and choosing to take sides with the present speaker as against the absent child, another participant says, "Well, she must have gone visiting around the market." Many such devices will have to be recognized before we can understand how conversations go.

Images

If Erving Goffman's game player, Harry, succeeds in thinking about his opponent's (or his partner's) ability, wishes, style, resolve, information, resources, and gameworthiness, it seems reasonable to say that Harry has a well-developed *image* of his opponent or partner. I want to get across the idea that knowledge of a person is different from other kinds of knowledge. One has knowledge of himself, and knowledge of family members and intimate friends; one also has knowledge of the different kinds of persons one is likely to encounter in daily life. All these images of persons, specific or generalized, are different from knowledge of tables and chairs because the added complexity of double contingency applies only to persons.

This concept is by no means new; on the contrary, it has been known in social psychology for half a century. Unfortunately, one tends to think of the human head as a kind of picture gallery, containing pictures of parents, siblings, and other significant persons. The inadequacy of this metaphor, however, is revealed when we consider the purposes the images have to serve. We use our image of a person not only to calculate the responses he is likely to make to a proposed course of action, but also to test what we ourselves are saying. As George Herbert Mead puts it, "A person who is saying something is saying to himself what he says to others; otherwise he does not know what he is talking about."[10] Furthermore, "To understand himself man needs to be understood by another. To be understood by another he needs to understand the other."[11] The point is that a picture cannot understand a person; the *image* we need is something more active.

Our thought processes are both active and intricate. When we try to find analogies for them nothing outside of man seems adequately complex. In the eighteenth century, the metaphor used to help understand this great complexity was that of fluids in networks of tubes, Later, electrical analogies were used, culminating in the switchboard metaphor when the telephone system was the most intricate object in technology. Today, the computer is the most complex machine, and thus the best available metaphor for thought. To use it is not to claim that man is a machine, or to claim that machines can think. But what better model do we have to aid our thinking about human nature?

A computer is a machine, and its behavior is determined by a combination of factors: by the physical construction of the machine itself, by the program of instructions supplied to the machine, and by the data on which the program operates. A program can ordinarily be subdivided into parts which are also programs or subprograms. Now one program can call on another; several different programs for making engineering calculations can employ the same subprogram for finding, let us say, square roots.

According to this metaphor, a person's head contains a number of programs called *Self, Mother, Father, Dick* (a friend), *Jane* (another friend), *Professor* (if the person in question is capable of distinguishing professors from other persons, but not one professor from another), *Plumber* (if the person has a general view of that trade), and so on, down to *Generalized Other*, the program the person calls on when all else fails.

All of these programs are active, in the sense that any one of them is capable of regulating conduct. No doubt *Self* is always the most elaborate, but, in fact, the metaphor suggests that all of the programs are basically rather simple, and use subprograms for almost every purpose. Most subprograms are suitable for use when dealing with most images. If I have subprograms for choosing foods from a menu for myself or others to eat, then I can use the same program for *Self, Mother,* and many of the rest. What I know about the person Dick, however, may qualify my program-image of him in such a way that I choose to use a somewhat different menu subprogram when choosing for him.

Now, when I speak to my friend Dick, in order to determine whether what I am saying makes sense to him, I am simultaneously using my image *Dick,* my capacity for understanding speech, and my subprograms for taking part in conversation. Naturally, if I know that Dick's knowledge is different from my own, that difference qualifies my image *Dick* and affects the way I speak. When, according to my image *Dick,* the person Dick might fail to understand what I am about to say, then I edit my speech, stopping and restarting until I think that what I say will be comprehensible. Thus the speaker's image of the hearer is a feedback mechanism, a device to check the communicative effectiveness of what he is saying. In view of the importance of feedback in many facets of human behavior, this speculation about the need for elaborate feedback in speech production seems very plausible to me. And it seems plausible to speculate further that the systems furnishing feedback for speech are the same as those which make us truly social, and that they utilize both specific and generalized images of other people.

The relations among self, role, and other images can be thought of in this way. As my father is a person I know well, my program-image of him is very rich. I built it originally to help me understand him, and to help me predict how he would understand and respond to me. But this program is like any other in my head, and can serve not only to help me predict how my father will react, but also to control my own behavior. If I let it do so, but keep it and *Self* well apart, I am playing a *role*. But if I let some of the habits that originally belonged to *Father* become attached to *Self*, I have integrated a part of what was originally an image of another into my own personality.[12]

Internalization

I wish to use the term *internalization* to signify the conversion of one kind of memory into another. Since I believe that only mankind has these two kinds of memory, the conversion, or internalization, is a uniquely human phenomenon, and accounts, I believe, for many deeply human characteristics. Once again I use the computer metaphor to aid under-standing.

A computer has three parts: a store, an operations unit, and a central control. The store contains programs and data. The operations unit contains a circuit to perform necessary or desirable operations, such as adding, putting a datum into storage, or jumping from one part of a program to another when the proper conditions arise. The central control selects an instruction from storage, causes the operations unit to carry out the operation called for by that instruction, and then goes on to choose and carry out other instructions in exactly the same manner.

Furthermore, the number of operations is not fixed. It is known that a computer with just three different types of operation, correctly selected, can do anything any computer can do, no matter how many different types of operation it has. The programmer can write a long sequence of instructions using operations taken from a short list and achieve the same effect as with a short sequence of instructions using operations taken from a longer list.

Now, suppose the buyer of a computer finds that his programs often require the calculation of square roots. Each time a square root is needed, the computer has to execute a whole sequence of instructions found in storage. For economy, the computer owner may decide to purchase a square-root operation from the computer builder. It becomes a part of the physical machine, and can then be performed on the basis of a single instruction. Building in a new unit, in this case for finding square roots, is called *microprogramming*.

The brain, I think, is likewise able to store information both in the form of data or programs in a general-purpose store and as part of its structure. To some degree, this distinction corresponds to the familiar one between knowledge and skill, between what can be forgotten and what cannot. Some examples of information stored in a general-purpose store are the lines and cues I will speak in performing a role on stage, the grammar of a foreign language learned in high school, a procedure for calculation learned for an examination, and the route from my hotel to the railroad station in a foreign city. In contrast, here are some examples of information stored as part of the structure of my brain: my *Self* and the roles that I regularly enact in real life; the grammar of my native language, not as learned in school but as acquired in the early years of life; the grammar of any other language in which I can communicate with near-native proficiency; the tables of multiplication and addition that I acquired once and for all in school; and the route from home to office that I drive daily.

To tell which way a person stores a given piece of information, we can test the permanence of his knowledge, its reliability, and its speed of access. If he knows something instantly, reliably, and permanently, he has made it a part of the structure of his brain.

The behavioral repertory of any species of animal other than man is limited. Animals can learn all sorts of tricks, but human culture is indefinite in its variety. Two major aspects of culture are social roles and language. No matter what one's native language, one can employ its resources to describe any situation or event, however bizarre or unanticipated, and if speaker and hearer have a common language, the hearer will understand. Language is thus unlimited in its expressive power, and it seems fair to make a similar statement about social roles and statuses. Man is capable of acquiring and enacting incredibly fantastic roles. Limits of physical endurance must be admitted, of course, and even limits of speed and memory. But at bottom, all of culture is based on the human being's ability to invent new operations (in the metaphor of computing) and to make them part of himself.

Storing data is a kind of learning, and very important in human life. But the conversion of stored data into the permanent structure of the nervous system, *internalizing*, is what makes culture, society, and language possible.

Mechanisms

It is time to return to our original question: By what mechanism does language engender love and other interpersonal attitudes? Let us see how much help we can get from the computer metaphor.

If the sociologist brings together in his laboratory a group of persons who

know nothing of one another and gives them some relatively trivial problem to solve, they are faced implicitly with the problem of how to treat
one another. Their solution is to create a social structure, perhaps
superficial and evanescent, but nevertheless correlated with certain of
their interpersonal attitudes. R. F. Bales set up such a laboratory and recorded what went on. He trained observers to assign each remark to one
of twelve categories. Instead of recording the content of each interaction,
he recorded its social effect. Thus one act might increase tension in the
group, another provide the group with information, and so on. Bales and
his assistants also recorded who emitted each act, and who was target.
After an hour's discussion, the participants expressed privately their
opinions of one another.

Bales obtained two kinds of results. He found that his groups had a
rather clear tendency to begin a discussion with remarks in certain categories, proceed with others, and conclude a little differently. Although no
category was impossible at any stage, the mixture shifted with time. In
each group, certain persons took leading roles, and became emitters and
targets for acts in some categories more than for those in others. And it
was possible to calculate, from the content of the discussion, approximately
what opinions the participants would hold of one another.[13]

The work to date on social interaction has been less than satisfactory
in several respects. First, the overall patterns of change in category use
are not precisely definable, but only detectable as broad tendencies. Second, small-scale sequences defy analysis. Third, the connection between
substantive and social content—between the overt content of the remark
and its social value—has never been explicated in detail; even the trained
observer has to rely on his internalized system of interpretation, judging
how he would react if he were a participant in the discussion. Fourth, the
calculation of interpersonal relations as revealed by post-discussion attitude
questionnaires is not exact enough.

We would like to do better. We would like to go outside the laboratory,
and predict when conversation would lead to mutual love, when to hatred
or some less powerful feeling. Plainly to do this would require a detailed
understanding of mechanisms.

More as a metaphor for what must be understood than as a plan for
real work, we might imagine a computer with several programs running
simultaneously with a group's discussion. The first program, using phonological laws and the sound system of the participants' language, would
convert their speech into alphabetical form. The second program, using
grammatical laws and the grammar of their language, would parse the text
of each remark as it arrived, revealing its syntactic structure. The third
program would use semantic and other laws and facts to obtain a canonical form for the remark. The fourth program would compare the canonical
form with an encyclopedia of factual knowledge. A fifth program would

analyze the remark in terms of conversational strategy. Additional programs would bind the remark into a growing internal representation of the discussion, build up models of each participant's image of himself and of the other participants, and finally derive from all of this predictions as to the opinions each participant holds about each of the others.[14]

Consistent with this metaphor, let us hypothesize about some kinds of linguistic interaction which might induce love.

(a) *Confirmation.* Person A expresses opinions or preferences, etc. Person B agrees, elaborates, justifies, and otherwise confirms these opinions. Some theoreticians believe that this behavior tends to induce love for B in person A, at least under favorable circumstances.

(b) *Praise.* Person A describes himself and person B expresses a favorable opinion of the description.

(c) *Self-fulfillment.* Person A takes pleasure in the execution of certain subroutines that belong to A's Self. Person B provides the external stimulus that leads to successful completion of those subroutines.

(d) *Familiar patterns.* Person A takes pleasure in being the object of certain behaviors; in this instance, the pleasure attaches to the fulfillment of his image-program of B rather than to an element of Self.

(e) *Forgiveness.* Person A describes himself in negative terms. Person B recites extenuating circumstances, denies the importance of the terms named, and otherwise helps A forgive himself for his faults.

(f) *Intermingling.* Person A, through familiarity and close interaction with person B, develops an elaborate program-image of B, one which shares many subprograms with A's Self. If A has a favorable opinion of himself, this favorable attitude applies to each subprogram, hence to much of the image of B. Self-love thus becomes the basis for love of another.

I feel sure that many more hypotheses could be found in the literature and restated in terms of the mechanisms I have sketched. Once a microscopic model is proposed, its parts can be used—as I have been using Self and other program-images—to account for macroscopic events. Experimentation must then follow to see whether the hypotheses it suggests are valid. It seems to me that it is time now to study human love in this kind of scientific detail.

Metacommunication

To be human, many have said, is to be able to use symbols. Human symbolic systems differ from animal communication in several ways. One is the human being's ability to talk about anything in as much detail as he needs to—even if the topic is altogether new. Another is his ability to talk about speech; this is *metalinguistic communication.* If social roles and statuses are, as I suggest, part of symbolic culture along with language, then talk about them is *metacommunication.*

Language has several functions, such as passing on information about the environment, expressing emotional states, and exerting social control. Still another function of language is self-modification—a metalinguistic function. Roman Jakobson believes that, to a greater or lesser extent, each instance of speech serves each of these functions; in other words, every speech act changes the entire system of the language.[15] His critics, however, call this view exaggerated, pointing out that most speech acts change the language so little that their effect is negligible.

We should take note of the difference between explicit and implicit metacommunication. It is easy to assign a word a definite meaning by explicit statement: "Let us use the word *antinomy* when the paradox is certainly irresoluble." In other situations, where we are less sure of ourselves, implicit variations in meaning give us flexibility without forcing us to be precise. Several schemes for writing computer programs allow explicit metacommunication between the programmer and the computer system, but none so far allows implicit metacommunication.

The pressures that keep our language constant are very strong. The pressures for constancy in social relationships are much weaker. Metacommunication, not only the ability to redefine words but also the pressures against linguistic change, may be what gives language its practical flexibility, enabling a community of users to keep their language almost constant and yet to change it enough to keep up with changing circumstances. A similar kind of metacommunication, I think, must surely be what gives human relationships their firmness, their resistance to collapse. What I mean is that at every moment the partners in a relationship implicitly point up each other's smallest deviations from the established pattern of conduct. In the beginning of a relationship, when neither partner is quite committed, the implicit metacommunication consists of proposals about the form the relationship might take. Person A tries out a role from his stock of program-images, person B does the same, and each gives the other signals which cause him to alter the roles and images whereby he analyzes himself and his partner. As this process goes on, either the would-be partners fail and give up, or else they come reasonably close to conformity to one another's images.

Note that this establishment and maintenance of social relationships is done by means of implicit metacommunication, for the most part without the partners specifically communicating about patterns, just as the two students in the Hays-Kennedy experiment established a pattern of common activity without specific communication on the subject. Ordinarily, each of us is a more complex system than he is capable of understanding. Thus we are usually capable of successful explicit communication about our houses, automobiles, jobs, and miscellaneous affairs, but not about our relationships with spouses, parents, children, and close associates. When these relationships are good, we carry on with implicit metacommunication. When they are bad, we may give up or call on a professional therapist. Few of us are able to analyze ourselves and our relationships unaided.

It seems plain to me that if man and his language were not such as to allow implicit metalinguistic communication, the implicit metacommunication that guides the creation and maintenance of social relationships would likewise be impossible.

Three Models

The places where language and social interaction meet are busy intersections. Sociologists, psychologists, psychoanalysts, philosophers of several schools, and linguists have all investigated them. If we put together metaphors from modern logic and information processing, theories of the structure of language and the organization of thought, and methods of observation and analysis of social phenomena, we could expect to come up with more detailed knowledge of how language supports social life.

Thinkers have dreamed of finding a single theory grounded in neuropsychology which would explain everything right up to human action, but they have generally considered such a theory unattainable. Language appears to be the place, if one exists, where such a theory might find a home. Indeed, it begins to seem feasible to link neuropsychology to psycholinguistics to interpersonal relations, although some experts still judge that these links will not be found for many years. Probably three models are needed. The central one should be a model of information processing in man, using concepts at the level of psycholinguistics. This model would fix certain psycholinguistic limits or conditions. The second, a neuropsychological model, would use concepts at the level of molecular biology and fix conditions that psycholinguistics would have to accept because the human brain, and not some other machine, is its underlying device. The third model, with concepts from game theory, sociology, and social psychology, would describe the systematic consequences of interaction among units (people) with human needs, desires, and information processing capacities; it, in turn, would derive its theory about how such units interact from the central model.

Even if this broad theory with its three models remains impossible for us and our immediate successors to implement, the role of language as a carrier of knowledge and feelings is being made clearer all the time by the collective work of the many disciplines that have a common interest in these phenomena. Hopefully, the practical result will be that the happiest conditions of interpersonal relationship can be achieved more frequently and the least happy can be treated more skillfully.

REFERENCES

1. A. L. Kroeber, *Anthropology* (New York: Harcourt, Brace and Co., 1948), p. 223.

2. Leslie H. Farber, "He Said, She Said," *Commentary*, LIII, No. 3 (March 1972), 59.

3. Ralph Linton, *The Study of Man* (New York: Appleton-Century, 1936), excerpted in *Sociological Theory*, eds. Edgar F. Borgatta and Henry J. Meyer (New York: Alfred Knopf, 1956), p. 174.

4. Talcott Parsons, *The Social System* (Glencoe, Ill.: The Free Press, 1951), pp. 10-11.

5. Erving Goffman, *Strategic Interaction* (Philadelphia: University of Pennsylvania Press, 1969), pp. 94-96.

6. John R. Searle, *Speech Acts* (Cambridge: Cambridge University Press, 1969), pp. 49-50.

7. Emanuel A. Schegloff, "Notes on a Conversational Practice: Formulating Place," *Studies in Social Interaction*, ed. David Sudnow (New York: The Free Press, 1972), pp. 75-119.

8. Harold Garfinkel, "Studies of the Routine Grounds of Everyday Activities," *Studies in Social Interaction*, pp. 1-31.

9. Michael Moerman, "Analysis of Lue Conversation: Providing Accounts, Finding Breaches, and Taking Sides," *Studies in Social Interaction*, pp. 170-228.

10. George Herbert Mead, *Mind, Self, and Society* (Chicago: University of Chicago Press, 1934), excerpted in *Sociological Theory*, p. 51.

11. Thomas Hora, "Tao, Yen, and Existential Psychotherapy," *Psychologia*, II (1959), 236-242, quoted by Paul Watzlawick, Janet Helmick Beavin, and Don D. Jackson, *Pragmatics of Human Communication* (New York: W. W. Norton & Co., 1967), p. 36.

12. The model discussed here stems mainly from oral suggestions by Sydney M. Lamb.

13. R. F. Bales, *Interaction Process Analysis* (Cambridge: Addison-Wesley Press, 1951).

14. David G. Hays, *Introduction to Computational Linguistics* (New York: American Elsevier Publishing Co., 1967); "Linguistic Foundations for a Theory of Content Analysis," *The Analysis of Communication Content*, eds. George Gerbner, Ole R. Holsti, Klaus Krippendorff, William J. Paisley, and Phillip J. Stone (New York: Wiley, 1969), pp. 57-67; "Linguistic Problems of Denotation," *Proceedings of the Tenth International Congress of Linguists* (Bucharest: 1967).

15. Roman Jakobson, "Linguistics and Poetics," *Style in Language*, ed. Thomas A. Sebeok (Cambridge: M.I.T. Press, 1960).

MARTIN KAY

Automatic Translation of Natural Languages

THE HISTORY OF man's attempt to build a translating machine for natural languages has not been illustrious. There has probably been no other scientific enterprise in which so much money has been spent on so many projects that promised so little. In the late fifties and early sixties, numerous people obtained, from one agency or another of the United States government, appreciable sums of money, in return for which they promised to deliver, in a very few years, a computer program or even an actual machine that could produce high-quality translations automatically. The events that brought these euphoric days to a sudden end are, by now, well known even to people who have no other knowledge of work in machine translation. Stimulated partly by the displeasure of some high-ranking civil servants and military officers at having received less than the best value for their money, the National Academy of Sciences in 1962 established the Automatic Language Processing Advisory Committee (ALPAC) and ordered it to investigate the entire matter of the federal sponsorship of research on machine translation.

In its report, delivered in 1963,[1] ALPAC was as kind to the designers of automatic-translation machines as it could possibly be. It concluded that there was no possibility of producing a satisfactory translating machine in the foreseeable future and recommended that no further funds be spent on contracts that had such development in view. The committee did not, however, see the development of such machines as forever beyond the wit of man and, in fact, expressed support of the funding of research that aimed at hastening the day when it would be reasonable to let such a development contract.

Reactions to the report were predictable. For almost ten years, any application for financial support for a project involving language and computers, however modest or sound, could expect a swift and categorical refusal. None of the positive recommendations of the ALPAC report were acted upon, and a disservice may thereby have been done to many serious and inventive research workers as well as to the country. Nevertheless, although the number of research projects in computational linguistics has diminished, the discipline has attained far greater maturity. It required dedication to stay in a field that no longer had a ready source of money and whose center of interest had become an object of abuse. However, researchers were now free to look closely at the theoretical problems that stood in the way of successful machine translation. This is not to say that the profession has lost its lunatic fringe. It is not difficult to learn something about how computers are programmed, and many people know a foreign language. Those who know a little of both will always be susceptible to revelations about how a machine might be made to translate. What is to be feared is the predilection that some government agencies are apt to show for proposals that come from precisely this lunatic fringe.

The first machine-translation system to be put into full-scale operation was installed in 1964 at the Foreign Technology Division of the United States Air Force, where it remained in daily operation until 1970. It was a very ingenious machine called the Mark II translator, and it was one of the most interesting products of the early period of work on machine translation. Unfortunately, its ingenuity cannot be accounted sufficient to repay its prodigious cost. A study by Arthur D. Little, Inc. found its translations time-consuming, expensive, and of poor graphic quality; furthermore, they were not very accurate, even after human editing.

The machine made use of a so-called *photoscopic store* consisting of a glass disk, about ten inches in diameter, on which information was inscribed in concentric circles in much the same way as a movie's sound track is represented on the edge of the film. During the life of the system, a vast Russian-English dictionary of stems, prefixes, and suffixes was amassed and new disks were made periodically to incorporate the new information. The logical capabilities of the machine, however, were rudimentary. Each stem and affix on the disk was accompanied by a pair of codes indicating classes of stems and affixes that could occur before and after it. Thus, when a Russian word was sought in the dictionary, various alternative classes might be found, and the one chosen would be determined by the choice made for the item immediately preceding it.

In the heyday of machine translation, Leon Dostert at the University of Georgetown had three independent projects under his supervision. After the publication of the ALPAC report, two of these projects continued elsewhere, though less vigorously, and were eventually quietly buried. The third was delivered as an operational system to translate Russian materials into English to the Atomic Energy Commission at Oak Ridge and to the European Atomic Energy Community (EURATOM) in Ispra, northern Italy. This system, which is usually referred to simply as the "Georgetown program," was designed for use on a standard, general-purpose computer, the IBM 7090. Its logical capabilities therefore far surpassed those of the Mark II translator, though the enhancement is not always apparent in the quality of the resulting translation.

The Georgetown program is very complicated. It consists of a large number of instructions that make use of several magnetic tapes on which various kinds of information are stored temporarily so as to make room in the main memory of the machine for other operations. In the course of translating a text, the program goes through a series of more or less well-defined steps called "dictionary lookup," "syntactic analysis," and so on. When this program was designed, work was just beginning on the formal properties of languages and the kinds of processors they might require, and what little was known was, in any case, largely ignored by the designers of this supposedly practical system. The absence of suitable formalisms is not to blame for the scarcity of impressive results from the Georgetown and other early systems, but it is to blame for their monstrous size and complexity.

Though the Georgetown system purported to be concerned largely with syntax, it incorporated neither the notion of a· grammatical rule nor the notion of a syntactic structure. The complexity of the syntactic part of the program was devoted to nothing more than resolving ambiguities in the assignment of words to grammatical classes. If a word to be translated could, in the abstract, be either an adjective or a noun, the process examined the word's context to determine in which capacity it functioned in the given sentence. The methods by which this was done were *ad hoc*, and they always provided a single answer to each problem regardless of genuine syntactic ambiguities in the sentence. Of course, an attempt was made to find the solution that would be correct in most cases. The grammatical classifications that were thus appended to the words in a text could be used later to determine which of a list of possible English alternatives would serve to translate the word and to help decide on the eventual order of the words in the second language. Such information about the structure of Russian and English as the program used was built into the very fabric of the program so that each attempt to modify or enhance the capabilities of the system was more difficult and more treacherous than the last. After a while, such a program becomes so complex that any further development is virtually impossible.

In the nearly ten years since the publication of the ALPAC report, much has been learned about linguistics and computer science, but few substantial inroads have been made into the basic problems that beset machine translation. Using the best knowledge that the profession has amassed, an automatic-translation system could be developed far more cheaply and easily today than was possible ten years ago, but there is little evidence that it would be able to produce translations of markedly higher quality.

It is generally agreed that any machine-translation system intended to produce results of high quality must carry out a syntactic analysis of every sentence in the text to be translated. The product of this analysis usually appears as a labeled tree representing the surface or preferably the deep structure of the sentence. Developing a structure of this kind has two important advantages. First, the function that a word or group of words fulfills in a sentence cannot usually be determined simply by examining neighboring words and phrases. It can be determined only by insuring that any function proposed for it is compatible with that proposed for every other word and phrase in the entire sentence. In other words, the most solid basis on which to assess whether a function has been correctly assigned is provided by a structural analysis of the sentence.

Tree structures are also valuable because they permit the definition of a simple but immensely powerful set of operations, known as transformations, in terms of which the structural changes that must be made to produce the sentence in another language can be stated. Suppose that a text is to be translated from a language like English in which the subject usually precedes the main verb and the object follows, into a language like Japanese in which the main verb invariably comes at the end of the sentence. The necessary adjustment in word order is easy to make if the syntactic analysis of the sentence identifies entities like subjects and objects in such a way that their relative positions can readily be altered.

Since there is no theoretical limit on the number of words that can constitute a subject or an object, the structure on which the rearrangement operations are carried out must have a way of connecting indefinitely many words into a group with a name so that it can be treated as a single item. Furthermore, subjects and objects can include other sentences with their own subjects and objects. Take the sentence, "Claims that John had passed the examination surprised the professor." The subject of this sentence is "Claims that John had passed the examination," which contains the second sentence, "John had passed the examination," which has its own subject, "John." The relationships of these various parts to one another can be conveniently represented in a tree diagram, as follows:

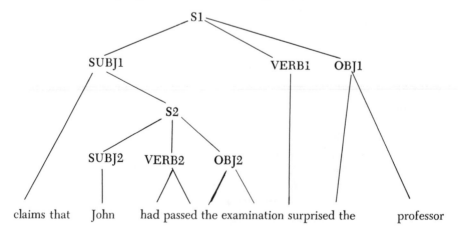

The labels S1 and S2 correspond to the first and second sentences respectively, and lines project down from each of these to labels representing the subject, verb, and object of the sentence.

Suppose, now, that the sentence is to be translated into Japanese. Two kinds of modification must be made. First, the verb of every sentence must be placed at the end, and second, whenever a subject or an object includes a noun and verb that make a complete sentence, that sentence must be placed before the noun it modifies. Arranging the English words in their Japanese order, we obtain, "John the examination passed had claims the professor surprised." The tree diagram representing this sentence is as follows:

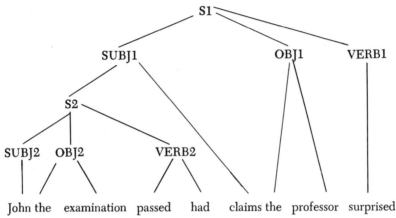

The new tree structure can be obtained from the original by treating the diagram as a mobile and changing the relative positions of the items that hang from particular places.

All the mechanical-translation systems that have been put into regular use are normally described as "machine-aided" translation systems. This is because the translations they produce are not, in general, comprehensible, but must be edited, often heavily, by a person who is familiar not only with the subject matter of the document but also with both languages involved. Therefore the production of a suitable translation by one of these systems can often be complicated, time-consuming, and expensive. All graphic material must first be removed from the text, leaving an indication of where it should be reinserted in the translation. If any of the graphic material contains matter in the foreign language, this must be specially translated and the appropriate amendment made to the tables, graphs, or pictures. The textual material must be represented in a form that the computer can read, and since optical character-recognition devices are still not equal to reading print, this must be done by a human operator at the keyboard. When the automatic translation has been done, a human editor must revise the translation, the graphic material must be reinserted, and a presentable copy must be produced.

In a letter published in *Science* on December 17, 1971, Dr. Walace Sinaiko described some tentative results of an informal experiment he has been conducting. In 1964, the Foreign Technology Division agreed to have a Russian paper translated for him, using the Mark II translator then in service. The Russian paper was itself a good translation of an English paper, made by a professional translator. Without any detailed knowledge of Russian, Sinaiko was thereby enabled to assess the quality of the product of the mechanical system, allowance being made for the scarcity of data (the original English paper contained only 1685 words) and the possibility that error had been introduced by the professional translator. Sinaiko was provided with the unedited output of the machine, making it easier to judge what its contribution to a satisfactory translation would have been.

Sinaiko had the same paper translated again in 1971 by the new system recently installed at the Foreign Technology Division, and he was given both the output of the machine and the final translation after human editing. In possession of two additional translations of the Russian text that he had obtained from professional linguists in 1964, Sinaiko was thus able to compare the raw output of the two translation systems, the final, human-edited output of the present system, and the work of the two professional translators.

The techniques that Sinaiko used to compare these translations were simple and informal. The two characteristics he concentrated on were (1) untranslated words and (2) translated words that had two or more possible meanings indicated for them in the translation. The differences between the raw output of the two machine systems were insignificant. The earlier system left 1.2 percent of the words untranslated, whereas SYSTRAN failed to find English equivalents for 2.3 percent. The earlier system provided alternative translations for 6.3 percent of the words, whereas the later system provided alternatives for 5.3 percent. These types of error, if errors they are, would not be found in the work of a human translator.

A comparison of the raw output of the machine with the translation that resulted from editing showed that about 35 percent of the English words printed by the computer were altered by the editor. Every one of the approximately eighty English sentences had some editorial modifications, most of them extensive. The most interesting statistic is the following: the manual translators worked at the rate of about 450 words per hour, whereas the editors working on the SYSTRAN output worked at the rate of about 400 words per hour.

Sinaiko was careful to point out that the results of this informal experiment are anything but conclusive. However, he observes, "It is apparent that little progress has been made during recent years. Moreover I do not know of any demonstrated advantages of MT over human translations."

Earlier I stressed that, while the last ten years have seen significant advances in the ease and elegance with which linguistic operations can be programmed as well as a bewildering array of new proposals in linguistic theory, no advance has been made that promises dramatically to improve the quality of machine translations. However, there may be ways that computer technology could serve translation other than those that have already been tried. At least two other ways have recently been suggested, one capitalizing on the recent development of machines that allow human intervention in the course of the computation, and one involving special artificial languages. If I seem unduly enthusiastic about the first of these, it must be remembered that I had some part in developing the idea.

The MIND system, developed at the Rand Corporation, is a package of computer programs that can be assembled in various ways to fill several linguistic functions. A version of the system was assembled in the latter half of 1971 that is intended to take over, as much as possible, the purely routine work involved in making a translation without ever attempting to solve problems for which it is not equipped. The program contains all the components that one would expect in a full-fledged translation program. There are facilities for analyzing the morphology of words, for obtaining their definitions, and for recording for each sentence all the information furnished by the dictionary about each of its constituent words. A thorough syntactic analysis of each sentence is performed that yields a *deep structure* (in the terms of modern transformational grammar) for each sentence. Transformational rules are applied to these deep structures to produce well-formed sentences in the second language. Finally, there is a component that provides the morphologically appropriate forms for each of the words printed out.

In addition, the system contains a component called a *disambiguator*, whose job is to mediate between the other components of the system with the help of a human consultant, to whom reference is made in all cases of difficulty or unresolved ambiguity. If a word has more than one meaning and the rules supplied to the system provide no basis for deciding which one applies in a particular context, the question will be referred to the consultant. If the rules allow more than one syntactic structure for a sentence, appropriate questions will be formulated to elicit the information necessary to decide among them. If it is necessary to know what a pronoun refers to before it can be correctly translated, the consultant will be provided with a list of possible referents and invited to choose the correct one.

These are the kinds of questions that cannot, as far as we know, be solved in a purely formal way. What is noteworthy about them is that they all arise in attempting to understand the original text rather than in attempting to compose a text in the second language. This suggests that a system of the kind just outlined might function very effectively with a human consultant who is familiar only with the language of the source document and its subject matter. If that is true, such a system might be made to produce creditable translations for technical documents without the services of a human translator or bilingual editor. Whether it can, in fact, do so still remains to be seen. The results of preliminary experiments in the translation of technical manuals from English into Korean are encouraging.

In the realm of language translation, one further line of investigation seems worthy of mention. Largely because of its sheer simplicity, it has usually been ignored or ridiculed in the past. We start from the premise that there are large numbers of people who need to read documents in some foreign language, Russian for example, but who have no knowledge of the language and no desire to learn it. Furthermore, we assume that many of the Russian documents would be read by such a small number of English-speaking people that it would be very difficult to justify the cost of making a translation. Let us further suppose that, though these people are unwilling to invest the amount of time required to learn Russian, they might be prepared to spend a tenth, or possibly a quarter, of this time to learn a skill of equivalent utility. They might be willing to learn a much simpler language into which, for one reason or another, it proved very simple to translate Russian. If, for example, there were some language into which Russian texts could be mechanically translated in a simple but entirely reliable way, and if this language were also very easy for native English speakers to learn, then these people would have ready access to the foreign materials they needed.

No language with the properties just described in fact exists. But there is good reason to suppose that one could be created. If a dictionary were made that provided a counterpart for each Russian word, prefix, and suffix, and if the process of translation consisted simply of replacing the Russian words and affixes by the counterparts listed for them in the dictionary, a new language would have been created with the grammar of Russian but with a different vocabulary. If the vocabulary were such that each item in it corresponded to one and only one Russian item, the translation process would be completely reversible, capable of reconstituting the original text exactly. Thus, no information from the original text would ever be lost, a property that no other kind of translation has.

Suppose, now, that the items used as counterparts for Russian words were chosen, wherever possible, to be English words, or English-like words, with meanings suggestive of the meanings of the Russian words. Though it is impossible to find English words with the same meanings as some Russian words, that difficulty is encountered less in technical documents where precise equivalents are usually abundant. This method would leave it to the human reader to learn the idiosyncrasies of the most common words with the widest ranges of meanings. In return, it would relieve the human reader of his most time-consuming task, that of finding equivalents for the precise words, which, though they individually occur relatively rarely, comprise the bulk of the vocabulary encountered in technical documents.

Lest what is being proposed here be confused with some early and notoriously unsuccessful experiments in machine translation, it must be stressed that we do not expect native English speakers to be able, without training, to read texts in the curious Anglo-Russian that would emerge from this translation process. We do, however, expect that this language could be learned in much less time than Russian or any other natural foreign language. The production of these translations would be entirely mechanical, and the algorithm required is trivial, so that the cost could be extremely low. In my view, the products of a simple system of this kind would fill the needs of the Foreign Technology Division at least as well as their present system does. Furthermore, the steps that would have to be taken to extend the system to other languages are straightforward, simple and cheap.

At present, linguists are devoting more and more attention to problems of meaning. This was, of course, the principal center of interest in linguistic studies until the end of the nineteenth century when there was a temporary shift of attention to the origin and development of language. One of the most vexing aspects of the study of meaning is that there is very little agreement on the question of what the problems are that need to be solved. Since almost anything that can be thought can be said, linguists have sometimes sought to exclude meaning from their field of study lest that field become too broad and amorphous. However, it is not clear that the study of meaning entails a study of everything that can be meant any more than that the study of logic entails an examination of every true and false argument. Some students of meaning have undertaken to provide a universally valid scheme for classifying words according to their meanings as Roget did in his well-known *Thesaurus of English Words and Phrases*. Such a categorization, for all that it is purely taxonomic, might be thought of as some kind of map of the territory over which the human spirit roams, or as the basis of a universal vocabulary into which the sentences of any language could be translated. To some scholars, the study of meaning has been effectively identified with the study of informal logic. Depending on how much rigor is introduced into this kind of study, it tends to take the form of an enriched, or corrupted, version of standard logical formalisms.

One of the principal points of contention among students of meaning concerns the question of whether there is, in fact, something that can eventually be captured and examined which is the meaning of a word or sentence. Every attempt to capture such an object leads, at best, to other words and expressions, possibly in some formal notation. Presumably the best that can be said is that the new set of words and expressions provides a more transparent representation of the meaning and shows the contributions of various components explicitly. But it cannot be claimed that anything set down on paper actually is a meaning. Some scholars have reacted to this situation by noting that the fact that words and sentences are meaningful is not grounds for assuming that there must be something which is their meaning.

The meaning, as Wittgenstein said, is the use. The meaning of a word or sentence is the total set of relations that it contracts with other words and sentences. When I learn a new word or a new fact about the world, the result is to change, however imperceptibly, the meanings of all other words and sentences in my language. While this view does not broaden the scope of linguistics so that it embraces the whole of science, it does claim for it much of the territory that was previously thought of as belonging to psychology and philosophy. In this view, a person's knowledge of the world is defined by his ability to describe that knowledge in language.

By what criteria should a theory of meaning in ordinary language be judged? Each theorist, of course, has his own answer. However, many people are prepared to concede that an ultimate test of a theory of meaning would be to incorporate it in the design of a machine, thereby enabling the machine to demonstrate the same kind of linguistic competence as a human being.

Allan Turing suggested that we could claim to understand the basis of human intelligence only when we could build a machine with which human beings could communicate and which resisted every attempt on the part of an interlocutor to determine whether it was, in fact, a machine. There is a growing number of students of language, most of them, to be sure, not claiming to be linguists, for whom the adequacy of a theory of meaning must be assessed in just this way. They would claim that the studies of meaning and of intelligence are all one.

The value of this approach to the study of meaning does not depend on the validity of the specific projects that have hitherto been based on it or on how readily we expect to be able to develop machines whose performance approaches the ideal. It does depend, at least to some extent, on such fundamental epistemological questions as whether it is ultimately possible to judge the grasp of meaning that a machine or organism has attained purely on the basis of its behavior. What would it be like to have a machine that not only could tell me that it was sorry I had a cold, but could also be sorry? Is it possible to understand the meaning of a word like "sorry" without being able to experience the emotion? To put the question somewhat differently, what conclusions would we be justified in drawing about the human faculty of language from a machine that had been enabled, by various kinds of cunning and trickery, to masquerade as a human being? Clearly there would be no necessary connection between the components of the machine and the components of human psychology. But this is to say nothing that cannot be said with equal justice of any linguistic theory that has been proposed. The test of a scientific theory must be behavioral. We cannot expect scientific models to operate for the same reasons or by the same processes as reality, but only to operate in a manner sufficiently analogous to enable us to extrapolate about reality from the behavior of the machine. Because of this ignorance of motive, the scientific value of a talking machine cannot be assessed objectively, but only on the basis of such subjective criteria as the parsimony and elegance of its structure.

The attempt to build machines that mimic human behavior belongs to a field that has come to be known as *artificial intelligence.* A contribution to that field that has recently attracted a great deal of attention is a computer program designed by Terry Winograd of M.I.T. This program enters into a conversation with its human interlocutor about a very carefully restricted domain of discourse. The program causes a picture to be displayed on a television screen depicting a table top on which a number of simple objects—cubes, balls, pyramids and boxes of various sizes and colors—are distributed. The machine can be instructed to move these objects about on the table top and it does this using its single "hand," a depiction of which can be seen entering the display from the top of the screen. It can, therefore, move only one object at once. It is possible to imagine instructions that require some ingenuity to carry out. Suppose, for example, that there are three blocks on the table and that the machine is told to stack them on top of one another. It may be that some of the blocks are initially supporting other objects which must first be removed. Obstructions must be removed from the upper face of at least two of the blocks before the stacking can begin.

Winograd's program may have to design quite a complex strategy in order to carry out a particular instruction, but, according to the view on which this work is based, it can only be said to understand an instruction fully if it can respond in this positive way. The program can also be asked questions about the disposition of the objects on the table and about its reasons for making particular moves. It may, for example, be asked, "Why did you put the green block on the red one?" to which the answer might be something like "Because you told me to stack up three blocks so that I had first to stack up two blocks."

Students of artificial intelligence have worked with very diverse models from robots that use a television camera for an eye and can move from place to place negotiating obstacles to programs that prove mathematical theorems and play chess. Hitherto, few of these efforts have involved a determined attack on obviously linguistic problems. Interaction with the machine has typically been through the medium of specially designed languages but, to the extent that a wider view is taken of problems of meaning, these projects can be seen as contributing to our understanding of natural language. For Winograd, it is a matter of the first importance that his program communicate in English and he describes his work as contributing to *procedural semantics,* an explicitly linguistic enterprise. For him, the meaning of a sentence is the procedure that it sets off in the head of the hearer and he takes it as his task to replicate that process in a machine.

Any machine that processes textual data in nontrivial ways must have certain basic capabilities. It must be able to recognize words, making due allowance for the ways in which their forms vary with number, person, mood, and the like. For each word, it must be able to retrieve information about its syntactic and semantic properties from a dictionary. It must be able to distinguish the correct syntactic structure from among the several possibilities in a grammatically ambiguous sentence. The details of how these processes are carried out depends on the theoretical stance of the designer. For some purposes, a strategy that is expensive in terms of computer resources may be preferred because it is considered a better model of the human strategy or because it is more perspicuous. On the other hand, if large amounts of text are to be treated, efficiency may be a prime consideration. For one purpose, it may be necessary to have all possible analyses of every sentence whereas for another it may be desirable to seek the analysis which is, in some sense, most probably correct.

Until recently, it was thought that each set of requirements demanded a new program and that there was no end to the designing of essentially different algorithms for basic linguistic processes. While there is, of course, no way of knowing what tomorrow's revelations may bring, it now seems likely that the best algorithms will turn out to be variants of a single overall strategy. Three strategies have been proposed for obtaining so-called deep structures for arbitrary sentences. By "deep structure," I mean the kind of structure assigned to a sentence by some variant of transformational grammar. It is an attempt to make explicit the underlying logical relations among words rather than simply to label subjects, objects, and the like. There has been rivalry among the proponents of three strategies, which were thought to be fundamentally different. However, it has recently become clear that the similarities are more striking than the differences. There appears to be a common core of operations that must be part of any algorithm for syntactic analysis.

The oldest of these strategies was the subject of Stanley Petrick's doctoral thesis at M.I.T.[2] It is a complicated procedure divided into several different stages and drawing heavily on the details of Chomsky's formalization of transformational grammar. The other two proposals make no direct reference to this formalism. William Wood's Augmented Transition-Network Parser[3] is inspired by parts of automata theory and, in particular, by the notions of automata theory with finite numbers of discrete states and of push-down stores. Kay's chart parser[4] capitalizes on the notion of general rewriting rules. It is, at least in principle, possible to write equivalent grammars for programs that follow each of these three strategies. In other words, grammars can be written which would cause the three programs to deliver identical analyses of the same sentences. However, the grammars would be written in entirely different notations; furthermore, they would cause quite a different sequence of events to occur in the machine. From this point of view, grammatical formalisms take on the aspect of high-level programming languages, each of which requires a compiler to translate it into the language of a particular machine. The difference is that, in this case, the machine is not simply a general purpose digital computer, but a special machine which might be called a *syntactic processor*. It is not necessary to construct instances of this special machine out of pieces of hardware because a general purpose computer can be made to stimulate it by supplying it with the appropriate algorithm in a suitable programming language.

That it is possible to design a single machine with reference to which grammatical formalisms appear as high-level programming languages is, theoretically, not surprising. Indeed, it is not difficult to prove that, if the formalism is adequate for syntactic analysis at all, then it must be possible to solve the problem in this way. What is interesting is that the proposed syntactic processor turns out to have a simple and elegant design and that this approach to the problem of syntactic analysis is efficient and practical. The difference between the syntactic processor and the general purpose computer is the difference between the theoretically adequate machines that are the object of mathematical study and the machines that are manufactured by engineers.

It will take time to discover the cash value of something like the syntactic processor. At best, it will be shown to incorporate important components of the human faculty of language. At worst, it will be a useful piece of engineering. In any case, it belongs to the field of computational linguistics.

The strategy of syntactic analysis is a real problem on which some modest headway has been made. But it is not a problem that belongs obviously either to linguistics or to computer science and it would probably never have arisen in the normal course of work in either of these disciplines. The same can be said of many problems in semantics. The computational linguist, however, sees problems of meaning in a different light from other linguists. To him, the meaning of a sentence is, as I have said, a process—a program that will be carried out in the head of the hearer. The computational linguist is, above all, a specialist in the processes of language and he is coming more and more to see semantics as the field in which his main contribution will be made.

REFERENCES

1. Automatic Language Processing Advisory Committee, National Academy of Sciences, National Research Council, *Languages and Machines* (Washington, D.C.: U.S. Government Printing Office, 1966).

2. S. R. Petrick, *A Recognition Procedure for Transformational Grammars* (Cambridge, Mass.: M.I.T. Press, 1965).

3. W. A. Woods, "Transition Network Grammars for Natural Language Analysis," *Communications of the ACM*, XIII (1970); W. A. Woods and R. M. Kaplan, *The Lunar Solences Natural Language Information System*, Report No. 2265 (Cambridge, Mass.: Bolt, Beranek and Newman, 1971).

4. M. Kay, *Experiments with a Powerful Parser* (Santa Monica, California: Rand Corporation, 1967), RM-5452-PR; R. M. Kaplan, *A General Syntactic Processor* (forthcoming).

PAUL KIPARSKY

The Role of Linguistics in a Theory of Poetry

OF ALL ART FORMS, literature, and especially poetry, has the greatest continuity of form in the Western tradition.[1] Since classical antiquity, the visual
arts and music have been changed profoundly through the introduction of
entirely new forms of expression and organization. Consider, for example,
how painting was changed in the Renaissance by the discovery of perspective, or how music was changed by the development of chordal harmony.
It is impossible, however, to point to any such spectacular enrichments of
technique in poetry. Styles and conventions have shifted, but no truly
new forms have emerged. Both of the fundamental stylistic elements of
poetry—figurative expression, using, for example, metaphor and metonymy,
and schemes of formal organization such as those of parallelism, meter,
rhyme, and alliteration—have existed from the beginning.

It is true that their relative importance changes all the time. In particular, the rules governing what must, may, and cannot be obligatory
in a piece of verse vary from one age to the next. For example, alliteration
was obligatory in Old English poetry a thousand years ago, but cannot
be obligatory today, and rhyme, which was never an obligatory formal
element in Old English, can and in certain forms of verse must be used
now. Many such seemingly radical changes in poetic form are actually
more or less automatic responses to linguistic change. Alliteration, for
example, seems to be found as an obligatory formal element only in languages where the stress regularly falls on the same syllable in the word,
which then must be the alliterating syllable. Old English was such a language, for the stress fell predictably on the root syllable. In modern English,
on the other hand, words with the same root can be stressed in many different places (take, for example, *ób li gate, ob líg a tor y*, and *ob li gá tion*).
When this kind of stress system was established in English, verse forms
with fixed alliteration were abandoned. The rhymed verse forms which
took their place were made possible, or at least more natural, by the evolution of English, specifically by the fact that English lost most of its inflec-
tional endings. Most richly inflected languages do not use rhyme, and
those that do, like Russian, tend to avoid rhymes that depend on grammatical endings.

When a particular element ceases to be obligatory, it remains as an optional element in the poetic repertoire of a language. In fact, optional elements of form in a poem are more significant than obligatory elements, precisely because the poet has chosen to use them. In plain rhymed verse, a pair of rhyming words may or may not be related in meaning.[2] Where rhyme is not obligatory, on the other hand, those words which do rhyme are almost always significantly related, as they are, for example, in the internal rhyme in Hopkins' line,

> And all is seared with trade; bleared, smeared with toil. . . .

Similarly, compare the obligatory and therefore only potentially meaningful repetition of lines in refrains or blues verses, with the free and therefore necessarily significant repetition of the line, in Frost's "Stopping by Woods,"

> And miles to go before I sleep.

In obligatory formulaic parallelism, like that found in the Finnish *Kalevala*, the parallel lines may contrast with or complement each other, but they may also be little more than paraphrases. But where parallelism is used as a free feature, it is always essential to the meaning, as in George Starbuck's "Of Late,"

> "Stephen Smith, University of Iowa sophomore, burned what he said
>   was his draft card"
> and Norman Morrison, Quaker, of Baltimore Maryland, burned what
>   he said was himself.
> You, Robert McNamara, burned what you said was a concentration
> of the Enemy Aggressor.
> No news medium troubled to put it in quotes.

As a further example, consider Starbuck's use of rhythm. Because he has not tied himself down to a fixed meter, he can use rhythmic variation to reinforce his meaning. The slow regular dactylic rhythm of the second line breaks down completely when McNamara's lies are cited in the third and fourth lines. The changed rhythm also contributes to the sense by directing an accusing stress onto the second "you" in the line,

> Yóu, Róbert McNamára, búrned what yóu said wás a cóncentrátion
> of the Énemy Aggréssor.

In such ways, "free verse" actually frees verse schemas for significant use; hence it can be a more difficult and a more expressive poetic form than regulated verse.

Perhaps our first impulse is to attribute the fact that the forms of poetic expression have not changed much to the sheer weight of the Western literary tradition. However, there are several reasons for believing that we must attribute it, at least in part, to the intrinsic nature of verbal art. In the

first place, from the available information it appears that all literary traditions, including those of primitive societies in many of which oral poetry plays an important role, utilize the same elements of form as Western poetry, and no exotically different ones. In fact it is not clear that there is any such thing as "primitive literature." Furthermore, many of the changes in poetic form, at least in the last 200 years, have been conscious innovations made by poets deliberately breaking with tradition. Yet even this conscious search for new forms has left the basic elements of expression essentially unchanged. Certain schemas have gone from obligatory to free or vice versa, and the grammar of poetic language has changed, for example, in its treatment of inversions. The reason, as I will try to show here, is that a good number of what we think of as traditional and arbitrary conventions are anchored in grammatical form, and seem to be, at bottom, a consequence of how language itself is structured.

The *theory of literature* usually concerns itself with classifying, analyzing, and comparing forms of verbal art which do, in fact, exist. But one could ask what characterizes existing forms of verbal art that differentiates them from forms which have never actually come into existence. Could we develop, in other words, a counterpart in the theory of literature to universal grammar in linguistics?[3] Although certain limits are implicit in traditional esthetics and rhetoric, neither poets nor students of literature have thought much about the intrinsic limits of poetry, any more than football players or spectators think much about gravity. The limits of poetic form are simply psychological givens, just as gravity is a physical given. In trying to define them we will have to make the effort, required wherever man studies his own nature, of not taking the "natural" for granted.

Our starting point will be the observation that various aspects of form all involve some kind of recurrence of equivalent linguistic elements.[4] They differ only in what linguistic element is repeated. Recurrence of *syntactic* elements is called *parallelism;* recurrence of *stress* and *quantity* (and, in some languages, *tone*), is called *meter;* and various kinds of recurrence of *vocalic* and *consonantal* sounds are called *rhyme, alliteration, assonance,* or *consonance.*

We can therefore conceive of poetic form in terms of certain *patterns,* such as *aa, aab, abab,* which are filled by *linguistic* (syntactic and phonological) *elements.* A pattern which is filled in a particular way may be termed a *schema.* A given pattern therefore underlies many potential schemas. For example, *abab* is a *rhyme schema* if *a* and *b* are units which are phonological sames of the kind we commonly called rhyme. If they are units of stress or quantity it is a *metrical schema.* For example, if *a* is an unstressed syllable, and *b* is a stressed syllable, the pattern *abab* represents iambic dimeter.[5] The same pattern, *abab,* can also be a *schema of syntactic parallelism,* such as that found in the first verse of Shelley's "Song to the Men of England."

Men of England, wherefore plow
For the lords who lay ye low?
Wherefore weave with toil and care
The rich robes your tyrants wear?

Understanding this distinction between the abstract pattern and the linguistic *sames* that are used to fill it will help us to approach in a more precise way the question of the intrinsic limits of poetic form.

The range of patterns in actual poetic use is small. Surprisingly enough, certain patterns of considerable formal simplicity are never utilized in the construction of verse. For example, one rarely encounters patterns which call for repeating sequences of more than three elements. The pattern *abcdabcd*, for example, is rarely used either as a rhyme schema, or as a pattern of parallelism. The choice of pattern, of course, depends in some measure on what sort of linguistic element is to fill it. For example, the pattern *abcabc* is common in short-term, line-internal recurrence, such as meter, but not so common in cross-line recurrence such as parallelism and rhyme, evidently because it is psychologically easier to keep track of as many as three elements if they recur fairly quickly. However, the fact remains that overriding constraints prevent the use of some potential patterns, regardless of the linguistic elements which might be used to fill them.

The range of linguistic *sames* actually in poetic use is likewise limited. One can easily dream up great numbers of plausible-looking principles of organization which no poet ever uses, and, more importantly, which even the most experimental poet would intuitively recognize as irrelevant were he introduced to a piece of work based on them. (Of course, if he were challenged to do so, he might detect them, by much the same process that a code is cracked.) For example, no one thinks of filling in a stanzaic pattern on the principle that the last words of certain lines must contain the same number of sounds. Nor do we find a type of rhyme in which the last sound or the last *n* sounds must be the same. (We will return to this question in the discussion of slant rhyme below). Naturally not, we might say. But a visiting Martian might find these nonexistent conventions no more peculiar than, for example, the Earthlings' custom of *rhyming*, whereby the last stressed vowel and anything that follows it must be the same.

To answer our Martian's objection would require a theory of poetic form that included a precise answer to the following two questions:

What patterns are relevant in poetry?
What linguistic sames are relevant in poetry?

Such a theory does not exist, although we do have certain useful bits and pieces. In what follows I should like to sketch out a partial answer to the second of these questions, in which I will argue that linguistics has a key role to play.

An initial tentative answer is this: *the linguistic sames which are potentially relevant in poetry are just those which are potentially relevant in
grammar.* Since one part of the theory of generative grammar is a precise
characterization of what sames are relevant in grammar, we can test this
hypothesis very specifically. In fact, the hypothesis is so rich that its implications can hardly be grasped yet, let alone fully tested. All we can do
here is to explore its consequences in particular areas. By doing so, we can
clarify some long-standing questions of poetics as well as some that have
thus far gone unasked.

Transformational grammar defines "grammatically relevant sameness"
in terms of syntax by analyzing the constituent structure of sentences. First
of all sentences are analyzed according to tree diagrams like this one:

(A)

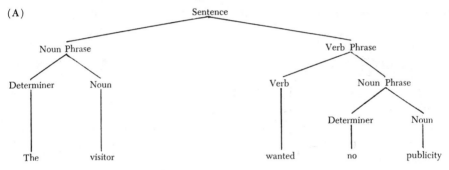

Such a tree structure shows how a sentence can be analyzed on various
different levels. For example, depending on which level of the tree one
looks at, the above sentence is described as made up of

Determiner + Noun + Verb + Determiner + Noun

or of

Noun Phrase + Verb + Noun Phrase

or of

Noun Phrase + Verb Phrase.

Such trees can be turned into other trees according to *transformational
rules.* The tree above is a surface structure and has undergone a number of
transformations; it derives directly, for instance, from another tree, shown
on the next page, which is one step closer to the original, or *deep structure,*
a tree in which the negation marker stands at the beginning of the sentence.
The transformational rule moves the negation marker "not" into the determiner "any" of tree (B), and the resulting "not any" becomes "no"
in the phrase "no publicity" of sentence (A). In this transformation, "any
publicity" is changed at the Determiner + Noun level of the tree. Other

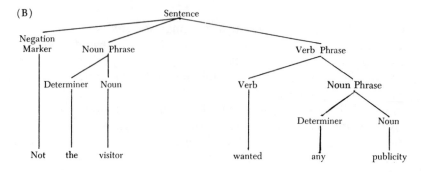

transformations, such as the passive transformation, would treat it at the Noun Phrase level.

A transformational syntax of a language provides a derivation from a deep structure via many intermediate trees to a surface structure for each sentence in the language. These derivations say what elements can and cannot count as the same with respect to syntax: two elements count as the same at a given stage in the transformational derivation if they are labeled alike in the tree for that stage. My hypothesis is that those syntactic elements which are counted as parallel for purpose of verse are, at some point in the derivation, counted as sames according to transformational grammar. Let me now map out existing varieties of syntactic parallelism in poetry, using the syntactic notions of constituent structure and transformational rules.

The poetry of both Walt Whitman and Dylan Thomas abounds in parallelism; this is one reason for the driving, incantatory quality which they have in common. But there is a big difference between the parallelism of the poets, as is clear from these excerpts.

> Where the striped and starred flag is borne at the
>   head of the regiments;
> Approaching Manhattan, up by the long-stretching
>   island,
> Under Niagara, the cataract falling like a veil
>   over my countenance;
> Upon a door-step . . . . upon the horse-block of hard
>   wood outside,
> Upon the race-course, or enjoying pic-nics or
>   jigs or a good game of base-ball. . . .
>   Whitman, *Leaves of Grass*

> A process in the weather of the heart
> Turns damp to dry; the golden shot
> Storms in the freezing tomb.
> A weather in the quarter of the veins
> Turns night to day; blood in their suns
> Lights up the living worm.
>   Thomas, "A Process in the Weather of the Heart"

The difference derives from the level of constituent structure for which the parallelism holds. Walt Whitman characteristically uses what we may call *loose* parallelism, in which only the highest syntactic constituents of the tree diagram are the same; although he uses a place adverbial in every line, each one differs from the others in form and complexity. In contrast, Dylan Thomas uses a *strict* parallelism, in which even constituents on the lower levels of the tree diagram are parallel. In other words, Whitman uses larger syntactic blocks to build his parallel structure. Now all form in poetry is potentially functional: this syntactic difference, for example, corresponds directly to the contrast between the "metonymic" Whitman and the typically "metaphoric" Thomas.

But parallelism can vary stylistically not only with respect to the level in the tree at which it is determined, but also with respect to the stage in the syntactic derivation from deep to surface structure for which it holds. Aside from actual repetition (as in refrains or blues verses) no syntactic parallelism is ever required to be complete on the level of surface structure. Even the strictest parallelism allows divergence of surface structure according to certain types of transformational rules that delete and reorder constituents. Thus, Dylan Thomas'

> The force that through the green fuse drives the flower
> Drives my green age,

is strictly parallel to

> The force that drives the water through the rocks
> Drives my red blood,

in spite of the fact that the constituents are crossed. Even in the obligatory strict parallelism of Finnish folk poetry, word order may vary freely.

Similar observations may be made about syntactic deletion. In Finnish folk poetry a verb is frequently "missing" in the second line. In nearly all such cases, the second line is derived from a structural parallel to that of the first by a transformational process (the *Gapping* rule) which calls for the deletion of a repeated verb in the second of two parallel sentences.

So far, we have discussed three variables pertinent to the analysis of poetic form:

1. The choice of abstract pattern: How is the recurrence of linguistic elements organized? For example, do we have symmetry *(abab, aabb)*, antisymmetry *(abba)*, or closure *(aab, ababcc)*? Is the structure hierarchical (stanzas) or linear (stichic verse)?

The other two variables have to do with how the abstract pattern is matched with linguistic elements.

2. The choice of linguistic elements: What are the syntactic or phonological building blocks which are subject to patterned recurrence? For example, do we have strict parallelism, where identity is maintained down

to the smaller constituents of the tree, or loose parallelism, involving only the major constituents?

3. The choice of the derivational stage: Where in the transformational or phonological derivation do we make the match between linguistic elements and abstract patterns? For example, do we define parallel structure before or after the passive transformation has been applied—that is, is an active sentence regarded as parallel in structure to a corresponding passive one?

These three variables are, in principle, independent of each other. Theoretically, either strict or loose parallelism in terms of linguistic elements could hold either at a point in the transformational derivation near the deep structure or closer to surface structure. However, there is in fact a close relationship among the three. The tighter the constraints on the abstract pattern, the stricter the parallelism tends to be, and the closer it holds to surface structure.

There is still a fourth variable, namely the grammar itself. Poetic language differs grammatically from regular speech. Poetry may use stylistic inversions not allowed in prose, as in "The force that through the green fuse drives. . . ." Such inversions are not imitations of Latin, as is sometimes claimed. Rather they are applications of transformational rules that have only limited existence in standard English prose. The extent to which special rules for poetic language have been acceptable is an important stylistic variable in English poetry. From Gray to Wordsworth, poets sought a more "natural" poetic diction and a major aspect of their effort was the conscious elimination of inversions. A hundred and fifty years later, however, inversions were brought back with a vengeance by E. E. Cummings, in whose hands they once again became an integral structural device.[6]

Poetic language differs, however, from Standard English in far more than word-order transformations. Perhaps the most striking characteristic of modern poetry is the stretching of grammar. This has led, in recent discussions of poetic language in the framework of generative grammar, to what has at times been a somewhat simplistic reliance on the concept of *ungrammaticality* or *deviance*. Metaphor, in particular, is frequently linked with a certain type of semantic deviance. However, it is clear that nondeviant sentences can have metaphorical interpretations: take, for example, "He came out smelling like a rose." In fact, the processes by which we give metaphorical interpretations to deviant sentences are the same as those by which we understand latent meaning in nondeviant sentences. Semantic deviance does not cause metaphorical meaning, but rather brings out what is already latent by blocking out a literal meaning, just as an eclipse of the sun does not "cause" the moon to shine, but makes its light perceptible by blocking out the sun. In general, then, deviance is a device of *foregrounding*. However, not all grammatical foregrounding involves changing the rules of grammar. Existing rules can also be utilized in new ways. For example, in Starbuck's poem, cited above, the striking phrase "burned what he said was himself" is not ungrammatical, but it is an unusual construction which may never have been used before.

We turn now from the syntactic to the phonological side of the language, where an examination of patterns has some rather surprising consequences, especially with regard to our habit of thinking of rhyme and alliteration as the simple repetition of sounds. We will find that the same four variables we distinguish in syntax also hold in phonology.

In addition to a set of transformational rules by which the syntax of sentences derives from a deep structure, grammar contains a set of phonological rules[7] by which the phonetic forms of words are derived from more basic underlying forms. The word "publicity," for example, which could be transcribed phonetically as /pəblísətī/, is derived, by a series of steps, from the more basic form /publik + iti/. The k is the basic form (which we can hear in the related words "public" and "publication") is converted to an s sound (indicated in the spelling by c) before front vowels such as i. Other rules place the stress on the third syllable from the end, and weaken all unstressed vowels except the last, which gets lengthened. Thus the *phonological derivation* of "publicity" is as follows:

/publik + iti/	basic form
publis + iti	change of k to s
publís + iti	placement of stress
publís + itī	lengthening of final i
pəblís + ətī	weakening of unstressed vowels

Investigation of the way such rules work has become the primary concern of phonologists in recent years, replacing their earlier preoccupation with problems of determining and classifying the phonemes of a language. This research is beginning to make clear that a surprising amount of the system of phonological rules of a language, which one might have thought was a rather arbitrary and unstructured part of its grammar, is actually determined by general principles. Phonological rules ring changes on a fixed repertoire of rules which, though very large in absolute terms, is still only a tiny portion of the huge total which could be imagined. Hence my hypothesis, that the linguistic elements which can count as sames in verse are just those which can count as sames in grammar, can be tested in phonology as well as in syntax. A comparison of the repertoire of phonological rules with the repertoire of metrical and rhyme schemas used in verse does indeed reveal a number of striking homologies.

Consider first this simple example. We know that "having the same number of sounds" is of no relevance whatever in versification, whereas "having the same number of syllables" is of fundamental importance. There is no explanation for this fact in the theory of prosody. But the fact has an exact counterpart in phonology. There are no known phonological rules which differentiate among words on the basis of how many sounds they have. The class of words containing exactly three phonemes (for example, "end," "shock," "Anna") is a linguistically irrelevant pseudoclass which plays no role in grammar. But there are, of course, rules which count syllables: in many languages stress falls on the nth syllable from the beginning or end of a word, monosyllabic words have special phonological properties, and so on. Therefore, it seems that rules of versification are based on facts which are at bottom linguistic, and that systems of metrics must be explained by phonology.

Consider rhyme and alliteration, which are often defined as involving "repetition of sounds." This definition is, in fact, inaccurate. It fails to cover, for example, the type of rhyme known as *slant rhyme*, which is widely used by Dylan Thomas and Sylvia Plath. In slant rhyme, consonants after the last vowel must be the same, but words ending in vowels are considered to rhyme regardless of what the vowels are.

In Sylvia Plath's *Medallion*, which uses terza rima with slant rhyme throughout, we find rhymes like

> wood/dead/crooked/
> him/flame/time
> light/that/trout
> ocher/fire/there

but we also find

> jaw/arrow/eye

where the requirement is satisfied without any "repetition of sounds."

Alliteration of consonants, as found, for example, in the old Germanic languages including Old English, is a mirror image of slant rhyme. In Old English, words alliterate if their stressed syllables begin with the same consonant (with the special proviso that *sp*, *st*, and *sk* behave as if they were single consonants). But words whose stressed syllables begin with vowels alliterate freely with each other (*Atol ȳđa geswing*, "terrible swirl of waves"). Thus the rule for alliteration (and its inverse, slant rhyme) is *not* that syllables must begin (or end) with the same sound, but rather that *if* the syllables begin (or end) with a consonant, then the consonants must be the same. If they begin (or end) with a vowel, they need not repeat the same sound.

How is it possible that certain words rhyme and alliterate without having any sounds in common? This question again has no answer in the theory of prosody. The fact that all vowels alliterate with each other has in fact provoked many ingenious but unsuccessful attempts to conjure up word-initial ghost consonants of some kind to "carry" the alliteration (which would imply similar ghost consonants at the ends of words to "carry" slant rhyme). But the problem is not merely that some rhyme and alliteration does not fit the traditional definitions of these concepts, but more importantly, that when the sound in question is a vowel the pattern which one would expect to be normal, that in which the first or last sounds are identical, does not seem to occur at all.

Let us turn to a grammatical analogue of rhyme and alliteration to see if corresponding phenomena are found there. Consider phonological processes of *reduplication*, which copy part of a word for grammatical purposes. It is interesting that we never find among them rules of the form "reduplicate the first (or last) sound of a word," just as we found no such rules for rhyme and alliteration. Rather, the typical form of reduplication is that of Gothic, where some verbs make their past tense by doubling their initial stem consonant, *if any*, and adding *ai* (pronounce like *e* in *get*):

saltan	"salt"	*sai-salt*	"salted"
haitan	"call"	*hai-hait*	"called"
slepan	"sleep"	*sai-slep*	"slept"
aukan	"increase"	*ai-auk*	"increased"
aikan	"renounce"	*ai-aik*	"renounced"
(ga) staldan	"obtain"	*(ga) stai-stald*	"obtained"

Note that this is very reminiscent of old Germanic alliteration, and even parallels the special treatment of *sk, sp,* and *st* as single units. Thus, the reduplication rules of phonology serve as well to circumscribe the kinds of rhyme and alliteration used in poetry.

Again, we have seen how a fact about the structure of verse derives from a fact about the structure of language. The question of how all initial vowels can alliterate with each other is a parallel question to that of how the *ai-* of *ai-auk* can be considered a reduplication of *auk*. Our answer is that language allows certain ways of organizing sounds, and that poetic form must draw on this organization.

More generally, consider how a word can be broken down into parts relevant to verse patterns. We can represent these patterns (or "analyses") by means of the standard notations used in phonology. For example, letting C stand for *consonant*, V for *vowel*, and # for *word boundary* (indicating whether the sound is an initial or a final sound), we can form the following notations:

#C	"a word-initial consonant"
#CV	"a word-initial consonant followed by a vowel"
V#	"a word-final vowel"
C_0	"any number of consonants"

Each of these expressions defines a class which might be referred to in a phonological rule.

The word "flash," for example, could pattern, for purposes of rhyme and alliteration, in the following ways:

#C	f.	
#C$_0$	fl.	alliteration
#C$_0$V	fla.	
VC$_0$#	.ash	rhyme
V	.a.	assonance
C$_0$# or C#	.sh	slant rhyme
#C$_0$ . . . C$_0$#	fl.sh	pararhyme (as in Wilfred
#C . . . . C$_0$#	f.sh	Owen's poetry)

Now each of these patterns is potentially a pattern in a linguistic rule as well as a rule of versification. The first three represent types of *reduplication* which occur in various languages of the world. The others are found in English in sound symbolism (*phonesthemes*).[8] Thus, an example of a sound symbolism pattern of the form C# is "fuzz," "buzz," "fizz," "razz," "jazz." An example of VC$_0$# is "smash," "crash," "bash," "dash." And #C . . . C$_0$# is illustrated by "pitter," "patter," "putter," or "tick," "tack," "tock."

We have seen that elements are considered to be syntactically parallel even after certain syntactic transformations have reordered or deleted constituents. In other words, to match them exactly we would have to imagine them as they were before they were so transformed. This phenomenon has a counterpart in phonology. It sometimes happens that phonological schemes such as meter and rhyme must be matched to linguistic forms *before* certain phonological rules have been applied to them.

We already made this assumption implicitly in speaking of the slant rhyme of vowel-final words like "arrow" and "eye." While it is true that these words end in a vowel in their basic phonological form, this vowel gets a consonantal glide sound inserted after it by a rule of English phonology, so that "arrow," as it is actually pronounced, ends with a *w* sound and "eye" ends with a *y* sound. For purposes of versification, however, we treat these words as if they really ended in vowel sounds—that is, we apply the rhyme schemes to them before the glide insertion rule is applied.

Examples in which poetic form "looks back" at phonological forms which are not phonetic, can be cited from many languages. In German, most poets rhyme *Mund* "mouth" and *bunt* "colorful" (both pronounced with *t*, but different in basic form, since when you add an ending, such as *e*, *Munde* is pronounced with a *d*). Some poets, however, like Stefan George, who strove to achieve unusually pure poetic language, consistently avoid such rhymes. In other words, Stefan George's poetry rhymes according to forms more basic than that in which final stops are unvoiced.

There are cases where a whole block of phonological rules must be peeled away in this fashion before the schema which underlies a given meter is revealed. This is true of the Finnish *Kalevala* as recited by the bards of Ingermanland, and of the *Rigveda* of ancient India. The complexity in these traditions of the interaction between phonological and metrical structure makes them a kind of laser beam with which we can probe into the way language is structured in the mind, via the way it is structured in poetry.[9]

Thus phonological identity in poetry is not a matter of phonetics alone, any more than syntactic identity is a matter of surface structure. In fact, we have arrived at the somewhat surprising conclusion that identity of sound is neither a necessary nor a sufficient condition for rhyme and alliteration.

These observations suggest that at least some constants of poetic form are dependent on the structure of language itself. The intrinsic structure of language, the raw material of poetry, is carried over into poetry. By virtue of the nature of the patterns that are relevant in poetry, the structures involved are primarily those which are universal rather than those which apply only to a particular language. Hence the homologies between grammar and poetry account, at least in part, for the universality of poetic form.

To be sure, that summary of my thesis is rather more sweeping than is justified by the concrete examples analyzed here. I have, after all, dealt only with external form, and hardly touched on such deeper questions as figurative language. Although I believe that it is in these areas that linguistics will make its greatest contribution to literary studies, I have here chosen more tangible aspects of poetic form since the linguistic approach can be more clearly illustrated with them. Furthermore, the linguistic semantics needed to tackle problems such as metaphor is only now beginning to exist. The current work which is being done in this area is highly encouraging, as are many other applications of linguistics to literary problems: Ohmann's syntactically based studies of prose style, for example, and the approach to the structure of narrative initiated in V. Propp's classic work on folktales.[10]

REFERENCES

1. This work was supported in part by grants from the National Institutes of Health (5 TO1 HD00111) and the National Institute of Mental Health (2 PO1 MH13390).

2. On the potential semantic function of rhyme, see W. K. Wimsatt, *The Verbal Icon* (Lexington, Ky.: Kentucky University Press, 1954).

3. An initial attempt, modeled on linguistic theory, is Manfred Bierwisch, "Poetics and Linguistics," *Linguistics and Literary Style,* ed. D. Freeman (New York: Holt, Rinehart & Winston, 1968).

4. This is expressed in Roman Jakobson's famous statement: "The poetic function projects the principle of equivalence from the axis of selection into the axis of combination." "Linguistics and Poetics," *Style in Language,* ed. T. Sebeok (Cambridge, Mass.: M.I.T. Press, 1960).

    Note the caesurae (obligatory clause boundaries at a certain point of the line) could be considered either as patterned recurrence of sentence boundaries, or perhaps better as a form of parallelism at the level of sentences. Enjambment may be considered simply as absence of "caesura" at the end of a line.

5. The distinction between the abstract pattern and its linguistic implementation in the domain of meter has been drawn particularly clearly by Morris Halle and S. J. Keyser, "Chaucer and the Study of Prosody," *Linguistics and Literary Style.*

6. In her unpublished Harvard dissertion, Irene Fairley shows that Cummings employs several syntactic systems, one of which is quite traditional in the form of its inversion rules.

7. A detailed analysis of the rules of English phonology is given in Noam Chomsky and M. Halle, *Sound Pattern of English* (New York: Harper & Row, 1968).

8. R. Wellek and A. Warren, *Theory of Literature* (New York: Harvest Books, Harcourt, Brace & World, 1961), p. 148.

9. P. Kiparsky, "Metrics and Morphophonemics in the Kalevala," *Linguistics and Literary Style,* "Metrics and Morphophonemics in the Rigveda," *Contributions to Generative Phonology,* ed. M. Brame (Austin: University of Texas Press, 1972); Howard Lasnik, "Metrics and Morphophonemics in Old English Verse," *Linguistic Inquiry,* forthcoming; Stephen Anderson, "U-Umlaut and Skaldic Verse," *Festschrift for Morris Halle,* eds. S. Anderson and P. Kiparsky (New York: Holt, Rinehart and Winston).

10. R. Ohmann, "Generative Grammars and the Concept of Literary Style," *Word,* XX (1964), 423–439; V. Propp, *Morphology of the Folktale* (Austin: University of Texas Press, 1968). For a new linguistic approach to the question of modes of narrative, such as "narrated monolog," see S. Y. Kuroda, "Where Epistemology, Style and Grammar Meet," *Festschrift for Morris Halle.*

Notes on Contributors

MORTON BLOOMFIELD, born in 1913 in Montreal, is Arthur Kingsley Porter Professor of English at Harvard University. Mr. Bloomfield is the author of *Seven Deadly Sins* (1952), *"Piers Plowman" as a Fourteenth Century Apocalypse* (1962), and the co-author of *A Linguistic Introduction to the History of English* (1963).

ROGER BROWN, born in 1925 in Detroit, Michigan, is professor of social psychology at Harvard University. His publications include *A First Language: The Early Stages* (1973), *Social Psychology* (1965), and *Words and Things* (1958). He received the 1973 G. Stanley Hall Award for Distinguished Contributions to Developmental Psychology, and the 1971 Distinguished Scientific Contribution Award of the American Psychological Association.

COURTNEY B. CAZDEN, born in 1925 in Chicago, Illinois, is professor of education at Harvard University. Before returning to university life, she taught young children for nine years. Her publications include *Language in Early Childhood Education* (1973) and *Child Language and Education* (1972).

CHARLES FERGUSON, born in 1921 in Philadelphia, Pennsylvania, is professor of linguistics and chairman of the Committee on Linguistics at Stanford University. He served for six years as the director of the Center for Applied Linguistics, and served as president for the Linguistic Society of America. He is the author of *Language Structures and Language Use* (1971), and an editor of *Studies of Child Language Development* (1973), and *Language Problems of Developing Nations* (1968).

EINAR HAUGEN, born in 1906 in Sioux City, Iowa, is the Victor S. Thomas Professor of Scandinavian and Linguistics at Harvard University. He has served as president of the Linguistic Society of America, the American Dialect Society, and the IXth International Congress of Linguists. He is the author of *History of the Scandinavian Languages* (forthcoming), *First Grammatical Treatise* (second edition, 1972), *Studies* (1972), *The Ecology of Language* (1972), *Language Conflict and Language Planning* (1966), *Norwegian-English Dictionary* (1965), *Bilingualism in the Americas* (1957), and *Norwegian Language in America: A Study in Bilingual Behavior* (1953, 1969).

DAVID G. HAYS, born in 1928 in Memphis, Tennessee, is professor of linguistics at State University of New York at Buffalo. He has served as chairman of the Social Science Advisory Committee of the National Science Foundation, and of the International Committee on Computational Linguistics. His publications include *Introduction to Computational Linguistics* (1967).

DELL HYMES, born in 1927 in Portland, Oregon, is professor of folklore and linguistics at the University of Pennsylvania. He has worked with the language and folklore of the Chinookian Indians of Oregon and Washington, and has been active in developing a social science approach to language. He is the chairman of the Committee on

Sociolinguistics of the Social Science Research Council, and the editor of the new journal, *Language in Society*. He is also the editor of *Reinventing Anthropology* (1973), *Pidginization and Creolization of Language* (1971), and *Language in Culture and Society* (1954).

MARTIN KAY, born in 1935 in London, England, is professor of information and computer science at the University of California at Irvine. He served as head of the Rand Corporation Linguistics Research Project from 1963 to 1972 and is a past president of the Association for Computational Linguistics. He is co-author, with Karen Spark Jones, of *Linguistics in Information Science* (forthcoming).

EDWARD L. KEENAN, born in 1937 in Somerset, Pennsylvania, is a senior research fellow at King's College, Cambridge University. He studied in France for two years, worked as a French-English interpreter for the United States Department of State, and did a year's fieldwork in Madagascar. He is the author of a number of articles on linguistics and on logic.

PAUL KIPARSKY, born in 1941 in Helsinki, Finland, is professor of linguistics at M.I.T. He has published articles on phonology, syntax, and historical linguistics in various journals and collections and is editor of *University Action Group Magazine*.

D. TERENCE LANGENDOEN, born in 1939 in Paterson, New Jersey, is professor of English at Brooklyn College and professor of English and linguistics at the Graduate Center of City University of New York, where he is also the executive officer of the Ph.D. program in linguistics. He was a student of Noam Chomsky's at M.I.T., and did field work on the Mundari language in India. He is the author of *Essentials of English Grammar* (1970), *The Study of Syntax* (1969), and *The London School of Linguistics* (1968), and the co-editor of *Studies in Linguistic Semantics* (1971).

ERIC H. LENNEBERG, born in 1921 in Germany, is professor of psychology and neurobiology at Cornell University. He has been studying the neurology of language since 1959 at Harvard Medical School, Rochester University Medical School, and Cornell Medical School. He is the author of *Biological Foundations of Language* (1967) and the editor of *Foundations of Language Development* (forthcoming) and *New Directions in the Study of Language* (1964).

WILLIAM G. MOULTON, born in 1914 in Providence, Rhode Island, is professor of linguistics at Princeton University. His particular interest is structural dialectology, working with Swiss German dialects. His publications include *A Linguistic Guide to Language Learning* (second edition, 1970), *The Sounds of English and German* (1962), and *Swiss German Dialect and Romance Patois* (1941).

PETER STREVENS, born in 1922 in Norwich, England, is professor of applied linguistics at University of Essex. He has taught phonetics, linguistics, French, and English as a foreign language in universities in West Africa, Edinburgh, and Leeds. He has served as the chairman of the British Association for Applied Linguistics, and is the author of *British and American English* (1972), *The Linguistic Sciences and Language Teaching* (1964), and, with M. A. K. Halliday and Angus McIntosh, of *Papers in Language and Language Teaching* (1966).

KARL V. TEETER, born in 1929 in Berkeley, California, is professor of linguistics at

Harvard University. He is the author of *The Wiyot Language* (1964), a grammar done on the basis of fieldwork with the last living speaker of Wiyot, a language now no longer spoken. He has worked on the history and dialects of Japanese, and is currently interested in the description and history of Algonquin languages, especially Malecite and Passamaquoddy, which are spoken in New Brunswick and Maine. He has published numerous papers and reviews dealing with his various linguistic interests.

Eric Wanner, born in 1942 in Wilmington, Delaware, is assistant professor of psychology at Harvard University. He is the author of *On Remembering, Forgetting, and Understanding Sentences: A Study of the Deep Structure Hypothesis* (forthcoming), and, in collaboration with D. C. McClelland, W. Davis, and R. Kalin, of *The Drinking Man* (1972).

Calvert Watkins, born in 1933 in Pittsburgh, Pennsylvania, is professor of linguistics and the classics at Harvard University. He is the author of *Indo-European Studies* (1972), *Indogermanische Grammatik III/1: Geschichte der indogermanischen Verbalflexion* (1969). *Indo-European Origins of the Celtic Verb* (1962), and of some sixty-five articles in journals and collections. In addition, he directed etymological research and contributed to the *American Heritage Dictionary of the English Language* (1969).

Index